Sex and Violence in Tibetan Buddhism

Also by Mary Finnigan:
*Psychedelic Suburbia: David Bowie and
the Beckenham Arts Lab* (2016)

Mary Finnigan and Rob Hogendoorn

Sex and Violence in Tibetan Buddhism

The Rise and Fall of Sogyal Rinpoche

Copyright © 2021 Mary Finnigan and Rob Hogendoorn

All rights reserved

ISBN-10: 0-9863770-9-0

ISBN-13: 978-0-9863770-9-9

Library of Congress Control Number: 2019932298

Cover photo: Patrick Pleul/dpa/Alamy Live News

Author photo (Hogendoorn): Marlies Dekker Fotografie

Cover design: Keith Carlson

Revised and Updated

Jorvik Press

5331 SW Macadam Ave., Ste. 258/424
Portland OR 97239

jorvikpress.com

Yak caravan moving through Kham, eastern Tibet, circa 1920

Mary Finnigan was born in Manchester, England just before the start of World War II. Marrying an older man at eighteen, she produced two children before moving to London and landing a job as a fashion writer on the *Daily Mirror*. Her print journalism career included feature writing at the *Daily Sketch*, *Daily Express* and freelance at the *Sunday Times* and the *Guardian*.

During a five-year holiday from the five-day week, in 1969 she met the legendary rock star David Bowie, who introduced her to Tibetan Buddhism. Her devotion to this comprehensive spiritual path has remained steadfast ever since.

Returning to her journalism career, Mary worked as a reporter, editor and producer at Visnews, Independent Radio News and the London Broadcasting Company.

Mary met Sogyal Lakar, aka Rinpoche, in 1973, helping him to set himself up as a lama before becoming sceptical about his credentials. With her journalistic training running in tandem with her appreciation for Tibetan Buddhism, she embarked on a campaign to match contemporary ethical values with the fundamentals of Buddhist view and practice.

Mary and her co-author Rob Hogendoorn pooled their skills and resources after meeting on social media. Mary lives in Devon, England with her husband Chris Gilchrist.

Rob Hogendoorn (1964) studied law at the Erasmus University at Rotterdam, Netherlands. After graduating as a Master of Law, he worked as a co-ordinator for the Centre for Applied Ethics at its Faculty of Philosophy, co-editing two books on environmental philosophy.

In 1993-1994, he spent a year among Tibetan communities in India, researching law from a Tibetan Buddhist perspective. After that, he focussed his research on the Fourteenth Dalai Lama's conversations with (mostly) Western scientists. To this end, he attended several Mind & Life conferences and summer schools and taught about Mind & Life during a Science for Monks workshop in Sera Monastery in India.

For the past nine years he has researched and published on sexual abuse by Buddhist teachers, both as an investigative reporter and an unaffiliated scholar.

The last four years he has focussed on researching the formative years of Sogyal Lakar, formerly known as Sogyal Rinpoche. He presented a paper on his findings during the 2018 meeting of the American Academy of Religion in Denver, Colorado.

Rob is married with three adult children. He lives in Maasland, near Rotterdam, in the Netherlands.

Acknowledgments

This book is the culmination of 40 years of research. During this time, it has undergone many changes of shape and direction, blown along by events and developments.

Many people have helped, encouraged and supported me. Nkag'chang Rinpoche and his wife Khandro Dechen are first among equals, closely followed by Evelyn Ruut, Tahlia Newland, Luc de Roeck, Linda Parker Solomon, Lama Tsultrim Allione, Lama Jampa Thaye, Tenzin Geyche Tethong and His Holiness Tenzin Gyatso, the 14th Dalai Lama of Tibet.

I would also like to thank Mike Farmer, Sangye Ngawang, Ian Baker, Sogyal Truth, Tenzing Abrahams, Guy Durand, Mireille Durand, Dominique Cowell, Victoria Barlow and Marion Dapsance for information, co-operation and collaboration. Sharing their stories with me was a painful experience for some of these people. I am forever grateful. Also, thanks to Diana Rockefeller, Stephen and Martine Batchelor, Professor Donald Lopez, Chris Fynn, Olivier Raurich, Norman Steinberg, Alex Studholme, Mick Brown, Alex Wilding, Gary Goldman, Lena Raab-Tsering, Gary Beesley and Nick Godwin. If there is anyone that I have forgotten, I apologise.

Several people who wish to remain anonymous have kept me up to date with advice and information. I owe them a huge debt of gratitude. I pay homage to my family – especially husband Chris Gilchrist and grand-daughter Alva Andersson Taghioff. They have been patient with my mood swings and long periods of silence during writing marathons. I owe deep appreciation to my publisher/editor/friend Peter Stansill.

Mary Finnigan
Devon, England, May 2021

I wish to thank the late Theo Dik, without whom everything would have been different; Oane Bijlsma and the other brave women and men I met for speaking truth to power; journalist Bas de Vries for his encouragement and consummate skill; our colleagues Nicole Le Fever, Anna Mees, Dirk Mostert, Wil van der Schans, Michael de Smit, Olaf Tempelman, Ilja Tuning, Koert van der Velde, and Jolien de Vries for their solid reporting on Sogyal Lakar and other abusive Buddhist teachers; scholars Henk Blezer and Jann Ronis for their help with Tibetan sources; Marijke Schaffers for her help with French sources; whistleblowers Marion Dapsance, Tahlia Newland, and Tenzin Peljor for their perseverance; Joy Vriens for his moral support; friends Rob van Eijk, Joest 't Hart, Richard de Jongh, Stuart Lachs, Joop Romeijn († 2020), Ron Sinnige, Eric Stols, Guus Went, and John Willemsens for stimulating exchanges through the years; and Ann Gleig and Amy Langenberg for inviting me to contribute a paper on Sogyal Lakar to the panel "From Rape Texts to Bro Buddhism: Critical Canonical and Contemporary Perspectives on the Sexual Abuse Scandals in Western Buddhism" of the American Academy of Religion in 2018.

Lastly, I am deeply grateful to my companion in life, Petra van der Pas, who cheerily puts up with my dogged pursuit of sobering facts while providing for all our family's needs.

Rob Hogendoorn
Maasland, Netherlands, May 2021

*This book is dedicated to victims of sexual abuse
and exploitation in all circumstances and across the world.
And to the courageous whistle blowers who kick-started
a cultural paradigm shift.*

Contents

Glossary 1
Preface to Revised Edition 3
Foreword.. 4
1 Top of the Game 7
2 Early Days and Turbulent Times... 11
3 School Days in India 21
4 Drugs, David and Dharma 29
5 Squats and Sogyal 37
6 Doubts and Setbacks 47
7 Fame 61
8 Seduction and a Lawsuit... 69
9 Mimi and Guy 79
10 Hubris and Nemesis 87
11 The Letter 93
12 The Aftermath.. 103
13 A Very Sick Man 119
14 Cracks in the Party Line 125
15 Another Letter 137
16 Damage Limitation 147
17 The Report.. 151
18 Breakthrough 163
19 The End of an Era? 167
20 Death of a Salesman 173
21 Post Mortem 193
References... 199

Sogyal in Kalimpong, northern India, with attendants (ca. 1958)

Glossary

Bardo – Intermediate state between death and rebirth.

Bodhisattva – A realised being who renounces nirvana in order to be reborn in the human realm to help other beings to enlightenment. Can also be applied to acts of selfless generosity.

Buddhadharma – The teachings and practices taught by the Buddha.

Chuba – Tibetan robe, worn by both men and women.

Dakini – Female deity. Male equivalent is "daka" (Sanskrit) or "pawo" (Tibetan). In Tibetan dakini is "khandro." Dakini is also used to refer to spiritually gifted human females.

Dharma – One of the Three Jewels of Tibetan Buddhism. Buddha (the enlightened one), Dharma (the teachings/path to realisation), and Sangha (the community of students). Tibetans also add the Lama (teacher/guru)

Dzogchen – The Great Perfection. The most subtle, apparently simple but extremely challenging peak of Tibetan Buddhist view and practice. Kept secret in pre-Chinese Tibet but now widely taught in the West.

Gompa – Tibetan for temple.

Karma – Loosely translated as "fate." Can best be understood via the aphorism, "As you sow, so shall you reap." Buddhists and Hindus believe karma is a continuum from one incarnation to the next.

Khata – Long white scarf presented as a token of respect and usually returned to the donor for the same reason.

Lama – Tibetan for guru.

Lojong – Tibetan Buddhist mind training practice.

Madhyamaka – Tradition of study and practice founded by the Indian sage Nagarjuna. Refers to the ultimate nature of phenomena and the realisation of this in meditation.

Mandala – Sacred diagram depicting realms of deities, humans, etc.

Mimayan – Non-human entities.

Ngondro – Tibetan Buddhist preliminary practice, said to establish the basis for more advanced techniques.

Nirvana – The state of permanent bliss experienced by realised beings.

Puja – Collective ritual practice.

Rinpoche – Title accorded to distinguished lamas. It means "Precious One" and is usually conferred on tulkus or (re)incarnated lamas.

Sadhana – Personal practice.

Samaya – Sacred vow which binds the guru-disciple relationship.

Samsara – The realm of illusion experienced by non-realised beings. The ultimate Buddhist experience is the realisation that samsara and nirvana are indivisible.

Sangha – Community of Buddhist students.

Stupa – Reliquary monument.

Thangka – Tibetan sacred scroll paintings, usually of deities and mandalas.

Tsampa – Roasted barley flour.

Tulku – Lama believed to be the (re)incarnation of his predecessor.

Vajra – "Dorje" in Tibetan. Ritual sceptre symbolising male energy. Also used to describe an indestructible spiritual relationship – hence vajra brother/sister/kin.

Vajrayana – The diamond vehicle. Esoteric Tibetan Buddhism. A synthesis of Indian Tantra and Tibetan shamanism. The powerful direct short path to enlightenment.

Yogi – Non-celibate Tantric/Dzogchen practitioner. Female: "yogini."

Yum – (Spiritual) wife, sex partner.

Preface to Revised Edition

How did it happen? A howl of pain, dismay and disillusionment from Rigpa students who had devoted decades of their lives to the organisation and its leader, Sogyal Lakar. They went public with their anguish following the publication of an open letter that stripped away more than 40 years of secrecy and denial. A letter that revealed a catalogue of abuse – so extreme and so far removed from core Buddhist principles that many people found it almost impossible to believe. Except that it was signed by eight members of the Rigpa elite who had been close to Sogyal for many years. Their credibility is beyond doubt.

The original version of this book told the story of Sogyal's rise to guru superstardom and the events that led to his demise. People who know a lot more about what happened behind Rigpa's public façade read the book and decided to speak out. Many new developments ensued after initial publication in 2019 – including Sogyal's death several months later.

The full horror of the depravity and abuse that took place behind a firewall of secrecy for such a long time came into focus as new witnesses spoke about their experiences. We owe them this revised and updated edition.

And we owe Tibetan Buddhism a more comprehensive account of what went so disastrously wrong at Rigpa, because this lesson needs to be learned so that nothing like it can happen again.

Mary Finnigan
Rob Hogendoorn

Foreword

This is not a conventional narrative. It took some time to figure out how to make it work because a significant segment of the book is based in the personal experience of one of the two authors. The other author did the research and analysis, which is of equal importance. We tried transposing all of it into the third person, but it became clear that this was an artificial device. So Mary Finnigan's voice is present throughout story, while Rob Hogendoorn's contributions are attributed as they occur.

We tell the story because we care deeply about Tibetan Buddhism. We hope that by highlighting some of the things that have gone wrong during the early stages of its transition into the developed world, the lamas from Tibet and their students will be able to move towards appreciating each other on equal terms. The lamas and their followers both have a lot to learn about how to cope with the cultural dissonance that could not be avoided when feudal-medieval old Tibet met modern Western liberal democratic values.

We have done our best to present facts, events and opinions as impartially as possible. We do not seek to blame anyone. The naïve, very needy adulation that many Western devotees are eager to project onto the lamas is a significant factor in the dysfunctional relationships that cause so much distress to so many people, including perhaps some lamas. They, in turn, brought their misogyny and their authoritarian attitudes with them from the Himalayas.

Most lamas do not pay attention to the emotional impact of the sexual liaisons they enjoy with Western women. Nor do they understand that sex involving a power imbalance is firmly established as a taboo in Western society – with good reason. Those magical men in maroon are so glamorous, so mysterious and so different, it is not surprising that so many people are spellbound by them, only to discover that their romantic expectations will never be fulfilled.

The book zones in on one opportunist Tibetan guru, who should never have been allowed to attract a following in the first place.

Sogyal Lakar, aka Rinpoche, stands out as a nasty piece of work, whose excesses tarnished the reputation of Tibetan Buddhism. People left his groups around the world in droves when the whistle was finally blown by members of his inner circle. Before he died in August 2019, we offered Sogyal the chance to contribute his point of view. He did not respond.

It must be said that there are many lamas who get on with the job quietly, ethically and effectively. The International Commission of Jurists cited estimates that there were 2,770,000 Tibetans in Tibet in 1953.[1] The most conservative estimate reckons that there were 3,000 tulkus in Tibet.[2] This means that one in every 900 Tibetans was a tulku. It is highly implausible that all of them were exceptional beings. Clearly some of them are (the Dalai Lama is a good example), but while most of the ones who teach in the West are usually well trained, not all of them are spiritually gifted.

The complete oral tradition of Tibetan Buddhism is on a knife edge between survival and fragmentation. As with all esoteric traditions, its effectiveness depends on transmission from teacher to disciple. Almost all the great lineage holders who were trained in Tibet are dead. The younger generation of tulkus have yet to prove their stature. If this formidable heritage is lost, it will be a tragedy of epic proportions.

The time has come for the lamas to adapt to the modern world – and for their students to nurture their common sense and critical awareness. We hope this book will contribute towards making that happen.

Sogyal and the Dalai Lama with Carla Bruni Sarkozy (first lady of France) at the inauguration of the Lerab Ling Temple, 2008

1

Top of the Game

It is a cloudy day in August 2008 in the Languedoc-Rousillon region of southern France. Hundreds of people, dressed in their best party clothes, line both sides of a narrow country road. Most of them hold a khata, a long white scarf, presented as a ceremonial offering to Tibetan dignitaries. A rainbow array of prayer flags flutter, and the breeze catches plumes of fragrant juniper smoke rising from pot-bellied stoves placed at intervals along the route.

A ripple of excitement runs through the crowd as a procession comes into view. Some people wave, others bow with hands clasped in the prayer gesture, others offer their khatas, holding them at arm's length towards a small elderly man wearing maroon monastic robes and a huge smile. Even at a distance he radiates charisma. He has acquired unique status on the world stage as the man who loves everyone – and many people nowadays accept that the joy on his face originates from a genuinely open heart. As he passes, Tenzin Gyatso, the 14th Dalai Lama of Tibet, reaches out to touch members of his adoring fan club.

The Dalai Lama strides alongside Carla Bruni Sarkozy at the head of a cluster of monks, security men and journalists, towards a multi-coloured, ornate portico. A monastic band strikes up. Monks in their red and yellow robes and ceremonial hats play shawms, oboe-like instruments that wail like the wind in a Himalayan storm. They lead the proceedings leading up to the inauguration of the largest, most grandiose Tibetan temple in the developed world.

Sheltered by the portico, Carla Sarkozy stands apart from the crowd – tall and elegant in a dark couture dress. She too holds a khata. Another figure sidles up beside her. He is short, balding, obese and clothed in a floor-length mustard yellow robe – a chuba, lay rather than monastic Tibetan attire.

His manner is obsequious, he is bowed in deference, but his face tells the phalanx of TV cameras, forest of microphones and those present in person that this is his finest hour. Here he is, Sogyal Lakar from a remote region of Tibet, introducing the Dalai Lama to the First Lady of France.

Sogyal is said to be recognised as a tulku and is known as Rinpoche, which means Precious One in Tibetan. He is the second best-known lama on the Tibetan landscape and he too is idolised by thousands of followers who belong to Rigpa, his organisation, active in France with six centres and six study groups, and with centres in 21 other countries around the world.

Carla Sarkozy appears somewhat awestruck. With a shy smile she offers her khata to the Dalai Lama. His big smile broadens even further as, according to Tibetan custom, he accepts the scarf and then returns it to the donor, draping it tastefully around Carla's neck.

A day of elaborate ritual follows, with the Dalai Lama tasting tsampa, tossing petals and cutting multi-coloured ribbons draped across the temple doors before entering to perform the consecration ceremony.

Once inside, more celebrities step out to meet the world's A-list holy man – French Foreign Minister Bernard Kouchner, Secretary of State for Human Rights Rama Yade, and former Prime Minister Alain Juppé. As the Dalai Lama moves inside the enormous building decorated with extreme oriental flamboyance, other public figures are on tenterhooks for their brief moment of eye contact with His Holiness. A famous actress here, an author there, more politicians – and a cluster of clerics, including Claude Azema, the auxiliary Bishop of Montpellier.

The name of the place is Lerab Ling, which means Sanctuary of Enlightened Action. Sogyal Rinpoche chose this name in honour of Lerab Lingpa, a 19th-century Tibetan Buddhist master whom Sogyal claims as his predecessor.

So how did a 63-year-old man in poor health, who left his native Tibet when he was just eight and had only a basic education in India, come to head a multi-national organisation with tentacles on five continents? How did he manage to raise 10 million euros to build a huge temple in southern France? And then persuade the wife of the President to provide the media focus for the opening day?

Christmas party at Lerab Ling

Sogyal with his uncle, the senior lama Jamyang Khyentse Chokyi Lodro (ca. 1958)

2

Early Days and Turbulent Times

To shed light on Sogyal's trajectory into guru superstardom – and his spectacular fall from grace – Rob Hogendoorn examines his origins in pre-Chinese Tibet, the culture that was the bedrock of Sogyal's ideas, inspiration and psycho-emotional circuitry.[3]

Sogyal was born in 1947 into the wealthy Lakar family in the province of Kham in eastern Tibet, now annexed into the People's Republic of China. His name is a contraction of Sonam Gyaltsen. Kham is a wild mountainous region inhabited by wild mountain people. They have a reputation as rough, tough, fiercely independent communities driven by clan loyalties and, until recently, frequently involved in skirmishes among themselves. Because of their proximity to China, they fought border wars at various points in history with both Chinese and Tibetan factions until finally overrun by the Red Army in the 1950s.

The Khampas were profoundly religious in those days and deeply attached to Vajrayana Buddhism. They still are to a large extent, despite rigorous and sustained efforts by the Chinese authorities to suppress religion.

There were lots of monasteries in Kham, financed by devout families who saw it as both a duty and a pleasure to support as many people as possible to dedicate their lives to the study and practice of Tibetan Buddhism. There were monks and nuns in the monasteries – and hermit yogis wandering the mountains, enduring extreme austerities to be alone and free to practise without interruption. When Tibetan Buddhism migrated to the West, starting in the early 1970s, many of the pioneer lamas who taught around the developed world came from Kham.

However, among the estimated 130,000 exiled Tibetans, Khampas are a small minority. This is why they tend to band together under duress, forming a bloc against the perceived hegemony of the Central Tibetans.

Kham is enormous and distances between towns, villages, hamlets and monasteries took days at least and often weeks or months to cover on foot, horse or yak. Prior to the Chinese takeover there was no motorised transport in Tibet.

Sogyal's family lived in a town called Rongpatsa. For several generations their wealth derived from their role as merchants strategically located on the trade routes between the Tibetan capital Lhasa and China. But by the time Sogyal was born their livelihood was threatened by a confluence of economic and geopolitical developments.

Two tea trade routes joined up just outside Rongpatsa. Local farmers and nomads stopped over at this junction to exchange commodities – alongside the caravans of merchants, officials and pilgrims trekking between Lhasa and China. Acting as middlemen in the Rongpatsa valley, the house of Lakar prospered for many generations via the lucrative long-distance tea and salt trades.

This traffic started to disappear during the early 1900s, when travel through India opened up via Sikkim and Darjeeling. New trade regulations and a boundary agreement with the British colonialists, together with the advent of paved roads and railway lines, made Tibetan business dealings with India fast, reliable and profitable. Boarding steamers in Calcutta, officials and traders would reach China months faster than by overland caravan through Kham.

War broke out in 1917 between rogue Chinese troops and the Tibetan frontier army. The Tibetans prevailed after a fierce battle on the Rongpatsa plain and the truce that followed effectively turned the Lakar territory into a border crossing point with China.

Continuous unrest, frequent troop movements and rumours of fresh hostilities swirled around Kham. The occupational hazards of long-distance caravan traders had always been daunting, but by the early 1930s the risks increased to the point where newcomers were no longer attracted into the business. Many of the Kham trading families abandoned their homes to settle in Sikkim and Darjeeling on the Indian side of the Himalayan ranges.

The Lakars did not join the ranks of the émigré community and were plunged once more into the field of fire. Chiang Kai-shek's Chinese Nationalist army became involved in a dispute between local monasteries. Heavy fighting broke out and the entire Rongpatsa region fell to the Chinese and so too did the city of Dege and vast tracts of Kham.

As a result of this, when Sogyal was born in the 1940s the Lakar estate was inside China, some 200 kilometres, or five days on foot, from the new Tibetan border. This radical re-alignment – combined with the absence of both Tibetan conscription and taxation and minus competition from other rich families – opened up fresh opportunities for the Lakars. They stayed in Rongpatsa for more than 20 years before leaving for Sikkim after the Tibetans were defeated.

During these upheavals one lucrative trade remained as a source of revenue. Tibetans prefer Chinese tea to Indian, so the tea business continued, and so too did the Lakars' prosperity. Throughout the turbulence the monasteries were key players, and as a prominent family the Lakar clan was enmeshed in the monastic power struggles and intrigues.

The Lakars were affiliated with Yakze Gompa of the Nyingma tradition of Tibetan Buddhism. Pema Lakar was the consort of Yakze Terton. The Nyingmapas are the oldest, unreformed order – some of them are celibate monks and nuns, other are married or take female consorts as Tantric partners.

Around this time Yakze Terton tried to rekindle his connection with his main teacher, Jamyang Khyentse Chokyi Lodro, the throne holder of Dzongsar Gompa near Dege. As the head of the monastery, he travelled the area on fund-raising trips.

During one of these journeys, Chokyi Lodro gave Yakze a Vajrayana empowerment at the Lakar home. While staying there, he met Sogyal's mother, Tsering Wangmo, when she was a child, and her sister, Tsering Chodron, who was still a baby. Yakze Terton suggested that a fortuitous connection was made and that the girls might one day become Lodro's sexual consorts in advanced Tantric yoga.

At that time Lodro was a celibate monk. He had a ferocious temper and exploded with wrath at Yakze's suggestion, refusing to speak to him for several days.

Inappropriate though it may seem to the modern world, Tibetan Buddhist lamas frequently abandoned celibacy to marry young girls from important and wealthy families. They did this in order to practise Mahamudra completion-stage sexual yoga. It was rare for ordained monks in the Gelugpa order to disrobe for sexual practices but widespread within the older Kagyu, Sakya and Nyingma schools in Kham.

Other reasons for taking consorts were to enhance visionary experiences and to remove obstacles to health and longevity. When the lamas fled from Tibet during the Chinese takeover in the 1950s and started teaching in the West, they brought these cultural mores with them.

There are reasons to assume that the Lakars' stance in the 1930s and 40s extended beyond adapting to changed circumstances. In the years preceding Sogyal's birth they forged strong political alliances with another prominent clan and the ruling Chinese Nationalists. In 1947 scions of both families liaised between Reting Rinpoche, the former regent of Tibet, and the Nationalist leader of China, Chiang Kai-shek.

When the 13th Dalai Lama died in 1933, the pro-Chinese Reting became regent. Power struggles were a feature of life in the highest echelons of Tibet's theocratic government. One faction whipped up corruption and abuse charges against Reting, who was forced to resign in 1941, just when the present Dalai Lama embarked on his monastic education.

Dispel any romantic ideas about Tibet as a tranquil Shangri-La. The political monks around the Dalai Lamas in the Potala Palace were ruthless and violent, constantly scheming to outmanoeuvre each other for status and influence, much the same as politicians the world over – except that in Western democracies nowadays they tend to avoid murdering their rivals.

Reting had no such scruples. In 1947 he orchestrated several botched attempts to assassinate Taktra Rinpoche, his successor as regent.

In addition, Reting requested Chiang Kai-shek's assistance to stage a coup that would overthrow Taktra's government. A Tibetan cabinet minister referred to Reting's representatives as "Gyagpon Donnam" and "Lakar Thutob". Sogyal's mother's family history confirms that her father was Thutop Lakar. Several other sources confirm the Reting connection.

Reting's envoys were not just errand boys. On their own initiative they submitted schemes to the Nationalists for disruptive activities against the Taktra regime. But Gyagpon Donnam blew the plot wide open by talking about it while smoking opium in the Nationalist capital, Nanjing. The Tibetan government cracked down hard on the conspiracy, ordering the arrest of Reting and his accomplices, one of whom committed suicide.

Reting was tried and found guilty of attempting to assassinate Taktra and of conspiring with the Chinese. These were capital crimes, but before the government could execute him, Reting died in his prison cell, probably of poisoning and presumably on Taktra's orders. There are rumours that Reting suffered a much more gruesome fate involving castration.

The chain of events that Reting initiated with the help of Thutop Lakar weakened Tibet and marked the end of Nationalist suzerainty – and in consequence contributed to the circumstances that led to the occupation of Tibet by Chairman Mao's Red Army.

The Reting affair suggests that by the time Sogyal was born in 1947, members of the house of Lakar were living in fear of what the future might bring. It was not safe for them to enter territory under the control of the Tibetan government until Taktra died in 1952.

In addition to Thutop's high treason, their wealth and connection with the Nationalists made them a conspicuous target for Chairman Mao's fanatical Communists. During those years they were also engaged in the black tobacco trade, which would invite dire consequences if they were found out. They did this to help out Chokyi Lodro with his monastery's financial difficulties. It was profoundly at odds with Buddhist values.

The Lakars had another big problem. After Thutop died there were no men in the household. Sogyal's father was said to be a man called Jamga, a member of the powerful Dilgo family. Jamga's marriage with Tselu was arranged by a local strongman, but he is only briefly mentioned as a family member. Thutop's brother died in a travel accident, which would ultimately leave Jamyang Khyentse Chokyi Lodro with a responsibility for the family – and for the infant Sogyal.

Lodro was not a well man. He suffered from violent fits, which were said to be caused by supernatural influences. He experienced protracted illnesses from the age of 49 onwards. In line with Tibetan beliefs, he eventually decided to take a young wife, in the hope that she would benefit his health and prolong his life. He chose the teenaged Tsering Chodron and married her in a brief ceremony around 1947 when he was 55. She appears to have accepted her fate stoically – probably because being selected as the consort of a high lama was regarded as a great honour. In feudal medieval Tibet a woman's right to choose a husband was non-existent.

Tsering Chodron's sister, Tsering Wangmo aka Tselu, decided for reasons that are not clear to take her infant first-born son to live at Dzongsar Gompa. It seems likely that her decision was more practical than spiritual and that Sogyal was not accepted as a tulku but rather as a child in need of protection.

Tselu's and Sogyal's reminiscences suggest that her son's stay at Dzongsar was temporary – but her account does not dovetail with Sogyal's description of his relationship with Chokyi Lodro: "All my earliest memories are of him," he writes. "He was the environment in which I grew up and his influence dominated my childhood. He was like a father to me."[4]

Tselu's and Sogyal's memoirs contain anecdotes about Sogyal's childhood in "Hor," which clearly references their home in Rongpatsa. This contradictory evidence suggests that Sogyal's account is slanted to enhance his credibility as a lama. All his biographical notes since he moved to the West in the early 1970s emphasise that Chokyi Lodro was his primary Buddhist teacher.

Chokyi Lodro's secretary-treasurer, Tsewang Peljor, was a frequent visitor to the Lakar home and in due course he took Tselu as his wife. Tselu's family history says nothing about her marital relations with either Jamga or Peljor. She sheds no light on why she separated from Jamga – or why she decided to have her infant son spend time in a monastery.

By the end of the 1940s the Lakar family's fortunes were waning. By the mid-1950s the trade they relied on had almost disappeared. Then came the seismic shift in Tibet's way of life when the Chinese Communists took over. Exorbitant taxes were levied on Tibetan traders – especially monastic ones – and the Communists soon had a virtual monopoly on Tibetan commerce, transport and communications.

As the Chinese consolidated their grip on Tibet, wealthy families, landowners and the monasteries had good reason to be alarmed – especially those who had collaborated with the Nationalists. It seems likely that the Lakar elders had been considering the possibility of an exodus to India or Sikkim for some time. Travel through central Tibet had been an option for them since the death of Taktra, and they were now encouraged by a general amnesty granted by the 14th Dalai Lama on his accession.

The Lakar history during the early decades of the 20th century does not indicate that they were concerned about maintaining a position on the moral high ground. They traded in tobacco and guns, they collaborated with the Nationalists and, together with Chokyi Lodro, they left Tibet well in advance of the formation of the patriotic volunteer force assembled in 1958 to resist Chinese rule.

Ostensibly, the reason for their departure to Sikkim was Chokyi Lodro's failing health. He divined that "an obstacle to his health" could be removed by going on a pilgrimage – and that he should travel simply, with as little fuss as possible.[5] He told his monks he would return. It was a smoke screen.

Dezhung Rinpoche, who was there at the time, relates a different version of what happened. He says that Chokyi Lodro "slipped away from his gompa incognito when he learned that all the main lamas in the Derge district were being summoned to a meeting with Communist officials in China."[6] Chokyi Lodro's close involvement with the Lakars would have been a serious risk factor – especially because of Thutop Lakar's attempt at collusion with Mao Tse-tung's archenemy, Chiang Kai-shek.

Jamyang Khyentse Chokyi Lodro left his monastery for good in the spring of 1955. He was disguised as an ordinary lama and travelled with a party of about 55 people. It included his attendants and members of the Lakar clan, including Tsering Chodron, Tsering Wangmo, Tsewang Peljor and eight-year-old Sogyal.

It was not the most auspicious start in life for an impressionable child. His mother had already put him into the care of an ailing, irascible despot, and he was now being uprooted from familiar surroundings and thrown into an alien culture and an uncertain future. The journey from Kham to their eventual refuge in Sikkim took a whole year.

Chokyi Lodro kept a travel diary, which helped his biographers trace the group's itinerary from Kham to Lhasa, to western Tibet and from there to Sikkim. According to Sogyal, the trek to Lhasa was a "tortuous three-month journey on horseback."[7] They often stopped over at monasteries along the way – and from time to time they pitched camp at sacred sites for several days in order to perform the appropriate rituals.

The present Dalai Lama was 20 years old at the time. It is understood that when Chokyi Lodro visited him, he was asked to do a divination "to determine the future security of Tibet." The advice came as an instruction to build an elaborate statue of Padmasambhava to avert misfortune. Apparently, the Tibetan government did not fully comply – a situation which Chokyi Lodro deplored as "not only improper, but catastrophically ill-judged."[8]

Sogyal has described the first time he met the Dalai Lama:

I was waiting on a balcony, lost in thought and looking out over Lhasa, when His Holiness's principle bodyguard, a tall, thick-set monk with an imposing presence, came to get me. I joined my master inside and as we were served tea, His Holiness asked me my name and my age. He then held me in a piercing gaze and told me pointedly to make sure I studied hard. It was a moment I have always remembered, for it was probably one of the most important of my entire life.[9]

So, this is how the relationship began between two of the most influential figures in the explosion of interest in Tibetan Buddhism that swept across the developed world during the 1980s and 90s.

Little more is known about Sogyal's personal experiences during the long, slow journey from Kham to Sikkim. He has, however, described their daily routine:

We would go to bed at dusk and rise before daybreak, and by first light the yaks carrying the baggage would be moving out. The tents would be struck, and the last ones to come down were the kitchen and my master's tent. A scout would go ahead to choose a good camping place, and we would stop and camp around noon for the rest of the day. I used to love to camp by a river and listen to the sound of the water, or to sit in the tent and hear the rain pattering on the roof. We were a small party with about 30 tents in all. During the day I rode on a golden coloured horse next to my master. While we rode he gave teachings, told stories, practised and composed a number of practices specially for me.[10]

Chokyi Lodro and the Lakars were dependent for their survival on the generosity of the Sikkimese royal family – but Lodro was not a happy man. He didn't want to live in Sikkim. If he couldn't return to Tibet, he would have preferred to live in India, but Sogyal's stepfather, Tsewang Peljor, applied some common sense to the situation and rejected both options. He said that if Rinpoche went back to Tibet, he would be thrown into prison by the Communists and die there. If he went to India, they would be separated from their Sikkimese benefactors. Without financial support, he said, as they owned neither houses nor land outside Tibet, they would all die of starvation.

Chokyi Lodro spent the last few years of his life in a state of permanent frustration. When he felt ill, he would scold and beat the people around him. His foul temper and the domestic violence within his household are recurring themes in oral history. The level of violence involved must have been obvious to the entire Lakar family.

To add insult to injury, Lodro blamed the Queen Mother of Sikkim, one of his most devoted benefactors, for his troubles – because of a prophesy that indicated he would face obstacles caused by an "old woman."[11]

Chokyi Lodro's interests and those of the Lakar family were closely aligned after they settled in Sikkim. They were financially dependent on benefactors for their survival, so the lama's attendants kept quiet about the prophesy, and Chokyi Lodro gave the Queen Mother many empowerments and teachings while the royal family hosted him and his entourage at the palace monastery in Gangtok.

After Chokyi Lodro's cremation in 1959 his remains were housed in a stupa there until they were moved to the resettled Dzongsar monastery at Bir, in India. His widow, Tsering Chodron, continued to live in Gangtok for almost 50 years before moving to Bir and finally to Lerab Ling in France.

A question now comes into focus. If Chokyi Lodro genuinely believed that Sogyal is the reincarnation of one of his teachers, why did he neglect to ensure that he received a comprehensive Buddhist education?

Sogyal and family on the Sikkim border, 1956, after their year-long journey from eastern Tibet

Sogyal with his uncle, Chokyi Lodro

Sogyal (standing at back) with young classmates at St Augustine's School, Kalimpong (1960)

3

School Days in India

Two of Sogyal's contemporaries in exile – Ngari Rinpoche and Sogyal's half-brother, Dzogchen Rinpoche – both received full traditional training, studying for years with some of the great masters. Chinese repression notwithstanding, Ngari Rinpoche was sent back to Central Tibet in 1958 to continue his religious education. Dzogchen Rinpoche attended the Institute of Buddhist Dialectics in McLeod Ganj, India, as a 12-year-old. His education there was personally supervised by the 14th Dalai Lama, who took care of his expenses.

McLeod Ganj was a small, dilapidated hill station above the town of Dharamsala in the state of Himachal Pradesh when the Dalai Lama settled there in 1960. Jawaharlal Nehru's government allocated him a spacious bungalow, built by the British colonialists, as his headquarters. He has lived there ever since. It is a far cry from the Potala Palace, but the presence of Tibet's revered leader and his entourage attracted worldwide attention. A rapidly expanding Tibetan settlement coalesced around him and McLeod Ganj became known as Little Tibet. It is now a major tourist destination.

Examination of the known facts about Sogyal's early life indicates that the window of opportunity for him to receive a traditional Buddhist education has to be framed between his infancy in Kham until the mid-1950s, the year-long trek to Sikkim and his subsequent enrolment in a Roman Catholic primary school in 1960. There is a stark difference between the rigorous training undergone by Ngari and Dzogchen Rinpoches on the one hand and Sogyal's sporadic studies on the other. In fact, Sogyal came nowhere near completing a sustained education of similar scope and depth.

However, Chokyi Lodro did appoint two tutors to instruct Sogyal. This study period could only have taken place between the arrival in Sikkim and the start of his Western-style education. Sogyal has suggested that he completed his monastic training before the family moved to Sikkim, but he contradicts this in *The Tibetan Book of Living and Dying*. His account of the "instruction" he received is uncorroborated and may well be wishful thinking. This version of his personal history confirms that he did not receive any traditional monastic training before arriving in Sikkim.

A later tutor was appointed for Sogyal, who took on the job shortly before Chokyi Lodro died in the summer of 1959. He began instructing Sogyal on Shantideva's classic *Bodhicharyavatara* in the presence of Chokyi Lodro's remains, but their relationship was short-lived. The tutor entered a long retreat soon afterwards and Sogyal enrolled at St. Augustine's School in Kalimpong in 1960.

In the light of these historical records, the only period that could have been devoted to continuous Buddhist education was roughly between 1957 and 1959. Within this short timespan Sogyal probably only learned basic reading, writing and memorisation skills in Tibetan – together with a rudimentary command of the vocabulary, logic and epistemology that children are expected to master before beginning their fully fledged Buddhist studies.

Contemporary reports do not suggest Chokyi Lodro's direct involvement in Sogyal's education – beyond allowing him to hang out in private or attend religious teachings or ceremonies in public, with Sogyal dressed as a monk or in ritual costume.

Even oblique references to formal Buddhist instruction by Chokyi Lodro are rare, as Sogyal himself admits:

> *As I grew older, he would let me watch when he taught. He understood that children learn more through watching than through direct teaching. As it all went on around me, I became very interested and very enthusiastic. I would watch the teachings with my master in the morning and in the evening when I was playing with my friends, I would put on a performance of what he had done, like a little theatre. He just had me by him all the time, which I really enjoyed. I would constantly ask him questions and he was always very patient. More than intellectual knowledge, through him I picked up the feeling, an intuitive understanding of the tradition."*[12]

Being close to Chokyi Lodro when he was young and impressionable must have affected Sogyal. The master lived in a constant state of superstitious anxiety. He had a volatile temper and suffered from seizures that he attributed to demonic forces caused by the movement of the planets. Lodro's biography contains many references that highlight his religious angst and obsessive fretting about evil omens and supernatural threats to his physical wellbeing. He constantly practised health-giving and lifespan-prolonging rituals and he self-medicated for common diseases such as a persistent cold.

Apparently, as a child Chokyi Lodro was very active and vivacious. But he grew up in an environment where physical violence against children was common practice.

His biographer Orgyen Topgyal recalls: "Usually Rinpoche's tutor was extremely strict and would slap or beat his charge at the slightest provocation. When I was a boy, we shaved Rinpoche's head and I saw 20 or 30 scars that remained from his tutor's most severe beatings."[13]

Beaten and traumatised as a child, it is no surprise that as an adult Chokyi Lodro turned out to be an iron-fisted and vengeful master. Violence was embedded in his DNA. He routinely administered physical punishments to his inferiors, both individually and collectively. As the regent of Khatok Gompa, he struck fear into the hearts and minds of its monastic population.

They said he was like an "invading force" because his sovereignty over them was absolute and indisputable. Chokyi Lodro was a tyrant who punished monks ten at a time. When a flogging was ordered, Rinpoche insisted on four or five hundred lashes and he always watched from the window of his residence when the punishment was delivered.

For some people, being hit on the head is alleged to be a healing method; Chokyi Lodro once knocked a lama nearly unconscious because his blood was said to be toxic. The beating allegedly induced a complete recovery. Orgyen Topgyal even alludes to the possibility that he may have assaulted his young wife. "I haven't heard that Rinpoche ever hit her, but people tend not to talk about such things."[14]

Chokyi Lodro frequently imposed his will on other people, forcing them into submission – sometimes at their peril. This happened shortly before the household was due to leave Sikkim on a pilgrimage to India in 1956. After much deliberation, a date for their departure was set, but they missed their train. That night Tselu Lakar gave birth to Sogyal's half-sister Dechen. The next day the master insisted that all members of the party must take part in a puja, Tselu included. Her husband, Tsewang Peljor, protested, but Lodro was adamant that she should be there "whatever the cost."[15]

Poor Tselu had a terrible time. Possibly afflicted with postpartum psychosis, she shrieked and shivered, jumped up and down, shook her head and shouted syllables with her arms flailing wildly. Throughout this extraordinary display Chokyi Lodro chanted without missing a beat, while his entourage watched in wonder. Presumably nine-year-old Sogyal was present. If so, his mother's behaviour must have left an indelible impression.

As a child Chokyi Lodro swallowed half a cup of liquid mercury by mistake. No immediate adverse effects on his health were observed at the time, which led his biographers to believe that he must have been an "unusual being" manifesting an "indisputable display of realisation."[16]

Later in life Lodro may have used Tibetan medicines that contained purified mercury. It is possible that he suffered from neurological symptoms consistent with mercury poisoning – for example, his emotional instability and autonomic nervous system dysfunction noted in anecdotal evidence.

Even if we give Sogyal the benefit of the doubt that he genuinely did absorb some of the "feeling" and "intuitive understanding" of Vajrayana/Dzogchen from uncle Lodro, it is beyond doubt that this relationship also included horror, dread and fear. It is not clear whether as a child Sogyal was physically assaulted by Chokyi Lodro, but the influences he must have experienced included domestic violence, the subjugation of inferiors by force and the alleged prolonging of a lama's life via sexual relations with a young woman.

Photographs taken between 1955 and 1960 show Sogyal dressed as a monk, but there is no evidence that he was ever ordained. Nothing in his personal history suggests that Sogyal experienced a religious vocation. Sogyal himself admits, "I was a naughty child, none of my tutors were able to discipline me."[17]

Aided by the formidable British woman Freda Bedi, in 1961 the Dalai Lama established the Young Lamas' Home School, set up to provide a comprehensive Buddhist and Western education for young tulkus who had escaped from Tibet. But despite his supposed status as a reincarnation, Sogyal was not invited to join them.

Sogyal's mother decided he should receive a modern Western education, that he should learn English and "know the ways of the outside world."[18] Aided by the Sikkimese royal family, they managed to get a place for him at the Roman Catholic St. Augustine's School in Kalimpong. When they took Sogyal to school for the first time they probably lied about his birth date, making him three years younger. The motive is obvious – it was Sogyal's only chance to receive an effective primary education.

Together with his brother Thigyal, Sogyal joined the class of 1960 at St. Augustine's. Thigyal and his other classmates were less than half his age. Presumably Sogyal was assigned to the first class as a 13-year-old because he was barely literate in English and had yet to master the Roman script. Tselu has held forth at some length about the difference between Sogyal and his classmates – pointing out his precociousness but glossing over his real age and the fact that he actually lagged behind other 13-year-olds.

Thigyal and Sogyal were boarders at St Augustine's, while the rest of their family continued to live in Sikkim. Thigyal recalls that Sogyal used to swap his uniform for monastic robes after school: "He used to be called Lama-la in school and had shorter hair than most other students."[19] Even so, Sogyal's schooldays are in stark contrast with his half-brother Dzogchen Rinpoche's formative years: the latter received private Buddhist tuition in their parental home from the age of six.

Sogyal has suggested that while studying at St. Augustine's he also took teachings from Dudjom Rinpoche and Dilgo Khyentse Rinpoche, who he describes as "his other primary teachers." But it is hard to see how they could have acted as Sogyal's personal tutors. Sogyal lacked a thorough grounding in Buddhism and was a full-time schoolboy. Dudjom and Khyentse Rinpoches were Buddhist heavyweights with responsibilities as leaders of Tibetan exiles in acute distress.

It therefore seems unlikely that his contact with these masters consisted of anything more than occasional audiences, together with other family members, or attendance at group teachings and empowerments. In *The Tibetan Book of Living and Dying* Sogyal mentions that he had "no personal connection" with the late great Dudjom Rinpoche until he was in his early 20s.[20] Dilgo Khyentse Rinpoche lived in Bhutan, more than 300 kilometres from Kalimpong, so he could not have taught Sogyal on a regular basis while the latter was at St. Augustine's.

The choice of this school does not indicate that Chokyi Lodro and Sogyal's parents were concerned about his Buddhist training. If it had been a priority, Sogyal could have combined a religious education with a modern one in English at Enchey High School in Gangtok – or received private tuition, like Dzogchen Rinpoche. It seems much more likely that the Lakar family wanted their eldest son to be groomed for a career as a businessman. Kalimpong was a commercial hub and its British-style schools attracted pupils from all over India and neighbouring countries.

Sogyal left St. Augustine's School in 1966, aged 19. He has said that he became a teacher there, albeit briefly: "I taught cathechism as well as other things."[21]

He subsequently enrolled as an undergraduate in philosophy at the University of Delhi's St. Stephen's College, one of India's most prestigious colleges. This choice also suggests a secular career path. St. Stephen's graduates are found in the civil service, arts, literature, business, education, journalism, law, social work, sport and film. Religious figureheads are conspicuous by their absence.

Sogyal's autobiographical statements contain very little information about his studies there, but there is no evidence that he was awarded an academic degree. His name is absent from the distinguished alumni list, which is remarkable, given the celebrity status he achieved in the West.

St. Augustine's and St. Stephen's were both affiliated with Cambridge University in England. This connection may have facilitated Sogyal's transition from India to Cambridge – though there are several differing accounts of the circumstances of his arrival there.

In the mid-1950s members of Kham's social and religious elite were keenly aware of Chairman Mao's expansionist rhetoric and of the Red Army poised for invasion on their borders. As anxiety levels rose, their primary concern was to facilitate escape into the Himalayan border regions for their revered high lamas.

The 16th Karmapa fled to Sikkim with a storehouse of treasure, including gold, silver, precious and semi-precious stones, together with the Vajra Crown. Known as the Black Hat, this item represents the authority of the Karmapa lineage. Dudjom Rinpoche settled in Darjeeling, Kalu Rinpoche in Kalimpong and others in Bhutan and Nepal. They were the pampered and protected lucky ones who made relatively easy journeys into exile.

Chokyi Lodro and the Lakar family's year-long trek was disguised as a pilgrimage. They did indeed visit many sacred sites and monasteries, but their destination was never in doubt. And the master never had any intention of returning to his gompa.

As Chinese soldiers slaughtered their way into and across Tibet, most Tibetans who fled for their lives lost all their material assets. Enduring extreme hardships, they struggled through the mountain ranges, dodging Chinese patrols. Many died along the way.

These perilous expeditions are described in vivid detail in John Avedon's book, *In Exile from the Land of Snows*:

> *On waking at sunset, Tempa's family gazed out over a vaulted world of jagged peaks and indigo sky, the sere, umber-coloured hills of Tibet beginning to glow in the fading light far below. After a brief meal of melted snow, dried meat and roasted barley, they moved upward again, the moonlight so bright on the snows and ice their eyes had to be shielded every few steps. By dawn, all were exhausted. Tempa's youngest sister had started vomiting from the thin air and altitude, the others had lost their appetites. Without eating, they fell asleep under an overhang in a depression between spires.*[22]

The 14th Dalai Lama's escape followed a similar pattern of high drama and great danger. There's an element of Tibetan magic around his escape from his summer residence near Lhasa. He consulted an oracle, who told him to go immediately. He did this not only under the noses of Chinese guards ordered to keep him under strict surveillance – but also, disguised as a soldier with a rifle on his shoulder, he slipped past a crowd of angry Tibetans that had gathered to protect him.

"I could sense the presence of a great mass of humanity as I stumbled on," he writes in his autobiography, *Freedom in Exile*. "But they did not take any notice of us and, after a few minutes' walk, we were once more alone. We had successfully negotiated our way through the crowd, but now there were the Chinese to deal with. The thought of being captured terrified me."[23]

So too did the escape from Kham led by the young tulkus, Trungpa Rinpoche and Akong Rinpoche, who later went on to found Samye Ling in Scotland, the first Tibetan Buddhist meditation centre in the West. They started out with a party of 300 refugees. By the time they reached India only 13 of them were still alive.

Some 80,000 Tibetans fled their homeland during the first wave of refugees in 1959. Many more followed them into exile. They found themselves destitute in an alien culture. Many fell victim to diseases like TB, which were largely unknown on the high-altitude Tibetan plateau. The young Dalai Lama shouldered an enormous responsibility for his refugee compatriots. It is widely acknowledged that he has made a good job of it.

When the Lakar family fled to Sikkim they arrived as paupers. From being bigwigs in Tibet they were now dependent on the goodwill of anyone who might be willing to support them. The Tibetan elite is notoriously haughty, so it must have been a painful humiliation for them. It was implicit in the clan code of conduct that Sogyal, as the eldest son, would be responsible for re-establishing the family fortunes. Indeed, one of the tropes passed around on the Tibetan Buddhist jungle drums is that his mother ordered him go west and make money.

Sogyal with the Dalai Lama during the latter's first visit to England in 1973

4

Drugs, David and Dharma

In 1973 Mary Finnigan received a letter from her friend, the late Zina Rachevsky, suggesting she might like to contact "a young Nyingma tulku called Sogyal," who was accompanying "a prince of Sikkim" while both were being treated for TB at a sanatorium in Cambridge. Zina had been in retreat for two years at a remote monastery in the Solu-Kumbhu region of the Himalayan foothills in Nepal. It is entirely possible that she was mistaken about the sanatorium. Sogyal's own version of events and other historical references state that he went to Cambridge to study Comparative Religion at Trinity College, in tandem with his role as companion to Prince Tenzin Namgyal of Sikkim.

Mary takes up the Sogyal story, starting with how her personal lifeline led to a meeting that triggered a tsunami of repercussions.

During the mid-1960s I went through a profound paradigm shift – from suburban single mother and mainstream journalist working for a national newspaper into a fully-fledged member of the Alternative Society.

This came about because I was busted for a tiny amount of herbal cannabis while working undercover on a story about drug dealing in London. In 1967 this was a new phenomenon and, as such, rich pickings for shock horror media content. In those days the fear and prejudice agenda focused on the hippie movement on the news pages, while fashion and lifestyle features extolled the glories of psychedelic music, art and design. I was an inexperienced young reporter at the time but still noticed the hypocrisy and double standards.

The arrest was a stroke of bad luck and bad timing, which landed me in prison for nine weeks. I actually received a nine-month sentence after my first lawyer bungled my defence. I replaced him with a solicitor referred by the hippie drug counselling organisation Release. He briefed a barrister called Michael Sherrard, who got me out of prison on appeal with an absolute discharge.

During my research into the London drugs scene, I met several members of what was then a small psychedelic elite. The majority of 1960s hippies were middle- to upper-class university-educated twenty-somethings. They launched the London Underground simultaneously with the cataclysmic social upheavals that originated in San Francisco.

I soon realised that my rebellious nature dovetailed neatly with their world view – which rejected pretty well everything connected with the binary black/white, right/wrong "straight" society perspective.

My new friends endorsed a more holistic approach, replacing conventional wisdom with a fresh collection of values drawn from oriental sources, primary among them what became known as the hippie bible – *The Tibetan Book of the Dead*. I was intrigued and became an enthusiastic convert.

The profound insight many of us gained from LSD was the most powerful driver behind the 60s social/political/spiritual revolution. This was the time when a whole generation of young people discovered drugs. There were lots of them available and we all tried one or more, but it was LSD that had the most potent effect on our psycho-emotional responses.

Out went a mechanistic world view and in came Gaia, with human beings and all life forms integrated into the vibrant totality of planet Earth – and its place as a tiny speck in the cosmos.

The drug culture was in its energetic infancy, proclaiming the gospel of love, peace and freedom to all with ears to hear and eyes to see. One aspect of the freedom component manifested as cheerfully guilt-free promiscuity. For the first time in human history women had access to reliable birth control via the Pill.

This *volte face* in attitudes, insights and behaviour was a lot to take on board for a young woman from an ultra-conventional background. It took some time to sink in, especially as I was still in recovery from the prison ordeal. So much change ran in parallel with so many new influences – in particular, musical ones. My taste was incubated in the classics, but a seismic shift occurred during a stoned encounter with The Byrds. Every cell in my body woke up and danced and after that it was a rock 'n' roll all the way.

I lived with my two children in a large flat with a 60-foot garden in the south London suburb of Beckenham. My new friends accepted invitations to visit, so our home soon turned into an outpost of big city hippiedom.

I sold a fine antique dining set, replacing it with a home-made revolving table about 18 inches high, some mattresses and a colourful collection of floor cushions. I bought oriental throws, candles, incense, beads and caftans. Mozart, Beethoven and Brahms LPs were neglected in favour of, to quote just a few examples, the Rolling Stones, the Beatles, Led Zeppelin, Pink Floyd, the Grateful Dead, The Incredible String Band and Bob Dylan.

One day in April 1969 a young musician called David Bowie took up residence with us as our lodger.[24] He was broke and out of work, and I was on a five-year break from the five-day week. From the start we did not observe landlady-lodger conventions. We shared the space and the cannabis – we cooked, ate and spent a lot of time together.

David spent most of his days composing new songs, but usually after dinner we rolled spliffs and talked – cosy, intimate fireside conversations. During one of them I was surprised when he told me he'd never done LSD. He hinted that the prospect of losing control during the psychedelic experience terrified him. This puzzled me, because up to that point I'd never had a bad trip and I enjoyed losing control.

Apart from my close contact with his prodigious creative output, I found David's experience of Tibetan Buddhism extremely interesting. I'd dipped into Zen meditation and I'd read *The Tibetan Book of the Dead*. The non-theistic, contemplative basis of Buddhism was calling me – I saw it as a logical extension of LSD, but David bypassed the chemical catalyst.

David told me about meeting the Tibetan lama, Chime Rinpoche, at the Hampstead Buddhist Vihara. Chime became David's meditation teacher, mentor and friend. One of only four lamas in the UK in 1969, he was a monk in maroon robes – although, in common with most lamas who migrated to the West, he disrobed soon afterwards when the temptations of the flesh became irresistible. When David Bowie died in January 2016, Chime recorded a tribute and prayers for him which can be viewed on YouTube.

David said that for a while he was serious about Buddhist practice. Never one to do anything by halves, he moved music to the back burner and went to stay at Samye Ling in Scotland.

Back in 1967 Samye Ling was in its infancy. It was acquired by a small group of students of Trungpa Rinpoche and his colleague, Akong Rinpoche. There was one building – a dilapidated Victorian hunting lodge called Johnstone House, set in several acres of land bordering the River Esk in Dumfriesshire. It was exotic, romantic, draughty and uncomfortable. Nearly everyone who went there fell under its spell.

David was no exception. For a while he considered being ordained as a monk, but the music and the poetry would not go away.

"On the cushion it echoed through my meditation," he said. "It was with me when walking in the hills and, sooner rather than too late, I realised I was not being true to myself."

David laughed when he told me it was a huge relief when he caught the overnight train from Lockerbie and headed back to show business in London.

I was infected by David's enthusiasm so, as his trajectory to mega-stardom took off, I visited Samye Ling for the first time, determined to get to grips with Tibetan Buddhist meditation. This happened soon after David and I organised the UK's first free festival in Beckenham in August 1969.

After the intensity of running an Arts Lab and putting on a festival with David, I was physically and emotionally exhausted. My ex took care of the kids and I took the overnight train to Lockerbie. A cheerful bloke called Jock met me at the station and as we drove through the lowland hills, I had a strong sensation that this was the start of a new phase and that I would finally get serious about Tibetan Buddhist practice.

It turned out to be a false start, because Trungpa Rinpoche had moved out and Akong was away on a visit to Tibet. The centre was functioning more like a rest home for burned-out hippies rather than a Buddhist retreat.

Akong had left his younger brother Jamdra in charge. Jamdra had Jimi Hendrix hair and slouched around in velvet bell-bottoms and an Afghan coat. He was thoroughly bored and miserable. Samye Ling was the last place he wanted to be. Jamdra was there because big brother had pulled rank. Jamdra was yearning to get back to sex 'n' drugs 'n' rock 'n' roll in London.

After meeting the 16th Karmapa, the head of the Kagyu school of Tibetan Buddhism and one of the all-time great contemplative yogis, Jamdra had a Road-to-Damascus experience. He abandoned hedonism, was ordained a monk, spent several years in retreat and is now known as Lama Yeshe Losal. He has been in charge of Samye Ling and its various offshoots, including island retreat centres, for many years.

Akong Rinpoche was murdered in 2011 by a disgruntled Tibetan while on a visit to his charitable projects in eastern Tibet. Trungpa Rinpoche went to America after marrying Diana Pybus, a 16-year-old English girl.

As I started to explore Samye Ling, Nick Jennings, one of my friends from the Beckenham Arts Lab, detached himself from a group of bright young things lounging on a ha ha wall and floated towards me wearing a Gandalf cape.

Nick gave me a tour guide introduction. We checked out the shrine room, complete with ornate altar, a giant Buddha statue, thangka paintings depicting serene tantric deities, alongside fearsome creatures with bloody fangs dancing on dead bodies in a halo of flames. I loved it on sight.

I'm not sure whether this instant sense of belonging occurred via fascination with the macabre, through past-life experience, or from my recent psychedelic explorations. Maybe a combination of all three. Whatever it was, it took root into my DNA and has remained there ever since.

I stayed at Samye Ling for two weeks and eventually encountered an American who taught me basic breath awareness meditation. It felt entirely natural to get up before dawn, shuffle into the shrine room with a few other people and sit for an hour cross-legged, straight-backed and shrouded in a blanket.

This experience established a pattern that has endured. I don't get up so early nowadays and as the years pass I do more physical yoga than silent sitting, but I am forever thankful for the karmic pathway which led me into Tibetan Buddhism.

I must admit that my appreciation for the Tibetan Buddhist tradition was severely challenged by the experiences and events that led to writing this book. But thanks to the quality of the transmission and teachings of my root lama, the late Chogyal Namkhai Norbu, I managed to stay connected. I also owe a thank you in this respect to my husband Chris Gilchrist, who supported me through periods of doubt and insecurity.

Through the roller coaster ride of the human condition, through periods of shock and disillusionment, I have managed to hang in there. I have witnessed extraordinary manifestations – in the true sense of the word, extra-ordinary. I have come painfully face to face with my demons – and because I have been taught Tibetan Buddhist skilful means, their power over me has diminished.

This probably seems opaque to people unfamiliar with the esoteric contemplative traditions. On the Tibetan landscape these traditions are known as the Vajrayana, the path of transformation, and Dzogchen, the path of self-realisation. It is not easy for anyone to make the transition from intellectual speculation into the dimension of direct insight – what those who are on this journey describe as Wisdom Beyond Words.

This powerful and sophisticated tradition developed over centuries, as indigenous shamanic practices met and merged with Indian Tantra, brought to Tibet by legendary masters like Padmasambhava. The reason it became so impressive and effective is because pre-Chinese Tibet was a theocratic society, with its central focus on enabling as many people as possible to study and practise Vajrayana/Dzogchen.

By modern democratic standards, Tibet was mired in medieval feudalism and was long overdue for radical reform. Sadly, when this came, Chairman Mao's Communist zealots regarded it as a moral obligation to destroy Tibet's religious infrastructure. Today, the survival of one of the world's most comprehensive Buddhist traditions hangs in the balance, largely dependent on Western patronage.

I returned to Samye Ling many times over many years, sometimes just to hang out there and meditate, sometimes to do solitary retreat. It took several visits and many hours on the cushion before I experienced what could be described as a contemplative breakthrough.

When it happened, Akong Rinpoche was back in charge. One afternoon I settled into a meditation box favoured by practitioners in the Kagyu tradition. It was comfortably lined with cushions and rugs. I was enclosed, relaxed and at ease. I have no idea how long I stayed there, but I do recall Akong coming into the room quietly to check up on me. It was dark when a thought came: "Wow – this is bliss!" That was when I emerged from a state beyond time, beyond words, beyond explanation.

I have a friend who works as a gardener in England during the summer months to make enough money to stay in retreat in India during the winter. Asked why he chose this lifestyle, he replied: "If you understand the value of Tibetan Buddhism, you really do have to give it top priority."

Trungpa Rinpoche advised wannabe meditators not to embark on the Vajrayana. "But if you must, do it one hundred per cent," he cautioned.

I do not want to give a false impression that Tibetan Buddhist meditation is easy – or that everyone attracted to it finds a way into profound levels of realisation. This is certainly not the case. Trungpa Rinpoche gave sound advice. Over the decades that followed my first encounter, I have established that some contemplative paradigm shifts embed into the mindstream, but mostly it's a rollercoaster ride. Just when you think you've made progress, everything you think you've learned evaporates, and it's back to basics. This is always personal, and the path is different for each individual. A wise and experienced teacher can, however, help you to stay motivated and give useful advice on overcoming obstacles.

In 1970 I set off on the must-have hippie experience. With an American friend I flew from London to Bombay, aiming to stay for six months in India and Nepal. I have been heavily criticised for this because I abandoned my children into the care of their father.

Our journey took us to the ancient holy city of Varanasi and from there to Kathmandu. There was lots of fun in Kathmandu. We met up with friends from London, hung out around the exquisitely carved pagoda temples that suffered tragic damage in the 2015 earthquake – and dropped acid on full-moon night in Swayambhu, close to the magnificent stupa, together with at least a hundred similarly intoxicated Westerners.

It was all exciting, but that was not the reason we were there. My friend Carolyn and I had been through the psychedelic experience, we had immersed ourselves in the delicious hedonism of sex 'n' drugs 'n' rock 'n' roll. At this point in our lives, we wanted to find out if it was leading us into another deeper, more challenging, and less physically and mentally dangerous arena. We were eager to learn and keen to find experts to teach us.

But even in Nepal we soon discovered that accomplished English-speaking Tibetan lamas were very thin on the ground. After asking around for several days, we were eventually directed to a woman known as "the Russian princess." It transpired that she lived on Kopan hill, above the Boudhnath stupa a few miles from the city centre. We took a bus to Boudha, paid our respects at the great stupa, and after asking directions set off for Kopan through an idyllic rural landscape.

The Russian woman was, in fact, a nun with an aristocratic Russian father, an American heiress mother – and certainly not a princess. Her name was Zina Rachevsky. Rumours about her colourful life story turned out to be true. A former international socialite, fashion model, film starlet and showgirl, Zina was a raving beauty who experienced a spiritual epiphany, renounced her attachment to the material world and was ordained a Tibetan Buddhist nun in the Gelug tradition by the Dalai Lama's junior tutor.

Zina's mission in her new life was to become a contemplative yogini – and to create an environment where Westerners could study and practise Tibetan Buddhism. It was early days at Kopan, but to our delight there were two very interesting lamas there – Thubten Yeshe and his disciple Thubten Zopa Rinpoche. They were happy to give us teachings, so we joined the small group of neophytes living on Kopan hill, a rural refuge with breath-taking views over the Kathmandu valley and the mighty Himalayan ranges beyond.[25]

We lived at Kopan for nine weeks in a wattle-and-daub farmhouse, and I have to say it was one of the happiest periods of my life. We went each day to take part in introductory teachings with the lamas. They explained the basics and gave us a sadhana, which involved visualisation of Chenrezig, the bodhisattva of compassion. Lama Yeshe was a unique and wonderfully eccentric personality. What he lacked in English vocabulary he made up for ten times over in wisdom and warmth.

I met Lama Yeshe several times afterwards. With Lama Zopa Rinpoche, he founded the FPMT (the Foundation for the Preservation of the Mahayana Tradition). Due to the quality of their transmission, Westerners eager to engage with Tibetan Buddhism flocked to Kopan, which mushroomed into a building complex that covered the entire hillside. These enthusiastic Buddhists from the developed world took the teachings back to their own countries and within a relatively short time the FPMT became a global organisation.

Meanwhile, Zina Rachevsky retired to a remote monastery in the Himalayan foothills. The woman who used be a member of the

Mary Finnigan after interviewing the Dalai Lama in Mcleod Ganj, India, 1997

super-wealthy international jet set settled into what can only be described as a hovel. A tiny one-room stone cottage with no running water, no electricity, and no sanitation. Zina stayed in retreat there for more than two years, keeping a detailed record of her contemplative experiences. She made some profound breakthroughs – and, amazingly, kept in regular touch with her friends in the outside world.

There was an immediate rapport between Zina and me. One of the mysteries around her is how she managed to send and receive letters. But she did, and when I returned to England we corresponded from time to time. In one letter Zina suggested a visit to the young Tibetan, Sogyal Tulku.

Zina died at Thubten Choling monastery in 1973. She was 47 and apparently succumbed to food poisoning. She was a fiercely determined pioneer Western Tibetan Buddhist. Her level of supercharged motivation is extremely rare, replicated by very few people I know of.

One of them is Diane Perry, an Englishwoman who was ordained as Tenzin Palmo and spent 12 years in solitary retreat in the Himalayas. Her story is told in Vicki MacKenzie's book, *Cave in the Snow*.[26]

Another is Freda Bedi, also English. She too became a nun closely linked to the late 16th Karmapa. Vicki Mckenzie and Norma Levine have both published biographies about her. And there's the legendary Belgian grande dame, Alexandra David-Néel, who described her time snowed into a retreat cave in Tibet as "an aristocratic taste for solitude."[27]

5

Squats and Sogyal

1973 was the year I gave up on Beckenham. For some time before I left, my London friends turned up grinning broadly and filthy dirty. They came for a bath and some home comforts, telling fascinating stories about their adventures opening up empty houses owned by the London Borough of Camden. It transpired that an entire district of Kentish Town was affected by planning blight and there were houses galore being claimed and squatted by my anarchic, idealistic middle-class friends – as well as people from a cross-section of the social spectrum who for one reason or another had become homeless.

Hoppy, Sue, Mike, Robert, Tony and others urged me to join in. I resisted for a while, but eventually it seemed like a sensible option. I had been on a five-year sabbatical from paid employment. I was broke, bored, restless and in need of a reinvigorating change.

My first squat was a rat-infested dump in a terrace of houses that were beyond redemption. But I joined an interesting group of housemates. There was an architecture student called Jack Taghioff who became my lover and the father of my third child. There was Rob, the son of a Hollywood film producer, and Nicole (forgotten her real name), a French student. Jack was super good at making wrecked houses liveable. He devised heavy-duty polythene double glazing, by-passed the company fuse and wired up the whole house to provide electricity, repaired floorboards, and laid carpet.

The Basset Street squat was short-lived but during my time there I met Cathy Graham, a journalist from New Zealand who worked at the television news agency Visnews (long since subsumed into Reuters). She arranged for me to meet the Head of News and from then I started to make a living again as a freelance scriptwriter.

I also met members of the embryonic Tibetan Buddhist community in London. Some of them were living in nearby squats and others came to visit. Then I remembered Zina's introduction to the Tibetan guy called Sogyal Tulku.

Around this time, we were evicted from Basset Street and, in an extraordinary stroke of good fortune, I was offered a spacious squat with a big garden at 56 Prince of Wales Road. Jack, Rob, Nicole and I moved into a massively improved lifestyle. The house had a separate toilet, a bathtub, gas, electricity, running water and a telephone. We each had our own bedroom, with communal living, kitchen and dining areas. By squat standards it was a palace. It had a very tight front door – but even so a local thief managed to steal our TV and then sell it back to us.

Jack installed a separate wash area with an electric water heater on the ground floor. In the basement he re-routed the plumbing to connect up with a gas geyser in the kitchen-cum-bathroom. We paid our utility bills and offered Camden money for the rates – but they were not interested in anything that could be construed as legal occupation.

I had more disposable income during my three years at 56 Prince of Wales Road than at any other time in my life. Jack and I bought an almost-new Minivan and one sunny spring day in 1973 I drove it to Cambridge for my first meeting with Sogyal.

Back then Sogyal was a slim figure with jaw-length black hair and an interesting face. He was not handsome, but I could see that women would find him attractive. He wore a white, open-neck shirt, dark trousers, and a welcoming smile as he strode towards me, hand outstretched. I noticed that the smile morphed into a fleeting head-to-toe appraisal, the look of a bloke on the alert for sex.

We strolled together in what I understood to be the sanatorium gardens, then sat on a bench in the sunshine and talked about Tibetan Buddhism. He spoke reasonably good but heavily accented English. He was quite solemn and certainly not flirtatious. In fact, apart from that first glance Sogyal never made anything even vaguely resembling a sexual advance to me. Given his reputation as a playboy even in those days, I was not sure whether to take this as a compliment to me as a serious Buddhist – or to mean that I did not measure up to his standard of feminine allure. Maybe I put him off by mentioning I was a journalist.

Sogyal said that as a Nyingma lama, his focus was on Dzogchen. This was the first time I'd heard the word. Intrigued, I asked if he could recommend a Dzogchen practice. He disappeared for a few minutes, returning with a small booklet which, he said, he would give me on loan on condition that I would return it. After I agreed, he explained its contents.

It was Dudjom Rinpoche's version of the *Guru Yoga of the White A*. I was impressed and very grateful.

Sogyal and I parted company amicably, exchanging phone numbers and with a cheerful "See you soon." Several weeks passed before I heard from him. I had photocopied the practice booklet and was beginning to wonder how I could return it, when one evening the phone rang. On the line from Cambridge, Sogyal announced that he was moving to London, with the intention of setting up a dharma centre. He asked if I would help him.

Tibetan lamas who spoke good English and were eager to teach Westerners were as rare as hen's teeth in London in 1974. Based on my first encounter with Sogyal, I was happy to oblige – though not confident I could be useful. After thinking it over I called some friends to ask if they would be interested in meeting a young lama who wanted to set up a centre in London.

In the mid-1970s many members of the first generation of hippies were settling down back home after their Oriental adventures and experiments with psychedelic drugs. Most of them acknowledged their interest in altered states of consciousness but realised it was time to stop using powerful chemicals. They had encountered exiled Tibetan lamas and monks (not all monks are lamas and not all lamas are monks) in India and Nepal and were keen to pursue their embryonic interest in the Vajrayana, inspired by the promise of authentic spiritual experience, leading to profound insights and what now (several decades later) seems like an impossible dream – enlightenment in one lifetime. At the time Chime Rinpoche was the only lama giving teachings in London.

Many of these travellers were drawn into the squatting communities that had sprung up across London because they offered ultra-low-cost living and the company of like-minded people. When I put out my feelers, the response was 100% positive, so I decided to introduce Sogyal by throwing a dinner party.

Among the people who came, several turned out to be Sogyal's first Western students. They included Judy Allan and Mike Farmer, who were already Tibetan Buddhist practitioners, an American Taoist-aroma-therapist called John Steele, my partner Jack, a Swedish yoga teacher – and Dominique Side, who fell instantly in love with Sogyal and has remained unwaveringly loyal to him ever since.

I encountered Patrick Gaffney sometime later, after Sogyal had moved to London and was staying with another pioneer Tibetan Buddhist in Swiss Cottage. Patrick met Sogyal while still an undergraduate at Cambridge – probably at one of a few lectures on Comparative Religion that Sogyal attended. Patrick's devotion to Sogyal is one of the wonders of the Tibetan

Buddhist world. Sogyal is on record saying that without Patrick as his right-hand man he could never have achieved his fame and fortune.

During the early days in London, friendships with Sogyal were informal and pretty much on a level playing field. But he already had a reputation as a womaniser, and it soon became obvious to his core group of followers that their new-found guru had a voracious sexual appetite. He moved in with Dominique Side for a while, but their amorous relationship was short-lived. She was devastated when she found out he was not monogamous.

Sogyal needed somewhere to live and a place to teach – ideally under one roof. But even in the 1970s buildings in central London large enough to fulfil this function were extremely expensive – way beyond the limited means of a bunch of squatters.

Sogyal taught for the first time in the karate dojo at the Polytantric, a squatted community centre in Kentish Town. It was cold and the room was draughty. Four of us sat on the floor, huddled around a one-bar electric heater – Sogyal, the late Judy Allan, her then-boyfriend Kristoff and me. It was the best we could do but we agreed that it was not sustainable.

Despite being one of the roughest environments in a very rough neighbourhood, the Polytantric had its moment of glory. Inhabited by some of the most damaged individuals in the squatting community, it was dirty, regularly trashed, and notorious for anti-social behaviour. Kristoff managed to achieve a minor miracle by converting the largest upstairs room into a karate dojo. It had a polished wood floor, functional windows, and several sturdy locks on the door. Kristoff was a heavy dude, karate trained and permanently shadowed by a bad-tempered dog. The druggies and crazies in the basement steered clear.

One day a buzz echoed through the squats: a legendary high lama, the 16th Karmapa, was visiting London for the first time. He had an awesome reputation that extended beyond the Tibetan Buddhist faithful. Kristoff accosted me in the street, asking if the Karmapa would accept an invitation to bless the dojo at the Polytantric. I replied that it was a very good idea and told him to direct the invitation via Akong Rinpoche.

Some hours later a dazed but delighted Kristoff came to find me with the news that not only was the Karmapa coming to the Poly but he was bringing his entire retinue, including four monks and at least 30 other people – and that it was happening that evening.

"He's going to do something called the Mahakala Puja," he said. "So I'll see if I can let people know and we'd better sort the place out a bit."

The activity that followed was nothing short of incredible. Within an hour Jack Taghioff had designed and printed a leaflet. Within two hours it had been posted through the letter box of every squat in Chalk Farm, Kentish Town and Camden Town.

An army of people appeared to clean and beautify the Poly. Nobody asked them to come, and very few of them had anything to do with Tibetan Buddhism. Nobody took charge of the operation, yet everything happened without a hiccup. When the cleaning was finished more people arrived with bales of silk, wall hangings, thangka paintings, quilts, cushions, rugs, ornaments, shrine objects, candles, incense, flasks of tea, and a variety of Buddhist statues.

Judy Allan and I went off to collect flowers. It was very early spring and there weren't many around. But the caretaker at Highgate Cemetery raided some graves ("the living need these more than the dead") – a lady carved branches off her beloved winter flowering tree, and all the flower shops in the neighbourhood gave us something. We returned to the Polytantric when we couldn't fit any more into the car.

We found it completely transformed. Every inch of wall space up the stairs, along the corridor and in the dojo had been hung with exotic fabrics. There was carpet on the stairs and along the corridor. In the dojo a platform was built and covered with quilts and cushions, with an altar in front of it. There was another big altar to one side. The room was softened with candlelight and scented with incense, and the ceiling was tented with silk. There were already masses of flowers and we only just managed to find space for ours. Ten minutes after we got back His Holiness the 16th Karmapa arrived. Those in the know kept their fingers crossed that the rickety staircase would not give way under his considerable weight. But he sailed up it, wheezing a little and blasting us all into bliss with his smile.

People were packed like sardines into the dojo and the overflow went down the stairs and out into the street. We had to leave enough room for Kristoff's karate teacher to perform – but first the Karmapa and his monks from the high Himalayas chanted the Mahakala Puja before an audience of London squatters who had taken part in a small miracle.

The Karmapa stayed for as long as his schedule would allow. He talked to us via an interpreter and asked penetrating questions about karate. After he left, everything came down off the walls, precious objects were reclaimed and the Polytantric was left as it had been before – though for a few days it was a little cleaner.

A year or so later the bailiffs moved in, the squatters were evicted, and the demolition gang got to work. But halfway through, everything ground to a halt, and for several months one wall of the dojo was exposed to public view. Painted on it was a giant multi-coloured Buddha.

The Karmapa's visit to the Poly could only be a one-off and, apart from the dauntingly orthodox Buddhist Society, there was no place anywhere in London where an ambitious young lama could set up his stall in order to meet the burgeoning demand for Tibetan Buddhist teachings.

Salvation came in the person of my then-friend Jeanette. Visiting 56 Prince of Wales Road one evening, she remarked that no-one would know it was a squat unless they'd been told.

"If we weren't here, this house would have been wrecked by now," I replied. "Vandalised beyond redemption." Jeanette fell silent for a while then said, "There's an empty house owned by Brent Council next door to where I live. Might be worth checking it out."

So it was that a posse of aspiring Vajrayana Buddhists set off to inspect the premises. It turned out to be beyond our wildest dreams. A large, apparently well-kept detached 1930s house set in spacious gardens on quiet, leafy Chatsworth Road in Kilburn, West London. We were experienced squatters, and after a careful recce broke into the house and claimed it in the name of the Nyingma tradition of Tibetan Buddhism.

It was a good thing we knew what we were doing, because a couple of days later Brent discovered that their valuable property had been squatted. To say that they were not well pleased is a huge understatement.

The council sent bailiffs to get rid of us. Three very large, very intimidating thugs stood on one side of well secured French windows. We stood defiantly on the other, trembling a bit but in full knowledge of our rights according to the law. There was slim, small Ann, teenage Felix in Tibetan monastic attire, and a couple more of us.

They glared at us and threatened to break the windows. We glared back and refused to budge.

"We are in," we said. "If you want to get us out you need a court order." The standoff continued for a few very tense minutes, then, grumbling insults under their breath, the bailiffs withdrew.

Brent's next move came a few days later. We were busy setting up the house to suit our needs when the electricity, water and gas disappeared. This was an illegal manoeuvre because in those days the utilities had a statutory obligation to provide services for occupied premises, regardless of their status.

Once again, our streetwise squatters knew their rights. One of us approached the Brent Trades Council, told them what we were doing – and although Jack Dromey, the head honcho, had no interest in Buddhism, he decided to support us. He told Brent his members would withdraw their labour unless our utilities were restored. We cheered the men who came round to turn them back on.

Chatsworth Road was a fine house, complete with parquet flooring, two bathrooms, five bedrooms, a fully functional kitchen, and a sitting room big enough to convert into a shrine room. While this was happening, we had our first experience of Sogyal the slave driver.

He moved in as soon as the house was habitable and from then on took up the role of director of works. He sat around and gave orders – we hammered floorboards, built shelves, moved furniture, fitted carpets and curtains, hung thangkas, built an altar, and made sure that everyone, including the boss, was fed. We did this as a team of volunteer labourers and we funded and/or donated the food, the materials and the furnishings.

We did this willingly and in high excitement. It was enormously good fun, despite the hard work. Our enthusiasm was infectious and, as news spread around the hippie grapevine that a Tibetan lama was setting up a centre in London, more volunteers showed up and offered to help.

One of them was my partner Jack, whose building skills were in high demand in the squatting community. Jack rose to the challenge but was not impressed with Sogyal's attitude. One day he hit his thumb while hammering nails. A stream of expletives later he said that from then onwards the esteemed lama would be known as Sir Joe Toolkit rather than Sogyal Tulku.

It's a pity there are no photos of the Chatsworth Road shrine room, because, considering the ultra-quick conversion and minimal resources, it was a work of art. I think Sogyal was grateful because, while we were adding the finishing touches, he put out a three-line whip to the titans of Vajrayana/Dzogchen. "Time to come to London," was the gist of it. "I have a place ready for you."

His appeal was spectacularly successful. There's no doubt about the effectiveness of Sogyal's role as a scout for Tibetan Buddhism's transition into the developed world. He came on his own with few contacts, no Buddhist education and no experience, but the big boys were waiting in the wings.

Dodrupchen Rinpoche was the first to accept the invitation. Born in 1927 in eastern Tibet, in 2017 he was still teaching at the age of 90. In September 2020 he was still alive but confined to a wheelchair in his residence in Sikkim. He was one of only a very few senior lamas to officiate at Sogyal's funeral and cremation in Sikkim.

I'd never heard of Dodrupchen, but his arrival must have resonated with more knowledgeable Buddhists because, when he came to Chatsworth Road to give a Guru Rinpoche initiation, the shrine room was packed to capacity. We sat knee to knee and elbow to elbow. There were not enough cushions for every bottom in the room, but none of us noticed the discomfort. We were present at a unique, magical happening.

Thus, one of the great lineage holders of the Nyingma tradition took us on a journey of self-discovery in an illegally occupied building. I think it fair to say that most of us there that evening "got" the initiation – a profound, almost shocking experience that took me totally by surprise. At the time I had no idea about the impact of authentic nonverbal transmission.

A succession of VIP lamas followed on from Dodrupchen Rinpoche. Among them Tara Tulku and his monks who were on a chanting tour of the UK, and the late, great Dilgo Khyentse Rinpoche. I "took refuge" with him – the Buddhist equivalent of baptism.

The response to these events exceeded all expectations, with capacity crowds turning up every time. Everything that happened at Chatsworth Road was publicised at short notice by word of mouth and had irresistible appeal, because nothing like it had ever taken place in London. We were trailblazers to a movement that gained momentum during the mid- to late 70s – and exploded across planet Earth in the 1980s.

During the early days in London, Sogyal acted mostly as a translator and assistant for the older generation of yogi-lamas who fled Tibet following the Chinese takeover in 1959. These included the head of the Nyingma order, Dudjom Rinpoche, a lama of legendary repute held in the highest regard by Tibetans and Westerners alike.

Sogyal baulked at inviting Dudjom Rinpoche to Chatsworth Road for his first teaching visit to London. Instead, he booked a venue just off Oxford Street in the West End. Pretty well everyone with an interest in Buddhism turned up for his teachings and empowerments. The hall held twice as many people as the shrine room in Kilburn and was packed to capacity.

The 16th Karmpa's yogic intensity blazed from him. Dudjom's realisation was equally impressive but more restrained. I warmed to him when he apologised for not always having a sharp focus on the nuts and bolts of the relative world. As an example of this, he described losing his luggage at an airport.

On 4 July 1975 Jack and I took delivery of our son Daniel. He was born after a short labour at University College Hospital's maternity unit in the West End of London. He was a sturdy nine-pound baby and from the moment I saw him I was ecstatically in love with him. I'd had my two elder children more along the lines of what the UK's Princess Anne described as an "occupational hazard" of being a wife. I wanted Daniel, so it was a much stronger emotional bond.

Sogyal came to visit while I was "lying in" after the birth – along with a group of friends. We were chatting around my bed when I noticed that Sogyal was no longer there – nor was baby Daniel. A quick investigation located Sogyal sitting in an armchair in the ward day area with my baby in his arms. He was crooning mantras softly. When he noticed me, he said that Daniel's full name should be Daniel Urgyen Dorje. Urgyen is one of the names of the founder of Tibetan Buddhism, the Indian yogi-magician Padmasambhava, also known as Guru Rinpoche. So that's how we registered him a few days later – Daniel Urgyen Dorje Taghioff.

The London Borough of Brent wasted no time in applying for an eviction order for Chatsworth Road. We knew it was imminent, so the hunt for new premises became top priority. At the height of the 70s squatting movement, some London boroughs were granting short-life tenancies for their unoccupied premises. The well-informed urban activists among Sogyal's ever-growing band of followers knew about this. They presented their case to the Brent Housing Department and in due course were allocated a large, ugly, dilapidated terraced house on Princess Road, Kilburn. It was a funky area, and the house lacked the bourgeois charm of Chatsworth Road – but it was legal and seemed likely to fulfil our needs for several years.

In Princess Road, Sogyal occupied the top floor, members of his band of wannabe Buddhist yogis and yoginis lived in other rooms, while the ground floor was transformed into a shrine room. The move marked the end of our honeymoon period with Sogyal – and the start of doubts that accumulated over the following years about his capacity to function as a role model.

From day one, the residents were confronted with Sogyal's insatiable appetite for sexual conquests. One of them recalled the steady stream of young pretty women summoned for "private teachings" to the guru's abode: "Some of them would stay for a while and leave quietly, but others would flounce out shouting loud protests and slamming doors."

People who have since left Sogyal's entourage speak about a "sense of pollution," and that the succession of females into and out of his bedroom made them feel ill at ease. No one at that time identified Sogyal's behaviour as a personality disorder, but more recently health professionals have stated that he was a sex addict, suffering from an obsession as powerful as drugs, alcohol and gambling.

When Daniel was only a few months old, Jack and I separated. Life at 56 Prince of Wales Road with a new baby in the house did not suit his style. Jack maintained that he never had any intention to settle down with me – but if he delivered this message, I did not hear it. I was very unhappy for a while with hormones in overdrive, a single parent in a squat, abandoned by the father of my child. But with a little help from my friends (especially the late Judy Allan) I survived the ordeal, hired an *au pair* and went back to work.

Mary Finnigan (right) with the late John Driver (centre) and friends circa 1979

6

Doubts and Setbacks

A few years later I acquired a new boyfriend. His name was John Driver. I use the past tense because he too sadly passed away in 2014. In the 1970s he was a highly respected – bordering on legendary – Tibetan Buddhist scholar-practitioner. He was fluent in both colloquial and classical Tibetan and Sanskrit.

In the 1950s while studying at Oxford, John was one member of a small band of pioneer Western Buddhists who headed off into the Himalayan regions of India in search of Tibetan texts which had not yet been translated into Western languages. John had a particular interest in Dzogchen. During his travels he met and studied with Dudjom Rinpoche, so he was aware of the quality of Dudjom's scholarship and realisation.

This elite band of Western practitioners included Dennis Lingwood, aka Sangarakshita, who founded the Friends of the Western Buddhist Order (FWBO), now rebranded as Triratna; John Blofeldt, who wrote several early influential books about Taoism and Buddhism; and Leslie Dawson, aka Anandabodhi, aka Namgyal Rinpoche.

Lingwood and Dawson allegedly had ulterior motives for their time in the Tibetan borderlands. Both gay, they had heard – so the story goes – that young monks trained as passive sex partners in Tibetan monasteries were now turning up in Darjeeling and Kalimpong.

During his time in India John Driver also worked at The Young Lamas' Home School run by Freda Bedi. Recently escaped from Tibet, Trungpa Rinpoche was the spiritual head of the school. John taught him English and later arranged a scholarship for him to study at Oxford.

In those days, the lamas were hyper-secretive about Dzogchen – it was regarded as too subtle and too powerful for all but a select few yogis (and even fewer yoginis) who had undergone many years of rigorous training. Despite this extreme reticence, John managed to get hold of some interesting texts, which he mentioned to Sogyal when the two were introduced at a

Buddhist Society gathering. Sogyal was instantly intrigued and somewhat in awe of John. He invited John to Princess Road – and that's how we met.

Shortly afterwards the late great Dudjom Rinpoche came to London again – this time Sogyal organised his followers to set up teachings for Dudjom at Princess Road. Once again, we were shoehorned into a room designed to accommodate a family, rather than a group of around 100 people. Dudjom gave Ritod teachings over three days. They consisted of detailed instructions on what to do and how to live and behave in strict retreat. The room contained many aspiring hermits, so we paid keen attention to every word.

There was only one problem: Sogyal was translating. John sat next to me, following the text in Tibetan. I soon noticed that his usual polite demeanour had undergone a change. As the teachings progressed his brow furrowed, his lips pursed and every now and again there was a sharp intake of breath. During the first lunch break John steered me into a café down the road. He was quite angry.

"Sogyal is not translating correctly," he said. "Either he's interpreting Rinpoche's words into what he thinks is suitable for Westerners or he doesn't understand what Dudjom is saying."

I was lucky. Each night as we lay side by side in bed, John perched the Tibetan text on his chest and re-translated for me what Dudjom had said that day. It was radically different from my notes taken via Sogyal.

Everyone else in the room had to make do with Sogyal's translation and was almost certainly unaware of its shortcomings. But this knowledge, combined with Sogyal's sex antics, rang alarm bells for me. They became louder and more persistent after a conversation with John. "He makes all sorts of promises about Dzogchen and how we will receive the highest teachings, but he never seems to deliver," I said.

"Of course he doesn't," John replied. "Because he can't. He's out of his depth. Apart from some stuff he picked up from his uncle, the lama Jamyang Khyentse Chokyi Lodro, Sogyal knows very little and what he does know isn't Dzogchen."

It was acutely uncomfortable for me to hear that I had apparently facilitated a charlatan to set himself up as an authentic teacher – and in the process deceive a lot of people. With John as an exception, we were all naïve and trusting in those days because we did not have enough knowledge and experience to make informed choices.

Around this time another Englishman with sharp intelligence and a keen interest in the Nyingma yogic tradition found his way into Sogyal's orbit. In those days he was known as Ngakpa Chogyam and had already spent time with Nyingma lamas in India. He was in touch with Dudjom Rinpoche. Chogyam describes his introduction to Sogyal in his own inimitable way:

"Once, when speaking with Kyabjé Düd'jom Rinpoche in Bodha, he told me there was a Tibetan fella living in London with whom I might like to associate. He might turn out to be a friend. The idea was that we could be of possible help to each other. He was more or less my age, so it could prove a mutually beneficial association. He could improve my Tibetan, I could improve his English, and he could point me in the direction of giving teachings in Britain. The Tibetan fella had no great knowledge or retreat experience – Düd'jom Rinpoche explained – but he'd been brought up in close proximity with several quite remarkable Lamas. There'd be things I could learn from him in terms of the living-detail of Vajrayana, things that only a Tibetan would know."

The closest proximity and by far the most influential was Sogyal's uncle, Jamyang Khyentse Chokyi Lodro. Sogyal was Chokyi Lodro's protégé and because of this was designated a tulku, in line with his status alongside a revered elder. This casts doubt on Sogyal's claim to be the re-incarnation of a lama known as Terton Sogyal – a doubt confirmed to Ngakpa Chogyam by another senior Nyingma lama, Chimed Rigdzin Rinpoche.

In this context, some Tibetans are uncharacteristically candid about the fact that not all tulkus are spiritually advanced and capable of passing on the subtleties of Vajrayana/Dzogchen. The esteemed Gelug lama, the late Song Rinpoche, is on record about this:

> *I have seen one or two small boys from big families who have been recognized as incarnations just on the hope that they would be able to hold the place, the riches of the people, of the person who recognized that child as an incarnate Lama. Without consulting the spiritual advancement, the inner attainment – I have seen one or two cases of such enthronements and they come from big families and do not have any spiritual advancement, the inner attainment.*[28]

Back in the early days of Orgyen Choling, Nkagpa Chogyam hung out with Sogyal, motivated by his devotion to Dudjom Rinpoche. He describes conversations with Sogyal about Dzogchen. He emphasises that these always took place in private:

"It became apparent that he didn't know the answers to the questions he was asking. It was embarrassingly transparent in the way he asked the questions. He confused terms. He framed his queries awkwardly, not because of his unfamiliarity with English – because he was actually quite fluent – but in terms of Dzogchen. He didn't know the lay of the land and so what he asked tended to sound like, 'Where exactly in Scotland is Wales to be found?'

"The other major give-away was the way he took lengthy notes. He explained these as being simply a 'record for his interest.' He was new to teaching in the West and wanted to know what people knew in terms of Dzogchen.

"His ignorance became more painfully obvious when I listened to him teach. I then heard my own explanations coming back to me, albeit in a Tibetan accent. I knew they were 'my' explanations because I'd developed an eccentric phraseology which was easily recognisable."

Around this time Sogyal made his first sortie into France, a move that set a chain of events in motion that led to the establishment of Rigpa as a multinational organisation. Disciples of Dudjom Rinpoche had coalesced into a small group in Paris. Sogyal pitched up there and was invited to teach.

However, it transpired that the Dudjom people were considerably less tolerant of his playboy lifestyle than his followers in London. Before long they asked Sogyal to leave, but by then he had acquired a taste for the pleasures of life in France. It must have been tedious for him to return to hippiedom in a shabby house in an unfashionable area of London after spending time with the Parisian bourgeoisie.

Mike Farmer was one of the people who met Sogyal for the first time at my dinner party. He was profoundly impressed with Dudjom Rinpoche, so he hung in with Sogyal's group for some time after others had moved on. He describes from direct personal involvement how Sogyal reneged on his apparent devotion to the Dudjom lineage:

> In May 1979, his Holiness Dudjom Rinpoche returned for a second time to give teachings in London, for a month. He taught at Chelsea Town Hall, Friends Meeting House and at Orgyen Chö Ling.
>
> At this time, Sogyal Rinpoche offered all his centres to His Holiness, who very graciously accepted them. Orgyen Chö Ling was then named Dzogchen Orgyen Chö Ling, as he had indeed given precious Dzogchen teachings there. One afternoon Sogyal Rinpoche went out on a tour of London with His Holiness's daughters. We "older" students were discretely asked to remain behind in 76 Princess Road, and we were asked to come into the shrine room. His Holiness was there, with Sangyum Kusho Rikzin Wangmo and Shenphen Dawa Rinpoche. It was very relaxed and informal. Shenphen Rinpoche was translating, and His Holiness started by saying how pleased he was to be teaching again in London, and how seriously he took Sogyal Rinpoche's devotion to him. He thanked him in absentia for making over his centres in London, America and France. However, he said that a few things

had to change. Sogyal Rinpoche had to settle down, not have so many girlfriends, maybe even marry, and do the extensive practices and retreats given in the Dudjom Tersar, which were absolutely essential for a teacher of the Dudjom tradition. He asked if we agreed, and, I remember this very well, His Holiness said: "As his students, what did we think Sogyal should do?" I think we were all a bit nervous – but the feeling came out that we agreed. So, a very long time ago, we had a warning from His Holiness that a few things had to change.

A year later I was in Kathmandu working as the architect for the design of Dilgo Khyentse Rinpoche's monastery, Shechen Tennyi Dargyeling. When I first arrived, Sogyal helped me very much by introducing me to Khyentse Sangyum, Dilgo Khyentse's consort, and from there on in, my work was made much easier. I thank Sogyal for both that and for introducing me to His Holiness Dudjom Rinpoche. While I was working on the Gonpa, I kept in close contact with Shenphen Rinpoche and Tulku Pema Wangyal. I remember one particular meeting with Shenphen Rinpoche and Tulku Pema, when they told me that His Holiness had given all his centres back to Sogyal, as the recommendations that His Holiness had outlined to us in London had not been followed. Indeed, Sogyal was giving mainly Longchen Nyingtig teachings... there is, of course, absolutely nothing wrong with the Longchen Nyingtig, but if you have proclaimed that you are a teacher of the Tersar, students were entitled to expect Dudjom Tersar teachings.

So, there then began a very difficult period. In France and America, there was hostility between the Dudjom and Sogyal groups. Many students (we were all a bit naive and inexperienced in those days) were terribly hurt. I was told by Shenphen Rinpoche and Tulku Pema that I should tell a very few people in London when I returned. I told Pete Fry and Bunny Burrows. Over the space of 24 hours, all my previous friends in Orgyen Chö Ling refused to have anything to do with me – I was proclaimed as being "sick" by Sogyal – and I was socially isolated. But the separation between Sogyal and the Dudjom Tradition did happen. And we had been warned.

Residents at Orgyen Choling recall no hesitation on the part of their teacher. "He refused point blank to obey the head of his order," said one of them. "Quite the opposite, in fact. He removed his group from the Dudjom mandala and changed its name to Rigpa, with him in charge and accountable to no-one."

The shocking truth to emerge from Mike's testimony is that, from the start, the embryo that grew into a global cult was fertilised by Sogyal's rampant ambition and nurtured by acolytes who knew beyond doubt that he was not the real deal.

In 1978 his student Jean-Claude Marol noted that the West did not welcome Sogyal as a lama whose renown as a Tibetan Buddhist master preceded him, but as an "ordinary student" who took an interest in Western culture.[29] Indeed, no contemporaneous records indicate that, before traveling to Cambridge in his early twenties, Sogyal conceived of himself as a Buddhist teacher at all – or was seen as one by the Tibetan exiles throughout India and the Himalayas. He himself has said: 'In some ways I went to Cambridge to learn about life in the West rather than to study.'[30]

The burgeoning Western interest in Tibetan Buddhism, however, caused the ordinary student Sogyal Lakar to abruptly transform – or rather, reinvent – himself as the Venerable Lama Sogyal Rinpoche.

After he began teaching in London, Sogyal and his associates launched a campaign to establish his public persona in the mainstream media.

Classified advertisements in newspapers in the late 1970s mostly highlighted Sogyal's skills as a meditator: "Tibetan Buddhist Meditation courses conducted by Sogyal Rinpoche, a highly accomplished Tibetan Incarnate Lama," an advertisement in the *Guardian* said. Two weeks later an advertisement in the Alternative Lifestyles section repeated: "Tibetan Buddhist Meditation conducted by Sogyal Rinpoche, a highly accomplished Tibetan Lama." In America, announcements in the *Santa Cruz Sentinel* and *The Press Democrat* simply described him as a meditation master.

Over time, Sogyal's association with Tibetan Buddhist hierarchs and monastic institutions was singled out. A report in the London *Observer* newspaper on Dudjom Rinpoche's first visit to Great Britain referred to Sogyal as his "representative" Lama Tulku Sogyal Rinpoche. That year, Sogyal was name-checked in a report on the Dalai Lama's intended visit to the United States. The *Los Angeles Times* dubbed him Venerable Lama Sogyal Rinpoche at the time – possibly mistaking him for a monastic. The *Capital Times* in Madison, Wisconsin, however, referred to him as a "filmmaker" named Sogyal Rinpoche.

This error probably originated in an encounter with Graham Coleman, which took place at my squat in Kentish Town. Graham was looking for collaborators for his Tibetan Trilogy film project. I introduced him to Sogyal, who latched onto it with enthusiasm, ending up as the principal consultant. He travelled with Graham to India and later around 17 cities in the USA on a film show tour.

The impression that he is a monastic turned out to be persistent. Years later, the *Arizona Daily Star* and *Santa Cruz Sentinel* still called Sogyal a Buddhist monk – as does sloppy journalism to this day. The distinction between lamas as monks and lamas who are not monks is largely ignored by writers and editors producing copy to tight deadlines.

By the 1980s references to Sogyal's supposed intellectual prowess and academic background became more pronounced. Suggesting that Sogyal was conversant with Western thought, it was mentioned that he had studied at Cambridge University – ignoring the fact that he did little more than attend a few lectures without ever graduating. A typical contemporaneous description ran: "Tibetan Lama, scholar and meditation teacher." In those years, Sogyal's appearances were frequently advertised as "seminars" and "courses" on psychological issues, such as "working with emotions," "depth of confidence," and "healing inspiration."

Juxtaposing his Tibetan and Western education, another advertisement claimed: "Ancient Wisdom, Modern Medicine: Sogyal Rinpoche Combines the Ancient Tradition of Tibet with the Modern Education of Cambridge."

A similar announcement in 1986 read: "Sogyal Rinpoche, a scholar and meditation master from Tibet, studied at Cambridge University and has taught throughout Europe, Britain and the U.S. Based on more than ten years' experience of life in the West, his teaching is widely appreciated for its humour, directness and relevance to the Western mind; he is the author of many articles on meditation and Buddhist psychology."[31]

His Tibetan pedigree notwithstanding, Sogyal appears to have engaged in spreading his bets by doing occasional lectures on Zen Buddhism. In this respect, he may have been influenced by his role model Trungpa Rinpoche, whose interests included Zen archery and flower arranging.

As time went on, allusions to his precociousness and traditional training as a child increasingly came to the fore. The biography for his first published work, *View, Meditation & Action*, reads:

"Tulku Sogyal Rinpoche, a Tibetan Lama, scholar and meditation teacher now living in the West, was trained in the Buddhist tradition by some of Tibet's most revered teachers and raised as a son by the great Jamyang Khyentse Chokyi Lodro in Dzongsar monastery in Kham Derge, Eastern Tibet. He is recognised as the tulku of Terton Sogyal, Lerab Lingpa, discoverer of the spiritual treasures of Guru Padmasambhava."[32]

A few years later, the American newspaper *Santa Cruz Sentinel* summed up: "Rinpoche is an incarnate lama from Tibet who has been trained by Buddhist masters since childhood."[33]

An inaccurate announcement in *The Press Democrat* elaborated on this: "Considered an incarnate lama by the old Buddhist masters in Tibet, he is thought by them to be the reincarnation of Terton Sogyal, who was the mind incarnation of Padmasambhava. A personal friend of the 13th Dalai Lama and his former translator, Rinpoche was reared in the Buddhist tradition by many of Tibet's most revered lamas who accumulated more than 2,500 years of knowledge. His closest mentor was a renowned lama, Jamyang Khyentse, who brought up Rinpoche as his own son in Dzongsar Monastery in East Tibet."[34]

As he became more widely known, Sogyal's personal characteristics, in particular his humour and westernised appearance, became selling points too: "Heralded as the incarnation of a past master and a personal friend of the 13th Dalia [sic] Lama, Sogyal Rinpoche has been taught by some of Tibet's most revered teachers. He now makes his home in the West, and his teaching, which is both humorous and open, is geared toward Western audiences."[35]

Over time, his apparent readiness to laugh, leading to descriptions of a "jolly" and "holy" man and the "merry teachings" of a "laughing saint" became a trope in itself: Sogyal was in fact tagged "the Laughing Lama from Tibet" for some time in the mid-1980s.

One of the first published reports on his teachings in the West illustrates how Sogyal added Oriental lustre to his jovial image by promoting the Lakar family's heritage as Buddhist benefactors.

Telling his listeners about the religious objects stacked on the dais behind him, he stunned them momentarily by explaining that in one casket there was a tooth of Buddha. "And this is very precious considering the only other one known is in Ceylon," he added. In two other caskets, the lama said with a giggle, were the mummified brain of a famous lama and "the underwear" of another renowned predecessor. They were part of a treasury of sacred objects, he said, bequeathed to him by his family, "which has been the main family supporting monasteries in Tibet for centuries."[36]

Typically short on specifics and evidence, the compound image of Sogyal's projected persona worked its magic with naïve Westerners. By the time he published *Dzogchen and Padmasambhava*, the most effective elements of Sogyal's public image as a spiritual leader in the West had been established. For example:

"Sogyal Rinpoche was born in Tibet and raised as a son by one of the greatest Buddhist masters of this century, Jamyang Khyentse Chokyi Lodro. He was recognized as the incarnation of Tertön Sogyal, Lerab Lingpa, discoverer of treasures (ter) concealed by Padmasambhava, and personal friend and lama of the XIIIth Dalai Lama. Rinpoche is also considered to be an emanation of Do Khyentse and of Lingtsang Gyalpo, a direct descendant of Gesar of Ling. After Jamyang Khyentse Rinpoche passed away, he studied with H.H. Dudjom Rinpoche and H.H. Dilgo Khyentse Rinpoche, his other principal teachers, and for a number of years he served as translator and aide to H.H. Dudjom Rinpoche, who was the inspiration behind his work in the West. He studied at Cambridge University and now has nearly twenty years' experience of living and teaching in the Western world.

"The clarity, ease and humour with which Rinpoche presents the teachings and practices of buddhadharma, along with his special gift for bypassing cultural barriers to reveal the vitality of the Buddhist perspective in today's challenging world, have led him to teach worldwide, and he is much sought after as a speaker at international conferences on a wide range of subjects, such as healing, psychology, the environment, peace, the arts and sciences. He is acknowledged as a pioneer in drawing out the common insights shared by the ancient Buddhist wisdom of Tibet and modem experience and research. Widely known for his work in the field of death and caring for the dying, Rinpoche is currently writing a long-awaited book on death, to be published next year, which will be the first of a series. Other titles will include a deeper investigation into the *Tibetan Book of the Dead* and books on meditation and Dzogchen."[37]

Over time, assertions about Sogyal's personal history as a Buddhist teacher coalesced into a public persona that took on a life of its own. Lacking alternative sources, uninformed journalists and advertisers tended to repeat Sogyal's own accounts by rote, often conflating historical events, garbling timelines, and amplifying storylines.

Bruce Best's portrait of Sogyal in the Australian newspaper *The Age* in 1986, for instance: "Brought up in Tibet and trained as a spiritual leader (lama), he has spent the past 10 years based in Britain, where he studied philosophy at Cambridge University, and in Europe."[38]

Clark Morphew's report in the *News Journal* in Ohio in 1993 provides yet another illustration: "Believing that Sogyal Rinpoche was the reincarnation of a deceased master, Buddhist monks took him at the age of 6 months and gave him to the care of probably the most venerated Buddhist master in the world, the late Jamyang Khyentse Chokyi Lodro. When Sogyal Rinpoche was able to understand language, he began sitting at the feet of his master, who treated him more like a son than a student."[39]

This flowery version of events is hardly compatible with the facts, including Sogyal's own accounts of them through the years.

Not only did incorrect claims about Sogyal's past go unchecked, the vague contours of Sogyal's self-representations in the media were perpetuated by ill-informed reporters and enthusiastic wannabe Buddhists. Sogyal's image was made to fit preconceived models of holy men/women and priests. The arc of the resulting narrative derived from three interacting forces: Sogyal's power of suggestion, professional reporters' lack of vetting, and starry-eyed Westerners' first impressions of some of the most charismatic Tibetan lamas of their day.

It was as if a gullible audience concluded that the impresario of an exceptionally gifted cast of performance artists must be a brilliant performer himself – and put him centre stage. To imagine the consequences of such a misapprehension, picture Colonel Parker replacing Elvis Presley at his 1968 Comeback Special.

These "established facts" have been accepted at face value and regurgitated by most observers ever since. Needless to say, Sogyal did not dissuade them from doing so. "Raised as a son" by Khyentse Chokyi Lodro became Sogyal's favoured credential, always on his lips. It also became a staple of biographical sketches in Western media. This was the result of years of carefully crafted image-building based on uncorroborated evidence of Sogyal's authenticity as a Tibetan lama. His runaway best-selling book, *The Tibetan Book of Living and Dying*, did not build this image, it exploited it.

Meanwhile, with an expansionist bit firmly between his teeth, Sogyal set off in 1975 to investigate his potential in America. His first stop was a visit to Chogyam Trungpa Rinpoche in Boulder, Colorado. After leaving Samye Ling, following a bitter dispute with Akong Rinpoche, Trungpa went first to Vermont and then to Boulder.

Trungpa was a formidably intelligent iconoclast who swiftly acquired a nationwide following, with a formula that shook Buddhist America to the core and generated enthusiasm wherever he alighted. In contrast to the more familiar austerities of Zen Buddhism, Trungpa offered Tibetan theory and practice in tandem with a hedonistic way of life. One of his early works, *The Sadhana of Mahamudra*, is a vivid example of the breadth and depth of his contemplative insight, coupled with his capacity to deliver it in modern Western language.

Sogyal discovered that he had a lot in common with Trungpa. They shared a taste for luxurious living, alcohol and pretty women. It must be said that young Western women stood in line to sleep with Trungpa and were usually eager to oblige with Sogyal. They became known as dharma groupies, and sex with a Rinpoche became almost as much of a status symbol as plaster-casting Mick Jagger.

According to Western ethics, men (and women) in positions of power and authority (police, priests, lawyers, counsellors, doctors) are supposed to resist such temptations, but it is hardly surprising that red-blooded young lamas recently imported into in an alien culture could hardly believe their luck. In old Tibet it was considered an honour to be selected as a yum of a high lama.

During the early days of the Tibetan diaspora there was considerable cultural dissonance – Western women and Tibetan lamas had widely divergent views on the nature of male-female relationships. Forty-plus years later, with only a few exceptions, little had changed. In general, Tibetan lamas are still misogynistic, and many Western women devotees are still eager to sleep with them.

When Sogyal returned to London from his first visit to America, his students gathered in the large basement room at 56 Prince of Wales Road, eager to greet our guru, fresh from his transatlantic adventure. Until this point, he had always been punctual. We waited. We chanted the Padmasambhava Seven Line invocation. We waited. We recited the Vajrasattva 100-syllable mantra a few times. Still no sign of Sogyal. Eventually I went upstairs to phone Princess Road to find out if there had been a misunderstanding.

There was no reply. Then, more than half an hour after the appointed time, there was a loud, imperative knock at the door. As I opened it, Sogyal strode past me in wrathful manifestation.

With a thunderous face and body language to match, our hitherto polite and friendly lama stomped into the basement and proceeded to harangue the assembled company in state of extreme exasperation.

He accused us of just about every possible crime and misdemeanour against the status of an important spiritual teacher. He said we were sloppy, lazy, and totally lacking in awareness of our good fortune. But most of all we had no ambition to create a suitable environment for a Rinpoche. From then onwards, he said, we were not to address him as Sogyal – anything other than Rinpoche would trigger extreme displeasure. The informal, matey period was well and truly over.

Patrick Gaffney tried to placate him with what he hoped were reassuring promises but only succeeded in causing the rest of us to squirm with embarrassment. One sensitive woman sobbed into her handkerchief. As abruptly as he had arrived, Sogyal got up and left at the end of his diatribe.

Around this time Sogyal launched into his habit of publicly humiliating his close followers – berating them for even minor errors in front of a roomful of people. Patrick Gaffney was the only one to be spared these ordeals.

The surge of enthusiasm for Tibetan Buddhism continued to accelerate, but in the late 1970s and early 80s there were still very few lamas actively at work in the big cities of the Western world. Sogyal's presence in London fulfilled a major part of the demand for teachings, so the timing of his arrival was spot on. News of Sogyal's activities – and the fact that he attracted some of the legendary elders like Dilgo Khyentse Rinpoche – spread like wildfire. It soon became apparent that the room at Princess Road was too small to accommodate the ever-increasing number of people turning up for teachings.

Sogyal must have commissioned some research, because he was quick off the mark to realise the potential of Tibetan Buddhism as a panacea for stressed-out city folk. As he set about repackaging the dharma for Western consumption, news of his activities reached the show business grapevine– and the ears of the actor John Cleese. A formidably intelligent man blessed with considerable emotional depth, Cleese was intrigued by Sogyal and impressed with his teachings. So much so that he donated £100,000 to Rigpa, which enabled them to obtain a lease on premises in Camden Town.

This was a much better-appointed space above a warehouse in a trendy location. Rigpa stayed there for several years until they outgrew it, as the mystique around all things Tibetan continued to attract new people. Rigpa's final move in London was to their present home in Caledonian Road, Islington. This is an extensive property with a very large, if somewhat claustrophobic, basement shrine room.

In the early 1980s John Cleese praised Sogyal in a video, joking about his own role as "a warm-up man for a Tibetan lama." Soon afterwards, rumours circulated on the Buddhist grapevine that Cleese was appalled by the escalation of Sogyal's sybaritic lifestyle. If this was true, he must have changed his mind, because in 2006 he was interviewed at Lerab Ling for an adulatory programme about Sogyal, broadcast on a Buddhist TV channel in Holland. The video is available on YouTube. It is truly nauseating in style, content, and production values.[40]

In 1979 Daniel and I were living in a council flat behind Camden High Street, allocated to us after the squat was repossessed. This was the peak period of my professional life when I did shift work on the news desk at LBC/IRN. In those days LBC Radio and Independent Radio News were joined at the hip with headquarters in Gough Square, just off Fleet St. It was also the year when my contemplative life went through a major upgrade.

My friend, the thangka painter Robert Beer, also lived in Camden Town. Visiting one day, I encountered the Tibetan Buddhist translator, author and later teacher, Keith Dowman, who spoke in appreciative terms about a lama called Namkhai Norbu Rinpoche. Because of the extent of his experience, Keith's recommendation had traction, so I passed it on to Jill Purce, the doyenne of the New Age/Spiritual/Therapeutic movement. Jill had an eclectic approach to spiritual teachers and, until she met Namkhai Norbu Rinpoche, had never made a commitment to a specific discipline or guru. She went to one of Norbu's retreats in Italy and came back ecstatic: "I'm going to bring him to London," she said.

True to her word, Jill set up a teaching retreat for Norbu Rinpoche at the squatted former Cambodian Embassy in St. Johns Wood. Re-named the Guild of Transcultural Studies, it had an enormous, comfortable reception room, ideal for a gathering of around 80 people. Norbu Rinpoche turned up with some of his Italian students. In those days he was based near Naples and taught in Italian, with a very big (literally) man called Barry Simmons translating into English.

I was one of roughly 20 people from Sogyal's following present on that occasion. From the moment Norbu started talking, we realised we had encountered an authentic Dzogchen master. When he led the Italians into The Song of the Vajra, every cell in my body exploded into recognition. It was electrifyingly familiar to me. I had met my root guru. Towards the end of the retreat Judy Allan, John Steele and I walked up Primrose Hill together.

"Is this as good as I think it is?" I asked after a long reflective silence. "It's better," they replied in unison. I remember hearing one of Norbu Rinpoche's students saying that most of them had a similar reaction to mine the first time they heard The Song of the Vajra. "He called us through the bardos with it," she added in a tone that implied that there was nothing remarkable about a lama guiding his flock through the after-death state.

There was a mass exodus to Namkhai Norbu Rinpoche from Sogyal's group but, such was the appeal of anything connected with Tibet, within weeks the defectors were replaced by a fresh intake. Devotees who remained faithful included Patrick Gaffney, Susan (Bunny) Burrows, Mike Farmer and Dominique Side. About two years later Mike also left to join Namkhai Norbu's Dzogchen Community.

This was the first of many setbacks that befell Sogyal during his 40-plus-year career that took him from a North London squat to the giddy heights of celebrity guru status – and first-class jet-setting, surrounded by an entourage of sex slaves, minders, clerks and gofers. And to that peak experience, when he introduced the First Lady of France to the 14th Dalai Lama of Tibet.

Sogyal snoozing on his throne while translation is underway at one of his teachings

7

Fame

If you ask a selection of Sogyal's many admirers about the qualities as a Buddhist teacher that have contributed to his success, two answers stand out: his charisma and his humour. Sogyal was an accomplished public performer who developed his presentation specifically to keep audiences entertained – that is one factor. Another is that he is credited as the author of the all-time best-selling Buddhist book, *The Tibetan Book of Living and Dying*, which has sold three million copies and been translated into 24 languages.[41]

More astringent observers of Sogyal's trajectory into guru superstardom point in other directions: to his lucky streak, his timing, his chutzpah, and his astute exploitation of zeitgeist. For example, from the mid-1980s onwards thousands of people in the developed world were ready to embrace the exotic spiritual path offered by exiled Tibetan lamas and ready to address the taboos surrounding death and dying. Sogyal was in the right place at the right time with the right message.

Gary Goldman, a former long-term Rigpa student, was one among the thousands who were profoundly impressed with the principles that underpin the book's message:

"I read it in one night," says Gary. "It was the most incredibly relevant thing I'd ever encountered…. I was almost overwhelmed by the concept of total compassion – of completely putting yourself in someone else's shoes, totally identifying with their situation."

In those days only a very few people had enough information available to make value judgements on Sogyal's capacity to transmit authentic Tibetan Buddhist teachings. In fact, he recalibrated Vajrayana/Dzogchen into what could be described as Buddhism Lite. He was aiming for mass popular appeal – and the cash flow that goes with it.

The source material for the Rigpa curriculum is authentic. I have shown it to several Buddhist scholar-practitioner-teachers who confirm this. There's also no doubt that many people attracted to Rigpa received what the Australian author Tahlia Newland describes as an "effective Buddhist education."

But Sogyal's "teachings" are a travesty of the real thing. He deploys the kind of tricks tried and tested by evangelists and cult leaders. One of them is involuntary hypnosis, another is love-bombing, and yet another is the narcissist's tactic known as gaslighting. This involves a barrage of attacks on people's self-esteem, followed by a *volte face* into saying how much he loves them. A technique deployed by control addicts, which systematically undermines the victim's self-confidence.

Sogyal's personal appearances are promoted as genuine Vajrayana/Dzogchen transmission. His audiences are duped into the belief that the love-bombing is giving them insight into "the nature of mind." Not everyone who attends is taken in, but the ones who are taken in appear to end up in a state of blind devotion. In a series of talks to Rigpa audiences in February and March 2018, even his supporter, Dzongsar Jamyang Khyentse Rinpoche, spoke about his serious misgivings around Sogyal's capacity to prepare his devotees for Vajrayana/Dzogchen teachings. This is a significant opinion, because Dzongsar is said to be the reincarnation of Sogyal's uncle, Chokyi Lodro.

As well as his lack of ability as a master of genuine esoteric transmission, there are many more dark strands beneath the surface of Sogyal's success story. His status as a Buddhist lama requires him to be an exemplar of two fundamental articles of faith: wisdom and compassion. Yet in 1994 an American woman known as Janice Doe sued Sogyal for sexual assault and battery. Ever since, allegations around his private life involving bullying, sexual violence and financial irregularities have surfaced from disillusioned former disciples.

Those in the know about the history of Rigpa make one firm assertion: that Sogyal could not have scaled the heights of success without the help of his long-term right-hand man, Patrick Gaffney. Patrick played an equal role with Sogyal during the Lerab Ling temple ceremony – highlighting his dominant position in the Rigpa hierarchy.

An early American seeker, Victoria Barlow, recalls meeting Sogyal in Boulder, Colorado in 1976: "Sogyal was enthralled by Trungpa's sexual conquests," she says. "He told me outright that he wanted what Trungpa had and aimed to achieve a rock star lifestyle." Around this time Sogyal sharpened his habit of publicly humiliating his close followers – excoriating for them for even minor errors in front of hundreds of people.

He was still doing it in 2011. A woman known as Lalatee who attended a retreat at Dzogchen Beara, the Rigpa centre in Ireland, was profoundly shocked by Sogyal's behaviour:

"I experienced what at best could be termed disrespect, at worst abuse of his colleagues and disciples. He was regularly late and often over-ran the sessions by several hours. He was insulting to the Irish people, about his assistants and to individual course participants. The last straw for me was when he called a senior assistant to come to the dais. She's a respected professional in her 60s doing amazing work with the bereaved and the dying.

"She was forced to kneel beside Sogyal, while he embraced her closely and put his hand on her chest. I could see that she was embarrassed and uncomfortable. Sogyal proceeded to stroke her face, looking deeply into her eyes. When she pulled back slightly, he turned to the 250 people present and said, 'This is none of your business, turn away'. So 250 people twisted round in their seats and looked away. If that is not crowd manipulation and abuse, I don't know what is. At the very least it shows complete disregard for Western social mores and ethical behaviour."

Also in 2011, another woman (Myra) attended a Rigpa retreat at Myall Lakes in Australia.

"Sogyal seemed arrogant and uncaring," she reports. "He was habitually an hour or more late and after he turned up would spend another hour and a half criticising his older students. Meanwhile, several hundred people who had already waited a long time had to witness this, not understanding what was going on. Many of them were new to Rigpa. Sogyal then gave his senior students orders about how he wanted the presentation to be prepared for the next day.

"I know they sometimes stayed up all night working on a new version, but next day when Sogyal arrived everything would be all wrong again, and there would be another diatribe."

Myra asked older students about Sogyal's behaviour: "One explanation given to justify it was that he aims to shock people out of their habitual thinking – that he's a Vajra Master and doesn't conform to the same samsaric standards as we do. I couldn't help thinking that if he's really a Vajra Master why does he need to follow a precise order of events? Why are the prepared readings and video excerpts so important? I really think there's something else going on."

There was a period of phenomenal expansion in the number of people seeking instruction in Tibetan Buddhism during the late 1980s and early 90s, especially in America. To some extent this was driven by the enthusiasm for all things Tibetan vocalised in public by high-profile show business personalities like Richard Gere, Adam Yauch and Goldie Hawn.

As news of the lush lifestyles enjoyed by lamas in the developed world spread to the austere monastic institutions in India and Nepal, more and more of them packed their bags and flew off to fulfil the demand. It soon became clear that not only would they live in luxury, but also that teaching Vajrayana Buddhism represented a major source of income for the Tibetan diaspora.

Most of the credit for the popularity surge has to go to His Holiness the Dalai Lama – especially since he acquired global celebrity status after he was awarded the Nobel Peace prize in 1989 for his non-violent struggle for the liberation of Tibet. He has consistently advocated policies of non-violence, even in the face of extreme aggression. He also became the first Nobel Laureate to be recognised for his concern for global environmental problems.

The Dalai Lama has travelled to more than 67 countries spanning six continents. He has received over 150 awards, honorary doctorates, prizes, etc., in recognition of his message of peace, non-violence, inter-religious understanding, universal responsibility and compassion. He has also authored or co-authored more than 110 books.

His most effective assets are undoubtedly his supercharged charisma, his engaging personality, and his willingness to share his knowledge and experience with all-comers. He is blessed with a capacity to be both transparently humble and totally self-assured. Like any human being he is not perfect, but he is arguably the supreme good guy role model alive on post-millennium planet earth.

When Sogyal set his sights on California, Victoria Barlow encountered him on his first visit to the West Coast. According to Victoria, he aired views which are diametrically opposed to his role as a champion of the Dalai Lama, who belongs to the monastic Gelug School. Sogyal is a Nyingmapa, an older, largely non-celibate tradition. "Sogyal loathed the Gelugpas and the Dalai Lama," she says. "I heard him in Berkeley being a staggering sectarian hater – he expressed real rage to all who would listen, trashing the Dalai Lama."

Despite his politically incorrect outbursts, Sogyal's style went down well with Californian audiences. This probably had something to do with the fact that Tibetan Buddhism was virgin territory for most Americans, so the lack of substance in his teachings was not immediately apparent.

The Dalai Lama only began touring the United States in 1979. The direct exposure of American audiences to him and other visiting Tibetan lamas of the highest calibre was usually brief and distant. Sogyal's interactions with aspiring devotees in the United States and Australia were more prolonged and intimate. They were driven by his exotic charisma and skill as an entertaining conversationalist, rather than real subject matter. His appeal lay in the Shangri-la myths and legends surrounding all things Tibetan. Sogyal's American audiences had few points of reference to give focus to their enthusiasm and, like many people in many countries, they were hungry for what seemed to them to be authentic access to an ancient esoteric tradition.

During a period of several years, Rigpa centres sprang up all over the world. In 2018 www.rigpa.org claimed 130 centres in 30 countries – although most of these are small groups meeting in each other's homes. The main ones are Lerab Ling in France, Dzogchen Beara in Ireland, Sukhavati in Germany and city centres in London, Amsterdam, Paris and Berlin.

One of the Californians impressed by Sogyal was Christine Longaker, who at that time was director of the Hospice of Santa Cruz County in the San Francisco Bay area. This smart woman made a connection between Tibetan texts dealing with death and the after-death state and her work in palliative care for the dying. She shared her insights with Sogyal, who swiftly realised that this could turn out to be his passport to fame and fortune.

He was right. From the mid-1980s onwards Sogyal set his acolytes the task of researching information on Western attitudes to death and dying – and linking these with *The Tibetan Book of the Dead*. This text is attributed to Padmasambhava, an 8th-century yogi credited as the founding father of Buddhism in Tibet. Originally translated into English in 1927, it was essential reading for hippies, and well-thumbed copies were passed around the traveller communities in India. Some found their way into San Francisco bookshops.

Once he had his research data, Sogyal started lecturing on spiritual care for the dying – challenging deeply entrenched taboos and attracting large audiences, including many people experiencing various stages of terminal illness and grief. It is beyond doubt that within a Western cultural context Sogyal helped to deliver a seismic shift. It was pioneered by the psychiatrist Elizabeth Kubler-Ross, but the addition of Sogyal's Tibetan Buddhist perspective was a radical new formula, which suggested that, rather than a source of fear, death can be treated as a source of inspiration.

The theories and practices expounded in Sogyal's lectures were collated into his version of the Padmasambhava treatise, but with a contemporary twist – living in tandem with dying, highlighting the two states as mirror images of each other. When *The Tibetan Book of Living and Dying* was published in 1992, it ticked every box on Sogyal's wish list. Almost overnight he became an international celebrity and, to top it all, in 1994 he accepted an offer from Bernardo Bertolucci of a role in his movie *Little Buddha*. Sometime later, worldwide book sales turned Sogyal into a personal millionaire.

But there are questions around the authorship of *The Tibetan Book of Living and Dying*. Rumours that Sogyal did not write the book have been circulating on the internet for years.

When approached for comment, the author, academic and mystic Andrew Harvey gave an inconclusive response:

"Sogyal participated totally in every level of the creation of the book and as the representative of his tradition was the indispensable transmitter of its wisdom. The process was a totally mutual collaboration in which Sogyal gave everything and had the final word on every word. It is a very hard process to describe. Any suggestion that Sogyal did not write this book is, I think, absurd and dishonouring of his genius and passion. Both Patrick and I worked tirelessly and, I hope, selflessly to honour Sogyal's brilliance and the wisdom of the tradition. And the book could not exist without the transcripts of Sogyal's talks that were its foundation."

Patrick Gaffney and Andrew Harvey are credited as editors – but Harvey's words do not confirm Sogyal as the author.

Graham, a former Rigpa member, recalls spending time with Harvey "when he was writing the book." Graham adds: "Could anyone who knows Sogyal imagine him being able to quote the German mystical poet, Rainer Maria Rilke? Or the Sufi sage, Jalaluddin Rumi? He simply doesn't have that level of education."

Andrew Harvey does – and comparisons between *The Tibetan Book of Living and Dying* and Harvey's own books reveal striking similarities in tone, structure and language. According to a well-known American Buddhist teacher: "Andrew Harvey was very upset at not being credited as co-author."

Buddhist teacher Ngakpa Chogyam also has doubts: "The book was cobbled together from more than a decade of Sogyal's teachings," he says. "I worked for a while on transcribing the tapes. There were a fair few mistakes, which I corrected as I went along – particularly about Dzogchen and precise definitions of Buddhist doctrine."

Joanne Standlee, a former director of Rigpa USA, gets straight to the point:

"Sogyal never wrote anything", she says in the Dutch film, *Guru in Disgrace*.[42]

John Cleese with student Janine Schulz at Lerab Ling, Rigpa's centre in France, 2008

Sogyal with some of his dakinis, ca. 2009

8

Seduction and a Lawsuit

In June 1993, less than a year after the publication of the *The Tibetan Book of Living and Dying*, a young and beautiful woman in a state of acute distress over the death of her father went to a Rigpa retreat in Connecticut, USA. After one of Sogyal's lectures she sent him a written question: "How can I help my father now that he's dead?" Sogyal's response was to invite her to his room.

The woman, Dierdre Smith (not her real name), says she was completely vulnerable. "I might as well have had a notice round my neck saying, Abuse Me!" She wept as she recounted to Sogyal the circumstances of her father's death from a drug overdose. "He asked me to massage him – I was in awe of him as the important guru, so I did as he wished. Then he told me he was my personal teacher and was going to help me. I was very excited about this and called my husband to tell him that everything was going to be OK.

"Sogyal asked me to come back the following day, with a picture of myself and of my father. It was all very paternal, and he kept saying I should trust him.

"It was about 10.30 at night when I arrived. He took his clothes off and got into bed. I was embarrassed and didn't know where to look – but he said I should feel safe because we were in a shrine. The room was lit with candles and there were pictures of Buddhas all around."

A long seduction followed that lasted into the small hours.

The reluctant, grief-stricken Dierdre protested that she did not want to cheat on her husband – but Sogyal persisted, insisting that having sex with him would benefit her father's karma: "He ground me down," she says. "It was the same thing over and over. Do you love me? Do you trust me? It must have gone on for about six hours. Eventually I was exhausted and gave up resisting. The whole thing revolved around surrender to him, and I was scared of losing the opportunity to heal my family."

Dierdre was told by Rigpa devotees that if you have negative feelings you destroy your relationship with the guru. With hindsight, she sees this as a cultish manoeuvre designed to smother dissent, but at the time she did not question this and other injunctions – including one from Sogyal swearing her to secrecy about the seduction.

Sogyal insisted that he loved her, wanted to take care of her and that she should see him as her family. He phoned her every day until they met again six months later. Dierdre flew to France at her own expense, expecting to be a normal student.

Instead, she was isolated in a separate house and told not to talk to anyone: "I only left the house to go to the teachings, where I saw 500 people prostrating themselves to the lama. The rest of the time I listened to him on tape, saying things like, 'Pray to me, see me as the Buddha, love me, trust me, be obedient to me.'"

For several months Dierdre put her everyday life on hold and travelled with Sogyal as his servant, sex partner and arm candy. She recounts how the smile on Sogyal's face and the unctuous charm of his public presentation vanished the moment they were hidden from view:

"There must have been about ten women in his inner circle," she says. "And it was our job to attend to his every need. We bathed him, dressed him, cooked for him, carried his suitcases, ironed his clothes and were available for sex. He was a tyrant. Nothing we did was ever good enough. He went into screaming rages and beat us. If I tried to question the way he treated us, he became angry. The only way to avoid this was to stay silent and submissive."

According to former Rigpa insiders, Sogyal's team of regular sex partner-attendants was the core group of a sub-sect of Rigpa known as Lama Care. This was set up specifically to make sure that women were available for sex with Sogyal wherever he travelled.

In common with other women who have spoken about their experiences with Sogyal, Dierdre recounts how she hardly ever slept, had no time to eat properly and lost 15 pounds during the first two weeks of her time with him.

"I looked pretty sickly," she recalls. Yet despite the brainwashing and the abuse the women in Sogyal's harem regarded themselves as highly privileged: "They kept on saying how lucky we were to be close to the guru, how we had special teachings and how much he loved us."

Indoctrination into the inner circle was designed as a life sentence. A young, vulnerable woman is programmed to accept Sogyal's god-like status and to be compliant with his wishes and whims, slave-like in her willingness to accept a punishing workload, and available for sex on demand. She is separated from her family and friends, discouraged from contact with the outside world, and persuaded to see Rigpa as her family, with Sogyal (confusingly as father-lover) in absolute power and control.

In most cases it worked. By the time these women realised they were being abused and exploited and deeply embedded in a coercive cult, it was too late for them to extricate themselves. Their investment was total and their chances of making lives for themselves outside Rigpa dwindled into non-existence. But in some instances, Sogyal's choices backfired on him. By 1994 it slowly dawned on Dierdre that she was being exploited.

"At first," she says, "I was willing to give up everything for the promise of healing my family, saving the world and being useful but, as these illusions started to melt away, I realised I had caused a lot of harm – I'd made myself sick and I'd hurt my husband."

During her last retreat with Sogyal, Dierdre found out about the scandals surrounding Chogyam Trungpa Rinpoche and his regent, Osel Tendzin (Thomas Rich), who infected several people with HIV.

"I was terrified I'd given my husband HIV," she says. "So, I told Sogyal I wanted to leave." He was very angry, probably because I knew too much about his promiscuity and his lies. I remember sitting on his bed with him, and he shouted at me, 'Get these crazy ideas out of your head' and at the same time he was hitting me hard on the head, one side and then the other."

So what finally drove Dierdre away?

"Mostly it was the beatings and because Sogyal kept on telling me I was a burden to him. It was bewildering, because at the same time he tried to persuade me to stay – saying that by serving him I was serving the world. But there he was with all these people attending to everything he demanded, and there was my husband who was alone and ill at the time, begging me not to leave him."

Regardless of Sogyal's threats (including aeons in the hell realms), protestations and persuasions, Dierdre left. But after returning to her long-suffering husband, she discovered that leaving was not as easy as physically walking out. Like many others who detach themselves from abusive relationships and coercive cults, she found herself dealing with a psycho-emotional hangover.

By this time a lot less naïve than she was when she first encountered Sogyal, Dierdre initially sought help from Jack Kornfield a well-known western Buddhist teacher. He wisely thought it best for Dierdre to talk to a woman, so he passed her on to a strong-minded Californian Zen teacher who had herself been a victim of a sexually abusive guru.

"It is harmful to both student and teacher," the teacher says, "because they end up slipping into a fantasy realm, rather than cultivating awareness of the Buddhist path. Americans are more sophisticated now – we know about the long-term damage inherent in relationships where there is a power imbalance."

Around the same time, one of Sogyal's victims who became known as Janice Doe, consulted a San Francisco lawyer, and on 2 November 1994 a suit was filed in the Superior Court of California seeking reparations from Sogyal Rinpoche aka Sogyal Lakar and The Spiritual Care for Living and Dying Network for assault and battery, infliction of emotional distress and breach of fiduciary duty.

The suit also charged that Sogyal had seduced many other female students for his own sexual gratification by preying on their vulnerability.

Three days later the story broke in several West Coast newspapers, following a report by an agency journalist, Don Lattin, which included comment by Victoria Barlow: "I went to an apartment to see a highly esteemed lama to discuss religion," she said. "He opened the door without a shirt on and with a can of beer in his hand." Once they were on the sofa, Barlow continued, "Sogyal lunged at me with sloppy kisses and groping. I thought I should take it as a compliment, so I surrendered to him – but it had a horrible effect on me and caused a lot of depression."[43]

News of the lawsuit spread like wildfire across the Tibetan Buddhist grapevine. At first the Rigpa hierarchy appeared to be caught like rabbits in headlights – frozen and incapable of anything other than whimpers of denial. Later, when the shockwaves had subsided, a letter was despatched to some students, acknowledging the existence of the lawsuit and containing a feeble attempt at damage limitation: "Allegations are only allegations. As far as we know, they have no foundation."

Journalists who requested interviews with Sogyal were told he was "in retreat."

A contemporaneous Rigpa press release (22 February 1995) stated:

The suit alleges that Rigpa is a cult, and that Sogyal Rinpoche is guilty of fraud, assault and battery. Rigpa is unable to comment on the allegations, as we would have wished, due to legal proceedings. However, we would like to point out that Sogyal Rinpoche and his teachings have moved many thousands of people, women and men, and there are many people who can say how he has helped them transform their lives in a very positive way. Many of the most eminent lamas of Tibetan Buddhism have recognised Sogyal Rinpoche as an authentic master and we have every confidence that this is so."

In January 1995, my feature about the lawsuit appeared in the British national newspaper the *Guardian*.[44] A few weeks later my broadcast version of the story ran on BBC Radio 4's Sunday Programme.[45] Sogyal was scheduled to lead Rigpa's annual UK Easter retreat, booked to happen at Harrow School, but someone at Harrow heard the BBC item and promptly cancelled the booking.

"Rigpa was stuck with more than a hundred people and nowhere to go," says Dominique Cowell, one of Sogyal's organisers at the time. "All we could do was cram them into the shrine room in London."

In February 1995, the UK's *Telegraph* Magazine featured a cover story on the Sogyal lawsuit by the journalist and author Mick Brown. In it, two English women spoke about their sexual encounters with Sogyal:

"It's a relationship that you haven't chosen, agreed to or discussed," said one woman. "Because he was my spiritual teacher, I trusted that whatever he asked was in my best interests… by sleeping with the teacher you get a closeness to him which everyone is hankering after… but in fact it caused me a lot of pain that I wasn't able to dissolve."

Another spoke about her distress at discovering that Sogyal was having sex with three other students, shortly after he initiated a relationship with her: "I came to the conclusion that Sogyal Rinpoche has used the teachings to attempt to keep me in a sexual relationship with him – one that I did not want to be in."

In common with other former Sogyal consorts, this woman "recognised that I was emotionally wounded and that my self-esteem was low, and that I no longer trusted myself or the spiritual path I had chosen."[46]

According to one former Rigpa insider, "An unsavoury witch hunt was launched to find out the identity of the women who spoke to Mick Brown."

In a manifestation of his disapproval, The Dalai Lama withdrew from participation in a Living and Dying Conference scheduled by Rigpa to take place in California. The conference was cancelled. Sogyal also had to cancel an appearance at a prestigious event in New York, the Art of Dying conference (31 March-3 April 1995). This time his excuse was "severe flu." The glorification of Sogyal suffered a serious setback and, to silence Janice Doe, Rigpa was forced to part with a large sum of money. Just how much money was involved in the out-of-court settlement is a closely guarded secret, but it is alleged to run into millions of dollars. Janice Doe signed a non-disclosure agreement.

It took about two years – and a huge workload for Patrick Gaffney and other members of the Rigpa inner circle – to re-establish Sogyal as a globe-trotting guru.

"People left in droves," says Dominique Cowell. "I remember noticing there was no-one around who had been there when I first got involved, except for Patrick and Dominique Side."

Sometime later, when Rigpa was struggling to deal with highly critical media coverage, they set up a series of Representing Rigpa seminars for senior members. One participant recalls being shown a video presentation by Sogyal in which he claims the Janice Doe lawsuit was the result of a conspiracy set up by "a group of seven American teachers who were jealous of my success with *The Tibetan Book of Living and Dying*."

I checked this out with one member of the alleged group of seven, Lama Tsultrim Allione. She confirmed that Sogyal's allegation is pure fantasy. "What actually happened was that Janice Doe first sought advice from Jack Kornfield, but he passed her on to me and to Yvonne Rand because he felt we would be better placed to advise her."

Around this time, I interviewed the Dalai Lama about the Sogyal lawsuit. He was quite clear about the issue of sexual relations between teachers and disciples. He condemned it as unacceptable and told me he had advised Sogyal to settle down and "take a lawful wife."

Sogyal's response to this was to have an affair with an American woman called Marianne Jurgaitis. She became pregnant and gave birth to Sogyal's son, Yeshe. Asked if he would marry Marianne, he is said to have replied, "That would be a step too far."

Marianne is the long-term partner of Pedro Beroy, a senior Rigpa administrator and professional money man.

Even though by this time Sogyal had been placing the Dalai Lama at the top of his totem for many years, he was clearly not impressed by advice from the boss on his private life.

"It was window dressing," says one former member of Sogyal's harem. "The Dalai Lama blessed the relationship, but Sogyal was never monogamous. One of his other women – Alison – saw herself as the 'wife' and she would not have allowed him to stop having sex with her."

There is no doubt that the lawsuit made the Tibetan Buddhist community in the developed world take stock of its situation. Even in 1993, before the lawsuit, a group of Western Buddhist teachers held a conference with the Dalai Lama. The statement the emerged from it included these words:

> ... *Each student must be encouraged to take responsible measures to confront teachers with unethical aspects of their conduct. If the*

teacher shows no sign of reform, students should not hesitate to publicise any unethical behaviour of which there is irrefutable evidence. This should be done irrespective of other beneficial aspects of his or her work and of one's spiritual commitment to that teacher. It should also be made clear in any publicity that such conduct is not in conformity with Buddhist teachings. No matter what level of spiritual attainment a teacher has, or claims to have reached, no person can stand above the norms of ethical conduct.[47]

Although the Dalai Lama told the meeting that sexual misbehaviour should be publicised and errant teachers made to feel "regretful and embarrassed," significantly, in the light of subsequent developments, he declined to endorse the statement.[48]

As the reinvention of Sogyal's credibility gathered momentum, leaks from within Rigpa indicated that he had no intention of changing his ways. Quite the contrary, in fact, because in 1996 Western Buddhist teachers met for the third time with the Dalai Lama and, to the dismay of most of them, Sogyal was a high-profile presence at the conference, holding forth vehemently about the perils of teaching Vajrayana without "authenticity, credentials and training."

"His chutzpah was breath-taking," says Yvonne Rand. "We could hardly believe what we were experiencing. It was only our respect for the Dalai Lama that stopped several of us from walking out."

When asked why Sogyal was allowed to take part, the Dalai Lama's private office came up with the lame excuse that they had to let all lamas know about the conference so they could attend if they wished.

Double standards perpetrated by the Tibetan diaspora headquarters in Dharamsala were becoming increasingly obvious to observers of Tibet, its religion and culture. At the turn of the 21st century the Dalai Lama had probably received hundreds of letters complaining about sexual and financial misbehaviour by Sogyal and other exiled lamas.

While some letters are acknowledged with anodyne expressions of regret, until 2017 there was no reaction on the part of the exiled Tibetan authorities to deal effectively with the alleged offenders. Apart from withdrawing from the Living and Dying Conference, the Dalai Lama never publicly criticised individual lamas – until the publication of the eight-signatory letter in July 2017 forced his hand.

When I asked why Sogyal was usually a guest speaker at events with the Dalai Lama, like the Kalachakra Initiation, Chhimed Rigdzin, an official in the Dalai Lama's private office, responded, "We don't invite him." I pointed out that they don't refuse him either.

As we pieced together Sogyal's timeline – from his birth in pre-Chinese Kham to the present day – it was impossible to avoid the conclusion that the exiled Tibetan hierarchy supported him wholeheartedly for nearly 50 years. This happened despite repeated alarm signals from many sources, together with the Janice Doe lawsuit and consistent media attention.

A web site called Tibetanlama.com is an outstanding example of the turn-a-blind-eye attitude towards Sogyal's well-documented character defects. Launched at the Kalachakra Initiation in Graz, Austria in 2002, it was sponsored by the exiled Tibetan businessman Sonam Topgyal. It went live soon after Sogyal had delivered his rant against unqualified gurus at the third conference of Western Buddhist teachers. The aims and objective of the site were firmly located on the moral high ground – clearly defined in its mission statement.

> *Our prime objective is to help the keen followers find the true contemporary masters of Buddhism, so that they are not misled. It is important to develop a clear identification of the true masters now to prevent the contamination brought to our religion by few imposters. Therefore, we are putting the information of all the great masters of Tibetan Buddhism (all the different schools of thoughts) on the website.*

Tibetanlama.com was endorsed by the Dalai Lama and promoted in various publications, including the Tibetan Review. Most of the lamas listed were probably well qualified and respectful towards their students. But guess who features prominently in the roll call of "the great masters of Tibetan Buddhism?" None other than our narcissistic charlatan, Sogyal Lakar, aka Rinpoche.

The site was online until 2011, when it was taken down without explanation, but not before being archived by the Wayback Machine at Archive.org.[49] After Rob Hogendoorn extracted Tibetanlama.com from the online vaults, we learned that it was originally set up to counteract the influence of Tibetan Buddhist organisations like the New Kadampa Tradition which uphold the practice of Dorje Shugden. Propitiation of this protector deity was vehemently discouraged by the Dalai Lama.

Sogyal's listing could easily have been removed without taking the site down – but it seems possible that the Tibetan elite realised they had made a serious error of judgement and decided to get rid of the evidence.

We emailed three senior officials in the Dalai Lama's administration to ask why Tibetanlama.com had been taken down. None of them replied.

2011 was an *annus horribilis* for Sogyal. My exposé blog about Sogyal, Behind the Thangkas, was launched that year, and the Canadian documentary *In the Name of Enlightenment* was broadcast, with damning interview material about Sogyal's sex addiction and violence from Victoria Barlow, Mimi Durand and myself.[50]

Sogyal dancing

Sogyal on the flight deck of an Air France 747 with the captain, Guy Durand

9

MIMI AND GUY

In 2006 Air France pilot Guy Durand was coming to the end of his career as a 747 captain. Since 2000 Guy ran his professional and spiritual lives in tandem. Off duty he spent his time as a serious – bordering-on-fanatical – student with Sogyal Rinpoche.

The extent of his commitment is illustrated by the fact that it spilled over into airtime – he accomplished the gruelling Tibetan Buddhist preliminary practice known as the ngondro by using his rest periods during long-distance flights to complete 108,000 full-body prostrations in the crew space behind the flight deck.

Guy worked his way through the Rigpa hierarchy to the point where he became a dharma teacher himself, alongside other members of the French elite, including Olivier Raurich, Philippe Cornu and the late Francois Calmes.

"I was looking for answers," he says, "trying to find a way to make my mind free and open. I have to admit that I was hypnotised by Sogyal for six years. As I became more involved, I distanced myself from my family and friends and devoted myself totally to Rigpa – with my time, energy and money. As a result, I became completely anti-social, turned-in on myself, and one-track minded."

Guy points out that following the Rigpa path is extremely expensive: "You have to buy ritual objects and constantly update study material. You pay for courses, study days, statues, food offerings for the temple – the list is endless. You have to sponsor people who can't afford retreats and, for those who can, the price is exorbitant. They never stop asking for money – and it's done with subtle persuasion – pretty speeches scripted specifically to make you put your hand in your pocket."

Other former Rigpa insiders confirm that there is relentless pressure to donate money. According to one of them, "I even heard Sogyal say to one man, 'Just shut up and give me your money.'"

The person who was probably most affected by Guy's obsession with Rigpa was his daughter Mimi. Aged 22 in 2000, half Japanese and outstandingly beautiful, she was already feeling parentally deprived because of Guy's professional absences. Determined to take every opportunity to be close to him, Mimi started attending Sogyal's teachings with her father – usually falling asleep against his back. Inevitably, Sogyal's lascivious roving eye alighted on Mimi, and in due course she was lured into the brainwashing process that led to his bedroom.

In 2009 Mimi spoke to me at length about her experiences with Sogyal in a series of recorded interviews. The way she was treated is identical in most respects to what happened to Dierdre Smith more than 15 years previously.

"We were at a retreat in Germany. He sent for me during his rest period and asked me to massage his hands and feet," she says. "Afterwards he gave me his schedule and his phone numbers – and almost immediately I was invited to join him for a holiday in Australia. This seemed like a nice thing to do, so I said yes.

"I was met in Sydney by a wealthy family, who were obviously under orders to look after me, and I was treated like a princess. They have a fabulous house where I was given a room, and they arranged everything I wanted – yoga classes, shopping, etc."

Did Mimi query this – and wonder why it was happening? "Not really," she says. "I assumed Sogyal was being paternal in an Asian way. But I still hadn't seen him. Then suddenly, in the middle of the night, he decided it was time to go to the beach."

A convoy of cars set off. Mimi found herself crammed into one of them with five other people, including Sogyal: "I didn't get a good impression," she says. "He virtually ignored me, which was not at all the Asian papa way – I think this was the moment when he started to manipulate my feelings."

The time at the beach coincided with Valentine's Day. Mimi was ordered to wear a best dress and turn up at Sogyal's house for dinner. At this moment she realised the whole set-up was somewhat bizarre. "There was Sogyal surrounded by five or six young pretty girls, and there were no other men," she says. "It was quite fun actually, we had nice drinks and we danced for him. Then at a certain point he asked me to go upstairs with him and massage his head. I made some sort of smart reply and he became angry. He said I was too proud, and he would have to break my pride."

A few months later Mimi got a phone call asking her if she would like to take part in a special training. "I accepted because it seemed to clarify my relationship with him. It turned out that the people involved were all women. We were put to work in the 'Lama Kitchen.' We called it hell because it was an underground bunker – a horrible place. A Swiss woman, Renata, was in charge of us, and the first three weeks were pure slavery – we worked non-stop doing the cleaning.

"We never saw Sogyal, but they gave us documents listing all the instructions he has given about caring for him around the world. There was nothing about Buddhism, but we were told the whole process was a teaching.

"They made us work so hard we didn't have time for proper meals. We had to grab food and eat standing up. We were constantly being told to run here or fetch this in a haphazard way – because basically Sogyal is not very organised. He says he wants something, and you have fifty people panicking to get it in five minutes."

As Mimi's induction into the inner circle unfolded, she was assigned work inside Sogyal's compound at Lerab Ling – two chalets and a garden surrounded by a high fence. The next stage involved being Sogyal's personal servant – bringing his food and looking after him in minute detail – in the same manner described by Dierdre Smith. "He made me the only person to interact with the other people," says Mimi. "By this time, I was sleeping on the floor in his room… every time he had a thought, I would write it down and communicate it. I had control of the phones and the walkie-talkies."

Sogyal was pampered like a medieval monarch, with a clique of women trained to respond to his slightest whim – day and night, 24/7. He was never alone and never lifted a finger to do anything for himself. After grooming her at record speed (other girls complained she had been fast-tracked out of hell's kitchen), Sogyal pounced on Mimi for the first time at a high-stress moment.

"We had arranged to go to dinner at a restaurant to celebrate one of the other girls' birthday," recounts Mimi. "Whenever Sogyal does something like this, it is a major operation involving anything up to twenty people. We have to send an advance party to the restaurant to make sure everything is exactly how he wants it. We have to polish up the big cars, pack his bags, wash him, dress him, and collect his pillows, tissues and so on."

"I was at the centre of the storm, co-ordinating the various strands, and at that time I had had only about three hours sleep a night for the past month."

When everything was ready and the people were waiting to leave, Sogyal and Mimi were alone in his chalet: "He ordered me to take my clothes off. I thought it was another test, so I did as I was told. He told me to get onto the bed and we had sex. As this was happening, he said, 'Look into my eyes, this is the moment you connect with your master.'"

"There were no preliminaries, he did not use a condom, my pleasure was not in the picture, and it was all over in about three minutes. Afterwards he made me swear to keep it a secret, even from the other girls, and said if I did not keep the samaya it would be very bad for my karma and for the karma of my family.

"It happened again, of course, especially at times of stress – before a teaching, for example, he has to have his fix. Sometimes it was every day, sometimes less often, depending on how many girls he was into, or what was happening. He is very selfish – he never asks what you would like, it's always him giving orders. Sometimes there is some petting afterwards and he reminds you how lucky you are. It's not comfortable being in the same bed with Sogyal because he's an anxious character and he doesn't sleep well. He keeps waking up and wanting things, medicines or food and so on.

"I blanked out my feelings for a while, but then I became very troubled, which was extremely difficult because I'd been sworn to secrecy and couldn't talk about it with anyone. Things started to go wrong with my body. My periods stopped. I was in shock. I had to sneak out of Lerab Ling to do the test because I was scared that I was pregnant.

"A lama called Dzigar Kongtrul Rinpoche, who was married to an American woman, came to teach at Lerab Ling. He was by himself in the courtyard and I needed to talk to someone, because I knew something was really wrong. So, I decided to talk to this lama, hoping he would explain it for me. I asked him, 'What's a consort?' He looked at me and he knew exactly what I was talking about. I burst into tears, and that bastard said, 'If you are the consort of a master you are very lucky' – and that was it. That's all he said.'"

Known as dakinis, the girls in the harem before Mimi's arrival, (Alison, Anna, Minu, Ny, Lillie, Jackie, Renata, Lorraine) gradually came to accept her as a team member. Eventually they announced that she should join them in an orgy. Mimi was not keen. The other women pressured her, insisting that they had to do whatever Rinpoche wanted: "They were terrified of being beaten," says Mimi. "During the time I was with him continuously, one of us would be beaten every day – because you forgot something or did something wrong.

"For one girl it was because the way she walked was too proud. I got a little less than the others – some would get a serious, really bad beating.

"He got irritated with me because when I did something wrong, I would hand him his back-scratcher to hit me with, and that would spoil the fun."

Mimi recalls that setting up the space for an orgy involved taking down the thangkas depicting Buddhas and other deities from the chalet walls, to reveal pornographic pictures concealed behind them.

A meeting took place during the summer of 2009 between Mimi and a former Sogyal girlfriend, Flora Sinclair (not her real name), who was with him for a while during the 1980s. During this encounter, both recalled their problems with sexually transmitted infections. "He gave me a yellow bottle of disinfectant and told me to wash with it after we had sex," says Flora. "I knew of three other women who were sleeping with him at the time – then one day I saw a different woman coming out of his room carrying a yellow bottle."

Flora recalls that her relationship with Sogyal started to deteriorate in 1985. "I felt I was being manipulated to provide sexual gratification. On one retreat in France, I discovered that he was being sexually promiscuous. I felt my trust had been betrayed. The final wake-up call came in a very unpleasant way.

"Rigpa was then based in Princess Road, Kilburn. His aunt was staying there. I had got close to her, often driving her around and having her to stay. Sogyal was being attentive to me and invited me to spend time with him in his room, which was next door to where his aunt had retired for the night. He wanted me in his bed, and I imagined that because his aunt was next door, he wouldn't have suggested it unless he was accepting me as part of his family.

"So, I got into bed with him as a consenting adult. However instead of normal sex, he forced non-consensual sex on me. I struggled but kept my voice down so as not to alarm his aunt. I was so confused that he could have done such a horrible thing when his revered aunt was literally on the other side of the wall. That was the last straw and, shortly after, I left Rigpa."

Mimi said that all the girls during her sojourn in the harem were constantly having to deal with STIs. "He never uses condoms," she says. "My gynaecological record during that time was a disaster zone."

Asked how she dealt with her situation, Mimi says the only way she could cope was to close down into denial: "I didn't think about it – I have a capacity to leave my body – I'm just not there," she says. "But I felt so ashamed because I allowed it to happen. We were constantly humiliated. I was the only one who did not have to ask him for money and was not obliged to wear Barbie Doll clothes that he paid for.

"One of the most humiliating things happened to Anna. Sogyal always had diarrhoea – his diabetes and his diarrhoea make him extremely irritable. We had to wipe his arse each time he took a crap. He also has haemorrhoids. Someone wiped his arse, then he asked her to stick a finger in and it hurt – so he went into a total fit and called in all the girls. He asked each of us to wipe him to see which one was the best. That was the only time I heard him say something nice about Anna – he announced that it was one thing she could do well."

Mimi's epiphany occurred when she was travelling alone on Eurostar: "I'd been distancing myself from Sogyal for some time. I could do this because I was not dependent on him like the other girls. I'd always kept up my singing lessons and had friends outside Rigpa. There I was in the tunnel and the defences I'd built up started to collapse. I remembered things. I realised I'd been raped and, from that point on, the more I remembered, the sicker I got."

Mimi went into counselling and, after initially keeping her experiences with Sogyal to herself, she eventually opened up with her therapist, who advised her to devise a closure ritual so that she could clear the psycho-emotional decks and move on: "I was really ill – I kept getting infections and I had a fever for about three weeks. I had nightmares every night – I was an empty carcass and I thought I was going crazy. Realising I'd reached my limit, I took my counsellor's advice and created a monstrous drawing and collage. I put myself in it and the other girls and I did a caricature of Sogyal like a Tibetan deity with lots of arms – but they were holding things like cash and the beating stick. Instead of clouds I put speech bubbles with the phrases in them that he used to intimidate and manipulate us."

Mimi took her artwork to Sogyal when he was leading the Rigpa UK Easter retreat. She also took two friends to ride shotgun – one of them a large man. "We went into his formal reception room and I handed him the drawing and burst into floods of tears. There was a long silence – then he asked me what I wanted. I tried to say that I wanted him to stop what he's doing, but he started to talk about money. I thought well, why not – I would like my expenses for the trip. I told him the ticket cost 450 Euros, so he got up and came back with an envelope. I left with my friends and when I opened the envelope, I had a moment of pleasure – he'd given me 350 rather than the full amount, so I knew I'd made him angry.

"After this a lot of important Rigpa people called me. There were all sorts of threats, and I heard that men were claiming I'd slept with them and were calling me a whore. But they should know that Sogyal is very possessive about the women he likes – he only lets the ones he wants to get rid of sleep with other men. I know now that many of the things he does are punishable by law. I am not afraid of him."

While the Sogyal-Mimi saga played out, Guy was participating in Rigpa's first three years, three months and three days retreat. This is a traditional Tibetan Buddhist training programme, designed to bring about deep contemplative realisation and yogic insight. The retreat, involving intensive practice and seclusion from the outside world, began on August 9, 2006 and ended on November 21, 2009.

However, true to form, Sogyal adapted the retreat to dovetail with his version of Tibetan Buddhism as a marketable commodity. One of Rigpa's websites described it thus: "The purpose of such a break is to re-emerge into the world refreshed and re-inspired, having further developed the mind's innate qualities of peacefulness and clarity, and deepened the heart's innate capacity for empathy and compassion."

It does not mention any of the profound aspects of Buddhist meditation – primordial wisdom, for example, emptiness or integration beyond duality. In comparison with the way other lamas present Tibetan Buddhism, Sogyal's programme could be equated with studying for primary school exams.

Guy Durand, retired from flight duty and free from family obligations, sorted his external affairs and settled into Lerab Ling with every intention of completing the retreat in the expectation that it would move his spiritual practice into a fresh dimension. Instead, he found himself in a situation where the emphasis on group rather than solitary practice was wholly unproductive.

"I had no experiences," he says. "At the start I went along with what was happening but eventually I gave up and, instead of doing Tibetan meditation, I concealed a Zen text in my prayer books and read that when I was supposed to be meditating."

The *coup de grâce* on Guy's involvement with Rigpa came when he read a letter from Mimi – three weeks after it had arrived. In it she confessed to her father that she had been in a sexual relationship with Sogyal. "I was very angry," he says.

Guy demanded an interview with Sogyal, who was initially wary but then admitted he had had sex with Mimi. He tried to shift the blame onto her – claiming that she had seduced him and that he was at first resistant but later gave in to her demands.

Guy was inclined to believe his daughter's version of what happened and this, coupled with his disillusionment with Tibetan spiritual practice, made him decide to leave the retreat – but not before he had shared his feelings with other retreatants. "We were not allowed to talk," he says, "but we found ways to communicate." As a result, some of the 200 people present also left the retreat – some shocked at the revelation, others realising that their pre-existing doubts were well founded.

During the time that Sogyal has been active as a lama in the developed world, the deep split between his public persona and his private life has been observed by several people who were not involved with him sexually.

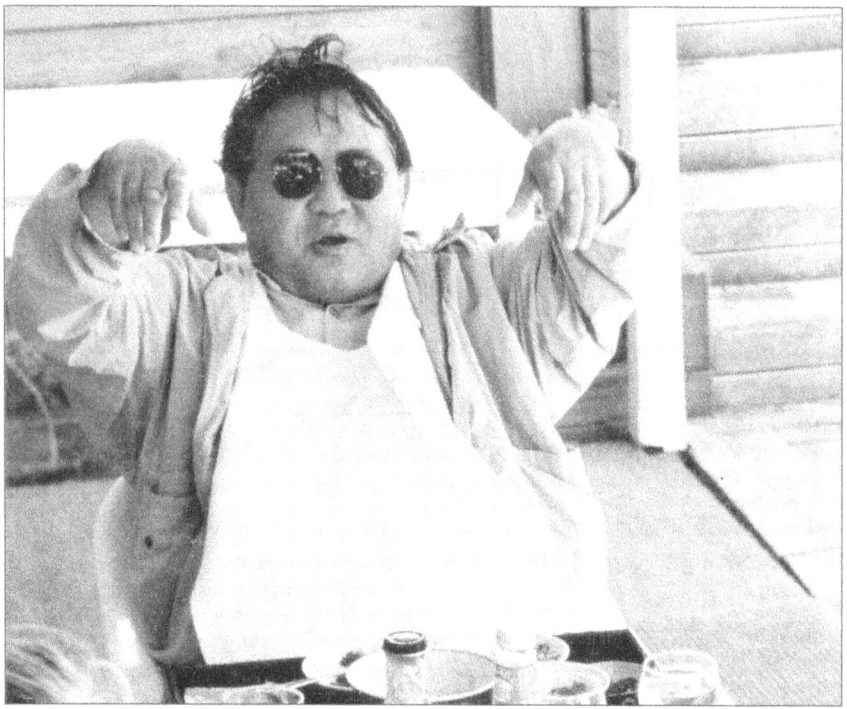

Sogyal enjoying a gourmet lunch

These include former assistants, a former member of Rigpa UK, an anonymous witness who was the manager of a Rigpa centre and Louella (not her real name), who cooked for Sogyal while he was teaching in Montreal.

Louella reports: "I was in his apartment all day. Most of the time, Sogyal was with his two dakinis, Mimi and Anna. I saw him furious and yelling insults at Mimi, saying things like, 'She's such a stupid woman'. He ran after her, trying to hit her as she ran away crying. When he noticed me there, he became very uneasy and tried to explain that he had to act like this because she had made a mistake.

"When he was taking a bath, he used to shout for Mimi. I asked Anna what was wrong with him. She replied that he needed Mimi to wash him. I was astonished at this – coming from a lama who claims to be as powerful as Padmasambhava. I left Rigpa because in my view the way Sogyal acts is autocratic and abusive, and Rigpa was becoming increasingly like a cult. Sogyal orders people around without any respect for their personal needs. Although I am still interested in Buddhism, I do not have confidence in Sogyal."

10

Hubris and Nemesis

The abuse witnessed by Louella and experienced by Dierdre and Mimi begs the question: why do Sogyal's dakinis tolerate his behaviour? A core group had been in this role for a long time, augmented by a steady flow of new recruits. Considering that beatings and other forms of abuse had been happening for many years, why did it take until 2017 for eight of his former long-term students to feel motivated to speak out?

In answer to the first question, it should be remembered that members of Sogyal's harem have very high status within Rigpa. They are the closest to the guru, and the propaganda line is that they are chosen for their spiritual qualities. On the second question, most of them are indoctrinated into keeping silent to "protect the dharma." Some are embarrassed by the fact that they allowed themselves to be duped by a con man and, after extricating themselves from his clutches, want to move on from the experience rather than re-live it (painfully) in interviews. Also, there is an element of sadomasochism in the relationship between Sogyal and his harem. Mimi maintains that one woman in particular welcomes the beatings.

These characteristics within the Rigpa elite were confirmed by Oane Bijlsma, a Dutch woman who was inducted into the inner circle as a hospitality manager but managed to avoid Sogyal's sexual attention. "It's a BDSM cult minus a safe word," she says.

In 2011 a woman who wishes to remain anonymous wrote about her experiences with Sogyal: "It's all so subtle and manipulative you just don't realise what's happening and you get ensnared in the dogma web. Fear and suspicion play a big part in controlling you.

"I remember I seriously started to have doubts about five years ago. I was ordered to give Alison a massage and she confided in me that she was SR's main consort and that he had a harem.

"She said after he made love to her, he just rolled over with no tenderness and she confessed how hard she found it and how jealous all the girls were of each other – that they are very competitive. She said she had been told to make a vow with two other main girls in the harem so that they couldn't have sexual relations with anyone else but were kind of married exclusively to him.

"The following Easter retreat I had lost a lot of weight – he likes them skinny – and had just come out of a long relationship. As soon as Sogyal knew this he started on me. He started to grab me and kiss me, but I would push him away. The worst time was when he'd eaten some Tibetan cheese and kissed me and poured the contents in my mouth – horrific. He also started to court another young girl who is married. She's his consort now.

"The following summer I was called into his chalet with Alison and Lorraine. He took Alison's breasts out and kissed them and took mine out but thankfully didn't do anything to me – I think it was to see how I would react. He kissed Lorraine, who is Patrick's partner, and then ordered me to give Alison a massage.

"That same summer he called me on my own into his chalet and said he wanted to open me up a little. I felt very trapped and frozen. I just stood there. He kissed me, then told me to lift my skirt because he wanted to look at my bottom. Then he asked me if I thought he was a good kisser – how pathetic is that? I eventually said I didn't want anything, and I left. After that I was ignored by Sogyal, and his entourage were horrible to me."

Marie Lefevre had a salaried job with Rigpa Paris, working for eight to 12 hours a day. She witnessed a number of circumstances and events which aroused grave doubts and caused her to leave. "I noticed that people are brainwashed and that Rigpa is run more like a business mafia than a spiritual organisation. They are obsessed with appearances – Sogyal urges his people to buy expensive clothes and products and to look smart. Money given by devout students is used to buy luxuries for Sogyal – and people who have outlived their usefulness are discarded in a very cruel manner."

After 36 years of high-profile activity as a spiritual mentor, it was inevitable that the dichotomy between the man and his message would become known. The Rigpa mystique started to unravel in 2009, when internet blogs in French and English (*Les Trois Mondes* and *Dialogue Ireland*) attracted testimonies from a wide spectrum of people disillusioned with Rigpa and distressed by sexual encounters with Sogyal.

A Google search for "Sogyal Rinpoche abuse" reveals a range of internet chatter along the same lines. It has to be said that some postings defend the man with obvious sincerity, while others are emotional outpourings from people who have invested their hopes and aspirations in a charismatic leader whose shortcomings are being revealed through the lens of public scrutiny.

In 2011 Sogyal's sex life came under mainstream media scrutiny again.

The Canadian production company Cogent/Benger's half-hour investigative television documentary titled *In the Name of Enlightenment* was broadcast on Vision TV in Canada on 27 May 2011, as an item in a four-part series on sexual abuse in religions. It featured among others, Mimi, Victoria Barlow, a Canadian former Rigpa student (Denise), the Buddhist teachers Stephen and Martine Batchelor, and me. Reports based on this documentary appeared in the *Irish Sunday Times* and the *Guardian* newspapers. It has been viewed 242,000+ times on YouTube and has generated more than 500 comments.

In October 2011, the French news magazine *Marianne* carried a six-page feature on one of Sogyal's teaching retreats at Lerab Ling. It was compiled from material gathered by an undercover journalist, Elodie Emery. The tone of the reportage alternates from coy to sarcastic to shock/horror and contains allegations that would not get past legal scrutiny at mainstream British media.[51]

It does, however, vividly illustrate the dysfunctional ambiance of a Rigpa event and it highlights Sogyal's bully-boy tactics, the pleasure he derives from making people squirm, and his ruthlessly cruel treatment of one Dutch participant who was stumbling towards an agonised confession of incest with his daughter in front of 500 retreatants. Emery also reported that Sogyal's display of self-importance included claims that people have been cured of cancer and blindness as a result of their devotion to him.

By 2012 Sogyal's hubris was running so far out of control that members of his inner circle could no longer sustain the level of self-deception required by their loyalty to him. Oane Bijlsma left Rigpa in 2013, to be followed a year later by the resignation of one of the most high-profile members of the elite.[52]

Olivier Raurich was president of Rigpa France. His defining moment occurred when Rigpa employed an expensive spin doctor to tutor senior figures on how to avoid answering awkward questions. Olivier spoke about his decision to Elodie Emery. The interview was published in *Marianne* and later translated into English:

I felt the tension ratchet up a notch within the Rigpa leadership. All the secrecy and manipulation of information weighed heavily on me. I had come for teachings on humility, love, truth, and trust, and I found myself in a quasi-Stalinist environment and permanent double-talk. His dictatorial side and anger worsened, and I was increasingly disturbed by it. He did not hesitate to brutally silence and ridicule people in meetings. Critical thinking is prohibited around him – the door is locked. Negative feedback never reaches him – only praise is reported because people in the close circle are afraid of him. It can make him angry, or he would humiliate those close to him. He can also be friendly and full of humour if everything conforms to his wishes.[53]

Cracks in the Rigpa façade widened even further with the publication in 2016 of Marion Dapsance's *Les dévots du bouddhisme*.[54] Originally written as a PhD thesis, her book examines Rigpa through a highly critical lens, based in her personal experience of Sogyal's teachings. The book attracted widespread publicity in France – together with an indignant refutation from Professor Philippe Cornu, a staunch Sogyal supporter and Rigpa teacher.

The Rigpa meltdown gathered momentum in The Netherlands. In November 2016 two women staged a silent protest outside the hall in Amsterdam where Sogyal was leading a city retreat.

On 13 June 2017, The Dutch investigative television programme *Brandpunt* aired a half-hour documentary on Sogyal and Rigpa which featured revelations of corruption from the former insider Oane Bijlsma, together with forensic analysis from Rob Hogendoorn highlighting the fault lines in Rigpa's modus operandi.[55]

Most of the spiritual seekers worldwide who still revere Sogyal choose to remain in denial. They have probably been advised against doing internet searches, on the basis that awareness of his hidden agenda would adversely affect their Buddhist practice. There are two taboos in Buddhist organisations – both of which have merit and both of which can be used as manipulative tools.

One of them is an injunction against gossip, effective when trying to establish a calm mental state but also useful to prevent the circulation of critical comment. The second is samaya, the indestructible bond of loyalty that is one of the key tenets of Tibetan Buddhism. It supports the relationship between teacher and neophyte but can be deployed unscrupulously as a threat – break your samaya and attract dire consequences to yourself and your loved ones.

Another pillar of Tibetan doctrine is pure perception. This entails seeing everything the lama does as perfect and beyond criticism. Fine, if the lama is fully qualified to teach and is guided by a fully functional moral and ethical compass. But it is also deployed by individuals like Sogyal Lakar as a manipulative tool, aimed at stifling dissent and keeping disciples in a state of mindless devotion.

Tibetan lamas who have taken empowerments from the same guru regard themselves as vajra brothers, bound by samaya. This is probably one explanation for the fact that most lamas teaching in the developed world closed ranks around Sogyal, regardless of their misgivings. A more cynical view hinges on the fact that Sogyal pulled in a great deal of money – some of which is channelled into Tibetan worthy causes.

There is a Tibetan prophesy attributed to Padmasambhava which goes like this:

When the Iron Bird flies and horses run on wheels, the Tibetan people will be scattered like ants across the world and the dharma will come to the land of the red man.

If it really was uttered in the 8th century, it is a potent illustration of the qualities of Tibetan Buddhism that have attracted a huge worldwide following and made the predication come true. Sogyal and his cohorts built an empire based on that tradition, but they turned their version of it into a personality cult around a celebrity guru, losing sight of core principles in their quest for ever-expanding power, influence and cash flow.

In my view it was inevitable that it would disintegrate. What took me by surprise was the high drama that kick-started the process.

Sogyal with members of his inner circle, Jackie, Kimberley and Mauro

*Sogyal with his close friend Namkha Rinpoche,
who is under investigation for sex offences in Switzerland*

11

The Letter

On the 14th of July 2017, a volcanic eruption that had been grumbling beneath the surface since the 1980s finally spewed toxic lava onto the worldwide Buddhist community.

Eight former long-term senior Rigpa devotees sent a letter to Sogyal, accusing him in graphic detail of a panorama of crimes and misdemeanours. Their mailing list also included 1,000 members of the upper echelons of the Rigpa hierarchy. It was intended for restricted circulation within the organisation, but in view of its contents it is not even faintly surprising that within hours of its despatch it went viral – initially around the Buddhist cognoscenti but quickly fanning out onto the internet. The corruption that had been festering under the carpet for decades was publicly exposed. The Buddhist version of omerta was blown wide open. The only way to get a handle on the colossal impact of the eight-signatory letter is to read it from start to finish.

Sogyal Lakar,

The Rigpa Sangha is in crisis. Long-simmering issues with your behavior can no longer be ignored or denied. As long-time committed and devoted students we feel compelled to share our deep concern regarding your violent and abusive behavior. Your actions have hurt us individually, harmed our fellow sisters and brothers within Rigpa the organization, and by extension Buddhism in the West. We write to you following the advice of the Dalai Lama, in which he has said that students of Tibetan Buddhist lamas are obliged to communicate their concerns about their teacher:

If one presents the teachings clearly, others benefit. But if someone is supposed to propagate the Dharma and their behavior is harmful, it is our responsibility to criticize this with a good motivation. This is constructive criticism, and you do not need to feel uncomfortable doing it. In "The Twenty Verses on the Bodhisattvas' Vows," it says that there is no fault in whatever action you engage in with pure motivation. Buddhist teachers who abuse sex, power, money, alcohol, or drugs, and who, when faced with legitimate complaints from their own students, do not correct their behavior, should be criticized openly and by name. This may embarrass them and cause them to regret and stop their abusive behavior. Exposing the negative allows space for the positive side to increase. When publicizing such misconduct, it should be made clear that such teachers have disregarded the Buddha's advice. However, when making public the ethical misconduct of a Buddhist teacher, it is only fair to mention their good qualities as well.

The Dalai Lama, Dharamsala, India March 1993.

This letter is our request to you to stop your unethical and immoral behavior.

Your public face is one of wisdom, kindness, humor, warmth and compassion, but your private behavior, the way you conduct yourself behind the scenes, is deeply disturbing and unsettling. A number of us have raised with you privately, our concerns about your behavior in recent years, but you have not changed.

Those of us who write to you today have first-hand experience of your abusive behaviors, as well as the massive efforts not to allow others to know about them. Our concerns are deepened with the organizational culture you have created around you that maintains absolute secrecy of your actions, which is in sharp contrast with your stated directive of openness and transparency within the Sangha. Our wish is to break this veil of secrecy, deception, and deceit. We can no longer remain silent.

Our deep and heartfelt hope is that this collective note might yield a more tangible result than any of our individual discussions with you have. We hope that long-lasting and sincere changes may come about rather than short-lived pledges.

Our primary concerns are:

1. Your physical, emotional and psychological abuse of students.

2. *Your sexual abuse of students.*

3. *Your lavish, gluttonous, and sybaritic lifestyle.*

4. *Your actions have tainted our appreciation for the practice of the Dharma.*

1. *Physical, emotional and psychological abuse.*

We have received directly from you, and witnessed others receiving, many different forms of physical abuse. You have punched and kicked us, pulled hair, torn ears, as well as hit us and others with various objects such as your back-scratcher, wooden hangers, phones, cups, and any other objects that happened to be close at hand. We trusted for many years that this physical and emotional treatment of students – what you assert to be your "skillful means" of "wrathful compassion" in the tradition of "crazy wisdom" – was done with our best interest at heart in order to free us from our "habitual patterns." We no longer believe this to be so. We feel that we and others have been harmed because your actions were not compassionate; rather they demonstrated your lack of discipline and your own frustration. Your physical abuse – which constitutes a crime under the laws of the lands where you have done these acts – have left monks, nuns, and lay students of yours with bloody injuries and permanent scars. This is not second-hand information; we have experienced and witnessed your behavior for years.

Why did you inflict violence upon us and our fellow Dharma brothers and sisters? Why did you punch, slap, kick, and pull our hair? Your food was not hot enough; you were awakened from your nap a half hour late; the phone list was missing a name or the font was the wrong size; the internet connection was slow; the television movie guide was confusing; technology failed to work; your assistant wasn't attentive enough; we failed to "tune into your mind" and predict what you wanted; or you were moody because you were upset with one of your girlfriends.

There are hundreds of examples of trivial incidents that have set you off and your response has been to strike us violently.

Your emotional and psychological abuse has been perhaps more damaging than the physical scars you have left on us. When we have worked for you while organizing and setting up the infrastructure for you to teach at different places around the world (Europe, North America, Australia, and India and Nepal), your shaming and threatening have led some of your closest students and attendants to emotional breakdowns.

You have always told us to be appreciative of the personal attention that you give, that you were "pointing out our hidden faults" in our character, and freeing us from "our self-cherishing ego." We no longer believe this to be so. It was done in such a way that was harmful to us rather than helpful, a method of control, a blatant means of subjugation and undue influence that removed our liberty. You have threatened us and others saying, if we do not follow you absolutely, we will die "spitting up blood like Ian Maxwell." You have told us that our loved ones are at risk of ill-health, or have died, because we displeased you in some way." At public teachings, you have regularly criticized, manipulated and shamed us and those working to run your retreats. You have told us for years that this is part of your unique style of "training" students and that this shaming is part of the guru-disciple relationship. We no longer believe this to be so.

As more students verged close to emotional breakdowns because of your "trainings," you introduced "Rigpa Therapy" for your closest students. Trained, practising therapists (who are also your students) were given the task of dealing with the pain that was being stirred up in the minds of those who you were abusing physically, emotionally and psychologically. During one-to-one sessions, the therapist heard from the student of your "crazy wisdom" methods and the trauma that it caused the individual. One such "Rigpa Therapy" method for processing the trauma was to negate the validity of seeing you, the teacher and instigator, as the source of the trauma. Instead, we were instructed to see old family relationship histories as the issue. In effect, our very tangible and clear discernment of seeing you as an abuser was blocked and instead we were blamed and made to feel inadequate. On the occasions when the "therapy" did not result in a student changing their view of you, you shamed the therapist into feeling that they weren't doing their job properly and were not skilled.

2. Sexual Abuse

You use your role as a teacher to gain access to young women, and to coerce, intimidate and manipulate them into giving you sexual favors. The ongoing controversies of your sexual abuse that we can read and watch on the Internet are only a small window into your decades of this behavior. Some of us have been subjected to sexual harassment in the form of being told to strip, to show you our genitals (both men and women), to give you oral sex, being groped, asked to give you photos of our genitals, to have sex in your bed with our partners, and to describe to you our sexual relations with our partners. You've ordered your students to photograph your attendants and girlfriends naked, and then forced other students to make photographic collages for you, which you have shown to others.

You have offered one of your female attendants to another lama (who is well known in Rigpa) for sex. You have had for decades, and continue to have, sexual relationships with a number of your student attendants, some who are married. You have told us to lie on your behalf, to hide your sexual relationships from your other girlfriends. Publically you claim that your relationships are ordinary, consensual, and proper because you are not a monk. You deny any wrongdoing and have even claimed on occasion that you were seduced. You and others in your organization claim this is how a Buddhist master of "crazy wisdom" behaves, just like the tantric adepts of the past. We do not believe this to be so and see such claims as attempts to explain away egregious behaviors.

3. Gluttonous lifestyle

Your lavish lifestyle is kept hidden from your thousands of students. It is one thing for you to accept an offering of the best of everything (that we may have) as an acknowledgement of our gratitude for spiritual teachings. It is quite another to demand it from us. Much of the money that is used to fund your luxurious appetites comes from the donations of your students who believe their offering is being used to further wisdom and compassion in the world. As attendants, drivers, and organizers for you, most of our time and energy is taken up providing a steady supply of sensual pleasures. You demand all kinds of food be prepared for you – at all hours of the night and day – by your personal chefs and attendants (who Rigpa pays for) who travel the world with you. You demand all forms of entertainment; this includes having detailed TV guide schedules for the shows that you often watch for hours on end each day; elaborate movie lists so you know what's playing in theaters near you at all times; continual supply of take-out restaurant food; drivers and masseuses on call 24 hours a day to serve you and deliver you and your companions to theaters, expensive restaurants, venues to shop and secretive places where you can smoke your expensive cigars.

With impatience, you have made demands for this entertainment and decadent sensory indulgences. When these are not made available at the snap of a finger, or exactly as you wished, we were insulted, humiliated, made to feel worthless, stupid and incompetent, and often hit or slapped. Your behavior did not cultivate our mindfulness or awareness, but rather it made us terrified of making a mistake. You tell your students that you spend most of your time engaging in Buddhist study and practice, but those of us who have attended you in private for years know this is not the reality. We feel it is unethical that ours and others' financial contributions to you – believed to be furthering the Dharma – are used to support this lavish lifestyle. Please stop living a duplicitous life. If you have no shame about your behavior then let it see the light of day. Allow the rest of your students to see who you really are, and let them make their own informed decision about whether you are the teacher for them.

4. *Tainted our appreciation for the practice of the Dharma.*

Please understand the harm that you have inflicted on us has also tainted our appreciation for and practice of the Dharma.

In our decades of study and practice of Tibetan Buddhism with you, we trained our minds to view you as the "all embodied jewel" and the "source of all the teachings and blessings" of the Buddha-Dharma. We trusted you completely. Yet, we struggled for years because your actions did not square with the teachings. Today, for many of us who have left you, the Lerab Ling community, and Rigpa the organization, our ground of confidence in the Buddha-Dharma has been compromised.

Some of us, who chose to depart abruptly Lerab Ling, left all of our possessions, because we were desperate to break away from your abuse and the community that supported it. Whether we departed abruptly or have faded away from you and Rigpa, we struggle to rekindle an appreciation for the transformative teachings and teachers we encountered. *Often when we sit down to meditate and practice, we feel polluted with trauma from our experience with you; some of us relate to the Vajrayana with deep suspicion; and some of us are at work rebuilding from scratch the foundations of our study and practice, recognizing that your manipulation was intermingled with all that we were taught. Others of us seek conventional therapy as a means for processing.*

So quite contrary to your aspiration to bring the true Dharma to beings, the effect of your methods is that our relationship to the Dharma has been tainted. We now see clearly the many ways that you betrayed our trust, manipulated and abused us and our Dharma brothers and sisters. We are not showing a lack of trust and respect, being a "trouble-maker" with "negative talk" as you often assert when anyone has dared to object to your methods. In fact, we have trusted you too long, given you the benefit of the doubt over and over again. When we've attempted to raise these concerns you've shamed us, and threatened to withhold the teachings from all the students because we had "doubts." You have encouraged us to defame others, in particular in France, who have spoken out against you in recent years. We have seen how you hold the teachings "hostage" and demand that students show their devotion through continuous "offerings" in the form of money and free labor. You tell us this is how to become an authentic Dharma practitioner. We do not believe this to be the path of the Dharma.

With regards to your abusive behavior, your sexual misconduct, and your lavish lifestyle, we see no clear or identifiable ethical standards or guidelines to which you are held. There is a vacuum of accountability. We hope that sending you this letter, sharing it with your peers, and the Rigpa Dzogchen mandala students, will serve to fill that vacuum. What you have taught in the last thirty years, and in particular The Tibetan Book of Living and Dying, *has brought immense benefit to so many people including those who write to you today. If we are wrong in what we write, please correct our mistaken view. If your striking and punching us and others, and having sex with your students and married women, and funding your sybaritic lifestyle with students' donations, is actually the ethical and compassionate behavior of a Buddhist teacher, please explain to us how it is. If, however, we are correct in our assessment, please stop your behaviors that we believe to be harmful to others.*

In closing we want to acknowledge that most of the public critique of you that is found on the Internet is factual. Some of us, who have held positions of responsibility within Rigpa, struggle with our own part in having covered for you and "explained" away your behavior, while not caring for those with traumatic experiences.

Our past motivation to see all the actions of our tantric teacher as pure obscured us from seeing the very real harm that you are inflicting. We are each taking a long and serious look at our own behaviors, trying to learn from them, and supporting each other on our journey. We can no longer stay silent while you harm others in the name of Buddhism. Our deepest wish is to see Buddhism flourish in the West. We no longer want to indulge in the stupidity of seeing the Guru as perfect at any cost. The path does not require us to sacrifice our wisdom to discern, our ethics and morality, or our integrity, on the altar of "Guru Yoga." Our heartfelt wish is that you seek guidance from the Dalai Lama, other reputable lamas of good heart, or anyone who can help to bring you back onto the true path of the Dharma.

With deep respect for the Dharma,

- *Mark Standlee, student for 33 years, Three Year Retreatant, former Director of the International Rigpa Online Courses & Rigpa US Teaching Services for 5 years, International Senior Instructor*

- *Sangye, student for 16 years, Three Year Retreatant, Buddhist monk for 14 years, Codirector of technology for Rigpa International*

- *Damcho, student for 15 years, Three Year Retreatant, Buddhist nun for 10 years, personal assistant to Sogyal Lakar*

- *Matteo Pistono, student for 19 years, former Rigpa US Board Member, author of* Fearless In Tibet: The Life of the Mystic Tertön Sogyal

- *Joanne Standlee, student for 18 years, Head of Sogyal Lakar's household in US for 15 years, National Director for Rigpa US for 7 years, Director of Zam America for 5 years, Rigpa Instructor*
- *Graham Price, student for 20 years, Sogyal Lakar's personal attendant and driver,*
- *Michael Condon, student for 21 years, Rigpa Instructor, Sogyal Lakar's personal attendant and driver in the US*
- *Gary Goldman, student for 23 years*

Gary Goldman

Sogyal's last public appearance in July 2017 with his Tibetan host Khenpo Sodargye on the first day of the Seventh World Youth Buddhist Symposium in Chiang Mai, Thailand.

12

The Aftermath

About two weeks in advance of the letter to Sogyal, several of his long-term critics were deliberating about issuing a news release. Our aim was to raise awareness of Sogyal's ongoing refusal to own up to his abusive behaviour by highlighting recent evidence published in France and online. We must have been telepathic. It was only after we were about to go public that one of the eight signatories to the Sogyal letter heard about our intention and wrote to us, advising us to hold fire.

Fortunately, we took this person's advice – and found out about our narrow escape from embarrassment on the morning of the 14th of July 2017. The letter hit my email from three different sources within a couple of hours, one of them from a member of our critics group.

It was impossible for me to avoid some *schadenfreude* moments when news came through that Sogyal had resigned as Spiritual Director of Rigpa and – surprise, surprise – was "in retreat." Sogyal's last public appearance was at the 7th World Youth Buddhist Symposium in Chiang Mai, Thailand between 30 July and 2 August 2017. We now know that he never left Thailand except for a brief trip to Nepal, where he was spotted circumambulating the Boudnath stupa. Sogyal's "retreat" lasted until his death on 28 August 2019.

For me, the letter triggered mixed emotions. On the one hand, I was ecstatically happy that he had been taken out of circulation as a teacher and that my long and at times turbulent campaign to get rid of him was vindicated. But on the other, there was a sense of failure – the eight insiders appeared to have achieved with one whistle blow what I had been striving towards for decades.

Despite the ebb and flow of conflicting responses, I winged off an email to Joanne Standlee, who had been pointed out to me as the signatory most likely to assume a leadership role:

I am writing to you about the very courageous, very impressive letter you and your co signatories have addressed to Sogyal and sent to many other people.

It has been hot in my inbox all afternoon.

Inevitably this will be picked up by the mainstream media. I will think carefully about how I frame the letter, with the aim of releasing it to the UK media. My intention at the moment is to offer it to the Guardian *as an exclusive. If they do not bite I will send it to all UK media, including the BBC.*

Although I appreciate your aim to achieve maximum impact with members of Rigpa, I have to say I do not appreciate being demonised. I also firmly believe that a wider constituency needs to be made aware of the dangers inherent in involvement with Rigpa.

I have had several FB Messenger exchanges with your co-signatory Sangye Ngawang. I urged him to appoint a spokesperson for the signatories who will be available for interview. I'm not sure if he took this on board because I think he was exhausted. I recommend that you do this in order to sustain your credibility.

Yours in the dharma

Her response was swift – and from my perspective, naïve and disingenuous. One or two Buddhist friends have described it as rude and insulting.

You have already done a wonderful job of getting the word out to new people and prospective students. This letter is intended to address a completely different and firmly entrenched audience.

The fact is you have been demonized and everything on your blog, everything you're associated with, gives ammunition to Sogyal Lakar with his students. I'm sorry for that but it's a fact.

The only way to effect change is to attempt to help our sangha friends to see the truth in a reasoned way. This was a private letter and we all would find it extremely aggressive, unhelpful and unkind for you to do anything with it. We could easily have gone to the press if that was our intent. If anyone from the media contacts us that will be our response. This was a private communication, we feel it is a violation of our privacy to have it shared in any way but that which we intended.

My sense is that none of us are willing to be interviewed, but in the interest of openness and transparency I will forward this communication to all of them, they can reach out to you if they feel differently.

Please consider that if none of us is willing to engage you will undermine your credibility. There is also the sense of the public harm you might cause to us personally, which is a very real thing for us.

I understand that we can't control the message, I'm appealing to your sense of fairness, and hope that you can respect our process.

To give credit where credit is due, according to the signatory Gary Goldman the eight spent a lot of time and energy figuring out the style and content of the letter. "We wrestled with it every day for two months," he says, "agonising over every word." Gary describes how the process evolved:

I had heard the rumours but discounted them, thinking that they were just the complaints of a few rejected women… SL wouldn't have been the first "celebrity" to have had contentious relationships with the opposite sex. Then I saw him flail Kimberly Poppe with his back scratcher in the car while driving in LA one day, for handing him a document printed in the wrong font. If we hadn't been on the freeway in traffic, I would have pulled over and made an issue of it. Later when I questioned Kimberly, she laughed it off, said he was just "worn out from teaching and traveling" and to let it go. Still…

After the Lerab Ling incident where he punched Anne Chöki in the gut, everything changed.

When we got back to LA, Michael Condon and I realised that both of us were seriously re-evaluating the whole Rigpa thing. SL's pomposity, his violent outbursts. Both of us had experienced them… at the time, I thought mine was quite funny but then I come from a military background, with all that entails. There was a very big change in the temperature. Word of that punching incident had begun to spread and honestly I do believe to this day that it really was the straw that broke the Lakar back. People started calling, asking about it and suddenly, it all started coming out into harsh daylight… the years of bizarre sexual abuse, the squandering of millions of dollars of donations, the luxurious lifestyle, the whole con game of teaching Dzogchen when he absolutely knew he was out of his depth despite Nyoshul Khen Rinpoche's private teachings, Rigpa "therapy", etc. etc. It was like a tsunami had hit us all. Funny... after getting away with years of privately physically abusing his closest students, a public punch finally brought him down.

Their discussions kicked off as an online group, sharing what they had seen and experienced. As the full extent of the horror came into focus, it became clear to them that Sogyal should resign. The idea of the letter emerged from their deliberations as the most likely way to achieve that outcome. Gary says several other people also wanted to sign.

The genie escaped from the bottle only a few hours after Sogyal and 1,000 other people received the letter. By the time Joanne responded to my approach, it was already frolicking gleefully in cyberspace.

As events following the release of the letter unfolded, it became clear that Joanne was mistaken on two significant points. The letter did not bring about the sort of change at Rigpa that the eight had intended. People certainly left the organisation in droves, which was a change in itself, but the culture within Rigpa was unaffected. And Damcho, one of the eight, was willing to talk to the media and gave an in-depth interview to Mick Brown at the *Telegraph* Magazine and to the *Canberra Times*.[56] Gary Goldman did the same for me. Damcho also spoke about her experience with Sogyal at a conference in Australia and for an online seminar.

ROB HOGENDOORN'S REACTION TO JOANNE WAS CHARACTERISTICALLY TRENCHANT:

For those of you who didn't know, I'm a Master of Law (LL.M.). So let's face the bare truth for a moment: the signatories themselves accuse Sogyal of 'crimes under the laws of the lands where you have done these acts.' I'm sure they understand what that means, because they use the observation as a threat.

And indeed, the signatories themselves present a long list of facts that are each criminal misdemeanours and felonies. Moreover, the signatories state that they've personally suffered and witnessed these misdemeanours and felonies for years, and covered them up. They admit that until now each signatory has been willing to hide these crimes from the public view. Also, they've not reported these crimes to the police, leaving the victims of these crimes out in the cold.

Why don't they report these crimes right here, right now?

All would be over for Sogyal within weeks, for he would be arrested.

Are the signatories, perhaps, acting under the assumption that they are laws unto themselves? That it's up to them to decide which crimes are to be reported and prosecuted, and which are not?

Has their stack of hubris not been depleted, yet?

Do they realize that there's a world outside Rigpa that deserves to be protected against their very way of doing things, enabling abuse and battery?

Instead, they expect the recipients of a leaked letter – which does not bear the stamp confidential – to keep these crimes secret, just like they did, and thereby become complicit in their cover up?

Those who were abused and traumatised in so many ways were victims not only of Sogyal, but of Rigpa and its leaders too.

The effects of sexual trauma, in particular, affect not just victims, but their children and grandchildren as well. Are some of the signatories afraid that they might be accused of criminal complicity? That they might be legally liable?

Joanne Standlee's diatribe addressed to me seems like blatant hypocrisy in light of her decision in 2020 to participate in the Dutch documentary *Guru in Disgrace*. She gives extensive interview material, describing Sogyal's violent attacks on helpless young women. She explains how the eight signatories decided that "Sogyal had to be stopped." And how Sogyal used to phone her, regardless of time zones, from wherever he was on his globetrotting schedule. She appeared to be flattered by his attention.

This movie is as close as you could get to an in-house production. It was directed by Jaap Verhoeven, Rigpa's former audio-visual co-ordinator – and features a cast of Rigpa enablers trying to atone for the error of their ways. One cannot help wondering if it was planned as a device to own up to Rigpa's knowledge of Sogyal's depravity. In this case, it may have been in collusion with the present Rigpa elite. Many of the participants sugar the bitter pill with appreciation of Sogyal's "teachings" and the joys of being involved with his organisation.

Simultaneously with the release of the letter, two blogs appeared online, both run by former Rigpa students. What Now? was the brainchild of Tahlia Newland in Australia, which morphed into Beyond the Temple. How Did It Happen? Is run by Bernie Schreck in America. Both were set up with the philanthropic aim of helping traumatised Rigpa devotees to come to terms with the seismic upheaval in their lives. Tahlia also set up a What Now? secret Facebook group.

On all three platforms there was a tsunami of debate and comment. People who had been members of Rigpa for many years had the rug pulled out from under feet that they believed were planted in fertile ground. People who had placed their trust and devotion in Sogyal were devastated to learn that the guru they idolised was in fact a very nasty piece of work.

The reason that so many Rigpa people were in shock is simple – they didn't know what went on behind closed doors. The vast majority of Rigpa's worldwide constituency only saw the kind, smiley, jokey lama who had mastered the dark art of deception. All the rank and file experienced was a fat man on a throne who was grumpy with his attendants – but who had also fine-tuned a portmanteau of evangelical techniques. They were encouraged to regard Rigpa as their family, which made the impact of Sogyal's betrayal all the more agonising. To the mostly kind and sincere Rigpa devotees it was like finding out that your father had been arrested for rape.

Rank and file members who asked awkward questions about Sogyal's ever-present young female entourage, or who expressed concerns about his bully boy tactics with his close disciples, were informed by senior students that his behaviour was Crazy Wisdom. In other words, the iconoclastic style manifested by great yogis like Drukpa Kunley, whose antics are vividly portrayed in Keith Dowman's book, *The Divine Madman*.[57]

But the version of Crazy Wisdom peddled about Sogyal is a far cry from the real thing. To clarify this point, I asked the English Nyingma teaching couple, Ngak'chang Rinpoche (formerly Ngakpa Chogyam) and Khandro Dechen, for an accurate description of Crazy Wisdom – what it is and what it isn't.

Vajra masters may manifest crazy wisdom – but their craziness is never prurient, predictable, hackneyed, clichéd, trite, or crass.

Yeshé 'cholwa (Wisdom Chaos) is the inchoate efflorescence of primordial wisdom.

Vajra masters may be divine madmen – or divine madwomen – but their "madness" is never self-oriented, self-indulgent, self-aggrandising or self-obsessed. sMyon Heruka (Mad Sainthood) is freedom from the bureaucracy of institutionalised experience.

Vajra masters may be wrathful – but their wrathfulness is never peevish, irritable, surly, petulant or aggressively impatient. Wrathful Lamas are never serene in public and sadistic in private.

Vajra masters may be the monarchs of their kyil'khors - but their majesty is never haughty, arrogant, imperious, or desirous of droit du seigneur. Vajra monarchs are vastly wealthy in terms of appreciation of the phenomenal world and therefore have no desire for excessive conventional wealth.

Vajra masters may be accomplished in karmamudra - but they reserve their skills for those disciples whose experience of the non-dual state pervades their practice, rather than for those who are merely young and conventionally beautiful.

Vajra masters may accept students' vows of vajra commitment – but imposters to vajra mastery can only steal the loyalty of those they dupe. Those who are duped only need to recognise they have been duped, in order to be free of those who merely pose as vajra masters.

Vows can only be broken when they have been entered into with authenticity. Deranged poltroons may pronounce two people married - but their pronouncements carry no weight in either religion or law.

Vajra masters are the living embodiments of Padmasambhava and Yeshé Tsogyel, like our own Lamas Kyabjé Künzang Dorje Rinpoche and Jomo Sam'phel Déchen. We, on the other hand, are not vajra masters - and cannot be viewed as vajra masters. We are merely convivial vicars of Vajrayana - and nothing we say need be taken too dreadfully seriously.

If they persisted with their inquiries, students were referred to a Rigpa "therapist," whose job involved convincing the doubters that it was their error of judgement because they lacked "pure vision" – or by criticising Sogyal they were in breach of samaya. What happened to them was tantamount to brainwashing. Some of the "therapists" were trained counsellors, who were undoubtedly themselves in breach of professional ethics.

Sogyal hypnotised his flock, then love-bombed them, so they came away from his "teachings" believing that he had shown them the nature of their minds. They came away with a high-octane feel-good buzz. And they came away hooked and wanting more.

So they never missed an opportunity to be present with the source of this delicious sensation – and every time they were present, they paid. And they donated. They bought books, pamphlets, photographs and tantric paraphernalia. They even had to pay for photocopied pages of ritual practices.

At its peak, Rigpa was pulling in membership charges, retreat fees, donations and retail takings from thousands of devotees all over the world. Most strands on Rigpa websites are designed to generate income. To quote three examples: there's Zam (the online shop), the Tenzin Gyatso Institute, designed to attract donations, and Rigpa Shedra, set up to collect tuition fees.

In this respect the eldest son of a trading family from eastern Tibet had fulfilled his brief. The Lakars were no longer destitute refugees. Largely sustained by volunteer labour with only a small number of poorly paid employees, the Rigpa business model was very successful for a long time.

Which is almost certainly the main reason for the position adopted by the governing elite after Sogyal fled into hiding in Thailand.

Most of Rigpa's paid workers had been in their jobs for decades. They knew no other life outside the organisation, so for them keeping the show on the road is a matter of economic survival. In this context it seems likely that the Buddhist principle of working for the benefit of all beings is of minor significance.

However, it seems likely that, even though he was no longer the front man, behind the scenes until his health went into a rapid decline, Sogyal directed every move.

"Of course he did," said one well connected former insider, "because Patrick, Dominique, Seth and the rest of the inner circle are incapable of making decisions on their own. They've been told what to do and how to do it for forty years."

As the letter circulated around the world, causing shock waves wherever it alighted, some well-meaning people saw it as an opportunity to influence reforms within Rigpa that would transform the organisation from an abusive personality cult into an effective, modern vehicle for the transmission of Vajrayana Buddhism. The first to go public came from Australia, in the What Now? blog on 17 July 2017. It is simultaneously heartfelt, practical and direct. It represents a blueprint for healing the wounds of the past and for progress into a healthy environment.

This group of 13 Australian Dz [Dzogchen] and Ng [Ngöndro] mandala students had two weeks warning of the contents of the recent email from long-term students on the issue of abuse in our sangha.

We have met twice in this period to process our mutual pain and concerns, and to begin a dialogue on what this means for the sangha.

In the first meeting we shared feelings of shock, confusion, anger, betrayal of trust, bitter disappointment and sadness.

All stated vehemently their continuing faith in the teachings, love for R, and gratitude for all he has done for us, but made a clear distinction between the teacher and the behaviour. We feel strongly that no one is above the law.

What follows are notes from the second meeting of the points that we all agreed on. As a small group, we were able to mobilise quickly, and we hope that the results of our discussion will help in the process of healing for all concerned:

Reaction to email.

No one doubted the truth of the testimonies. They recognised that these were all long-term dedicated and respected students.

There was agreement that those who wrote the email and those who support their stand should not be seen as troublemakers. We greatly appreciate that they have the courage to break the silence and feel that the sangha needs this kind of openness.

Some feel that this is the purification we have to have, that it is a direct result of Vajrasattva practice, and that facing this and dealing with it will ultimately be beneficial for R's health and the strength of the sangha.

Reaction to contents of the email.

All students have zero tolerance of abuse, no matter who the perpetrator is. They believe that this level of abuse simply cannot be condoned or hidden away.

They were quite clear that damage has been done and that it must never happen again.

After 2 week's consideration, 4 plan to leave R, others say their decision will depend on how R and the senior students handle the situation.

Students feel that if nothing substantial is done within R to address this issue their staying will make them complicit in the abuse (which would presumably continue), and their ethics will not allow them to stay under those circumstances.

They agreed that this behaviour is damaging for the dharma, as well as for the students abused and for every student in the sangha.

We feel that samaya goes both ways. We have the responsibility to help SR make a break from this negative pattern for both the sake of our samaya and his.

Feedback for national and international role holders and students close to Rinpoche.

Our trust in those who run the organization has been shattered. It is difficult to trust anything that comes from those closest to R because they have allowed the abuse to go on, their ethical standards to be compromised, and have not given support to those who felt abused. We don't want to see those who have been terribly hurt by SRs actions further damaged by "victim blaming."

We have seen, and in some cases experienced, verbal abuse by older students, and this concerns us greatly. This modelling of abusive behaviour also must stop.

Though some aspects of communication sent out as support for this challenging time do support an open approach, the attachments some of us received are either irrelevant or sound like a public relations exercise of damage control. (One student called it 'circling the wagons,' as if against attack.) Advice from 'spin doctors' is not helpful.

We don't want R's behaviour explained away, we want it addressed. Teachings on Crazy Wisdom and Pure Perception do not help. We may be poor students with little capacity, but we will not compromise our ethical standards and we want an organisation that supports this.

We want those running the organisation to listen to us, not the other way around.

We want access to SR in future. At present those around him keep him in a bubble where it is almost impossible to meet with him, ask questions or have our concerns heard.

What we want to see happen.

We want a code of ethical behaviour drawn up that applies to everyone in R, including SR, and structures put in place for any future abuses of those ethical standards to be heard and addressed. We took heart from the story of how Lama Norlha Rinpoche's sangha handled their problems. We feel that this is the way to move on from this situation with dignity.

We want SR to speak to us directly in a situation where any student can ask a question, but what he says must be based on his understanding that his behaviour is not acceptable in the Western world and cannot be excused with ideas of 'seeing the master purely' or following the crazy wisdom tradition.

Specifically:

He should acknowledge that he has behaved wrongly and hurt us. We pray that he can genuinely state that he regrets this, and that he will not repeat such actions in future.

To complete the four powers of purification, we consider that a period of personal retreat without an entourage, but with support from his peers such as Mingyur Rinpoche and professionals who can help him to manage his urges, would be beneficial for him and allow us all a fresh start on his return.

We offer our feedback along with our sincere gratitude for everything you, both SR and the Senior students, have done for us over the many years of our devotion. We pray that you will hear the words of us simple and very concerned students and take the appropriate action to heal this situation with integrity for all our sakes and particularly for the sake of the future of the buddadharma in the West.

Perhaps our modest contribution could help show the way.

In private, other former members of Rigpa communicated their views on how to deal with the situation – some of them expressing anger and dismay, with challenging questions directed at the ruling elite. Some received polite but non-committal acknowledgements, some were ignored. The Australians were told to forward their message to Sogyal. They did this but did not receive a response. One prominent long-term student sent several emails to Patrick Gaffney. They were ignored.

It is easy to imagine the dismay that reverberated around senior Rigpa personnel across the world – reeling under the shock, feeling helpless, and needing support and reassurance. The absence of reaction from the authority figures following the release of the letter spoke volumes. To the Buddhist community, watching with fascination from outside the arena, it seemed that Patrick Gaffney, Dominique Side, Philip Philippou, and the other members of the insider cabal were catatonic.

On 18 July 2017, a letter from Sogyal was addressed to the eight signatories. It was reproduced in the What Now? blog. Sogyal would have dictated the theme, but it was certainly written by someone else, on the advice of lawyers and crisis management consultants. Sogyal never acknowledged causing harm but in this instance he did express remorse:

> *I have only ever tried to serve the Dharma and to teach students to the best of my ability and I can sincerely say that I have never, not for one moment, had any intention other than a genuine wish to benefit others. My conscience is clear on this. But I have to see that hurt has arisen and my intentions and actions have been perceived in another way. You cannot imagine the distress this causes me. Therefore, from the bottom of my heart, I humbly ask your forgiveness. Since reading your letter I have been thrown into deep reflection and I'm firmly resolved that if this is the way that my actions are perceived, then I do need to take real action.*

On the 19th of July, the Nyingma lama Orgyen Topgyal, one of Sogyal's closest cronies and a frequent Rigpa teacher, wrote an open letter to Sangye Ngawang, one of the eight signatories. When he read this letter, Sangye was suffering from post-traumatic stress disorder and in a fragile state. He had recently disrobed, after being a monk for 14 years. He was in charge of Rigpa's IT and subjected to systematic abuse from Sogyal during this entire period. He put up with it in the belief that his work was of benefit to beings.

The tone of Orgyen Topgyal's letter combined sarcasm with false modesty and disdain. But by far the most psycho-emotionally damaging accusation was that Sangye had broken samaya – the sacred vow of allegiance to the master and the teachings.

> *… I was told two days ago that eight of Sogyal Rinpoche's most important students have turned against him. These eight people were all people who had followed and attended Sogyal Rinpoche for 15 years or more, and who were intimate with him, like family. These people say that he fooled them – not for one or two days, or one or*

> two months, or even a year or two but for many years. I find this quite strange.
>
> I am not saying that posting this letter was a mistake. I don't think that either. But it's really too late for you to turn against him now, after so long as his student. We are all quite old, we don't have that much time left. And the reality is that to turn against Sogyal Rinpoche, your teacher, after having followed him for years is a samaya breakage. I know that much.

It took a month of deliberations before the management team issued a formal letter, signed by the Rigpa Boards from all countries, in tandem with a letter from Sogyal addressed to the Rigpa sangha.

The Board's letter outlined plans to set up an independent investigation into the "allegations of abuse," consultation to establish a code of conduct and the introduction of a "spiritual body" to "guide and advise Rigpa." To many observers it was too little, too late – and it sounded an alarm bell that, far from owning up to the mistakes of the past, Rigpa was positioning itself towards business as usual. It was obvious at this point that radical change was not on the agenda.

It was also becoming clear that the inner-circle henchmen and -women were intending to stay in control. The same people who had participated in, condoned and concealed Sogyal's depravity for decades. The marionettes who danced to Sogyal's tune.

Sogyal's letter announced his retirement as Spiritual Director – with the caveat that it had "always been my intention to hand over the guidance of Rigpa to my most trusted students." But the paragraph that follows these words appears to be both closer to reality and in direct contradiction to them:

> Please understand that I am not and never will abandon you! I will continue to share teachings with you and to guide you, while on my retreat, and beyond. I will keep you in my heart and prayers each and every day. I have a solemn commitment to help bring you to enlightenment and I will never renege on that!

The rest of the content of both letters was, at best, anodyne. They were widely condemned because they did not mention the victims of abuse, let alone acknowledge their suffering, and they did not include an apology. These omissions were also probably advised by lawyers.

The Rigpa teaching schedule is organised into three levels: meditation, Vajrayana preliminary practice (ngondro) and Dzogchen. Students advance through them, and it so happened that about 1,000 members from all three levels were gathered at Lerab Ling, for the 2017 annual retreats, soon after the release of the eight-signatory letter. The formula for the event combines Buddhist teachings with a jolly social occasion.

"People treat it as a holiday in the south of France," says Oane Bijlsma, who spent a summer working at Lerab Ling. "Tourists come and pay for guided tours of the temple. I sold snacks to them. Rigpa members come for one retreat but stay on to hang out there with their friends."

Traditionally Sogyal would give the keynote address but on this occasion he was holed up in Thailand. Confronted with a crowd of people who had paid good money to be there, the Rigpa elite had to cobble a programme together at very short notice – which included taking on teaching roles themselves.

One component of this unprecedented situation was the need to inform the assembled company about what was going on and how the organisation intended to deal with the problems involved. It fell to the hapless Patrick Gaffney and Dominique Side to attempt to explain.

Their performance was recorded on video and a saboteur in their midst sneaked it onto YouTube. It didn't stay there for long, but long enough for Rob Hogendoorn to archive it.

From the outset, it is painfully obvious that Patrick and Dominique are out of their depth. They are awkward, hesitant and insecure. Their facial expressions are studiously blank, but their eye movements betray the turmoil below the surface. I felt sorry for them, genuinely concerned that they were pitched in to act as spokespeople in a situation where they couldn't say anything of substance. They are in uncharted territory, and it is obvious that they are navigating around several elephants in the room. Admitting that things had gone horribly wrong, for example, or that the eight-signatory letter is factually accurate – or that they had any idea about how to proceed towards a resolution.

Patrick waffles on for a while, repeating platitudes and pious Buddhist aspirations. He mentions several times that "Rinpoche's retreat is going well." He offers some vague reassurances about future developments. Then he hands over to Dominique to lead a prayer session. Hundreds of people left the meeting minus any concrete information or guidance.

Sogyal with Kenchen Namdrol and the brothers Mingyur Rinpoche (right) and Tsoknyi Rinpoche

Sogyal's mother, Tsering Wangmo

13

A Very Sick Man

Another bombshell hit the Rigpa community when the latest bulletin from the guru announced that Sogyal had been diagnosed with colon cancer and had undergone surgery. This news did not come as a shock to former Rigpa insiders who knew that Sogyal had been having digestive problems for some time – probably caused by a diet that consisted almost entirely of red meat.

There was a mixed reaction on social media. Some people were sceptical, suggesting that Sogyal was pulling another stunt, this time to attract sympathy. Others mentioned karmic repercussions, but many people felt sorry for him and wished him well. Sometime later Sogyal made an announcement on his Facebook page that he had refused chemotherapy and was relying instead on Ayurvedic and Tibetan medicine. It was accompanied by a photo of him that revealed massive weight loss. Sogyal has shrunk from obesity to slimline – which tended to confirm the truth of the cancer.

Another revelatory aspect of Sogyal's Facebook page is that more than 1,700 people posted adoring goodwill messages every time a new post by or about him appeared. Sogyal still had a fanatical following, despite the overwhelming evidence against him. Even after his death, many of his fans remain in deep denial, choosing to believe that the eight-signatory letter is a pack of lies motivated by jealousy, or that it was part of a conspiracy to "steal" Rigpa.

Tahlia Newland's What Now? blog morphed from a soft line of regret, coupled with support for Sogyal's victims and some intense soul-searching, into a much tougher, critical tone. The shift of emphasis emerged slowly, in tandem with increasing awareness of the breadth and depth of betrayal suffered by all concerned. Tahlia examines the ramifications of many over-arching principles, including Wake Up Tibetan Lamas, Are You Destroying Your Religion? Is Vajrayana A Cult Religion? And Should A

Spiritual Teacher Attack Your Hidden Faults? Tahlia's musings in both text and video reveal her capacity for insight into complex issues.

For example: "… And we're still asking What Now? Why are we still asking? Because unfortunately this isn't over. It won't be over until there's no possibility of abuse occurring in Tibetan Buddhism again. It won't be over until the lamas realise that we won't stand for it, that saying silence and obedience in Vajrayana isn't justification for abuse and cover-ups."

The French media had been reluctant to publish items about abuse in Tibetan Buddhism – largely, one suspects, because of deeply embedded respect for the Dalai Lama. But when the eight-signatory letter came to their attention this tradition was abandoned – initially by *Midi Libre*, the paper local to Lerab Ling – but later across the media spectrum after Agence France Presse ran the story. One of Sogyal's persistent critics, the journalist Elodie Emery, wrote visceral material for the news magazine *Marianne*. France's Channel 5 Television carried an in-depth report.

Detailed investigative coverage also appeared in the UK's *Telegraph* Magazine, Germany's *Süddeutsche Zeitung*, the Dutch *Telegraaf* newspaper and in Australia the *Sydney Morning Herald* and the *Canberra Times*.

A dam burst of revelations about Sogyal's behaviour followed. Former Rigpa insider Dominque Cowell told French TV about witnessing Sogyal leading a naked woman crawling round a room on a collar and lead, while he brayed like a donkey. She was known to have mental health issues and later took her own life.

Gary Goldman was one member of a group of American Rigpa students who decided to go to a Dzogchen Mandala retreat at Lerab Ling in France in 2015. Gary's intention was to be as inconspicuous as possible, but Sogyal insisted that the group must sit at the front of the gathering of about 1,000 people. They were about 15 feet away from Sogyal, with a clear line of sight. One day their guru made a grand entrance, complete with Nyingma headdress ("more like a crown"), ornate robes and a fanfare of drums, cymbals and horns.

"Later during the retreat, Sogyal made his way to his throne where a nun called Ani Chokyi was waiting to assist him."

Gary is a former US army officer who saw action in Vietnam, so he is not easily knocked off his perch. But what happened next shocked him to the point of disbelief:

"Ani Chokyi moved towards Sogyal to adjust the step stool," he recalls, "and at that moment Sogyal punched her in the stomach. I had a moment of cognitive dissonance – did I really see that?"

The nun gasped, burst into tears, and ran from the stage.

Gary recounts that Sogyal called her back and talked to her. Later Ani Chokyi claimed it was not really a punch, just a gentle shove and part of her "training."

"I've been in some fist fights", says Gary "and I know that's not true. It knocked the wind out of her."

After discussing the incident, the Americans sent an email expressing their distaste at what happened. The next day Sogyal did not turn up to teach. Patrick Gaffney conveyed a message that he was staying away because "you don't like my teachings." He did stop sulking, though, and returned to complete the retreat.

This was probably the first time Sogyal acted violently in public, and it was the trigger that led to his nemesis. When the American senior students Mark and Joanne Standlee were told about it, the process of reflection and evaluation unrolled, which culminated in the July 14, 2017 letter.

Many disaffected members of Rigpa commented on blogs about Sogyal's sexual exploitation and violent tantrums. The former monk and IT expert Sangye Ngawang recalled how Sogyal smashed a mug into the forehead of an attendant – because he didn't like the taste of the tea he'd been offered.

In an interview for Bodhi TV in Holland, Sangye recalled an incident when Sogyal flew in to rage because his shortwave radio wasn't working. "He thought it was Seth's fault, so he was hitting him with a Tibetan book in a wood frame. I was helping Seth and trying to explain that sometimes the signal is weak, and you have to go to another place to receive it – so he turned his anger onto me and started hitting me hard with this heavy book."[58]

And so it went on until everyone following developments was in no doubt about the validity of the accusations in the eight-signatory letter. A mysterious observer using the screen name Sogyal Truth is outstandingly persuasive. This person is quick off the mark with inside information in tweets and in videos on YouTube. It is obvious that s/he was a member of the Rigpa elite.

His/her most powerful contribution to the body of evidence against Sogyal was published on You Tube in March 2019. It is an audio recording of Sogyal justifying hitting a member of his inner circle. It was made in 2004 at Sogyal's chalet at Lerab Ling, shortly after Sogyal had hit a devotee called Herve for the first time. It consists of two short sentences.

"Each time I hit you I want you to remember that you are closer to me... closer to me. The harder I hit you the closer the connection."[59]

The recording was handed to the lawyer Karen Baxter when she was conducting her inquiry into Rigpa's activities. It is quoted on page 18 of her report. Ironically, it was made at Sogyal's request.

Our memories were refreshed by the revelations. I had forgotten some details about Sogyal's bizarre habits – like holding meetings with his henchmen and women while sitting on the toilet. And chewing food, then transferring it mouth to mouth to an adoring devotee. But it was the attitudes within Rigpa that I found most worrying. Rather than recoiling in disgust, devotees regarded swallowing Sogyal's slimy mouthfuls as a "blessing." Notices appeared in Rigpa communications giving lists of clothing used by Sogyal that were up for sale. They included "underpants – lightly washed" and other body contact items. This was as close as most students ever got to "the master." The second-hand underwear was eagerly snapped up and treasured as "relics."

Prior to the release of the cataclysmic letter, Rigpa had strayed a long way from the conventional dharma centre model. Vajrayana Buddhism is a guru-centric tradition. But as Ngakchang Rinpoche and Khandro Dechen point out in their analysis of Crazy Wisdom, it only works if the guru in question has realised deep contemplative awareness that includes humility and genuine interest in and compassion for her/his students.

Sogyal had been "teaching" around the world for more than two decades when an opportunity arose to brush up his knowledge of Dzogchen. This happened when a highly regarded Nyingma lama, Nyoshul Khen Rinpoche, made himself available to fulfil that role. Sogyal and other younger lamas took extensive teachings and empowerments from him.

It has to be emphasised that while the other lamas had probably undergone traditional training and done at least one long solitary retreat, Sogyal did not have this background in study and practice. As a result, he enhanced his credibility via Nyoshul Khen Rinpoche but largely by parroting information rather than through his own realisation. The fact that his abusive behaviour remained unchanged is testament to that.

The Tibetan Buddhist establishment was not exactly quick off the mark to respond to the letter. It was an unprecedented challenge to their global popularity, so how senior figures reacted was an important consideration during the weeks that followed. Until 14 July 2017 public awareness of the fault lines in Buddhism was largely confined to the cognoscenti who were interested in Sogyal, plus a handful of journalists and most Buddhist practitioners. The majority of the latter constituency knew what was going on at Rigpa but, with some exceptions, preferred to turn a blind eye.

Most of us were also aware that many other lamas have sexual relations with their female students. In fact, the lamas who do are probably more numerous than the ones who don't. But the difference between them and Sogyal's sadistic sex addiction is obvious – because women sexually involved with the likes of the late Chogyal Namkhai Norbu, the late Geshe Damcho or the late Chimed Rigdzin Rinpoche were generally happy with the arrangement and usually discreet. But I accept that there is a strong argument against any form of sexual (i.e., emotional) involvement when a power imbalance is involved. Hence the democratic society taboo against sex with doctors, therapists, gurus, lawyers etc.

An exception to the Tibetan rule of silence was June Campbell. She blew the whistle on the late Kalu Rinpoche, who was one of the most highly regarded missionary lamas in the developed world. A lot of Tibetan Buddhist practitioners were horror-stricken at the revelations in her book, *Travellers in Space* – and even more appalled that she had ignored the fatwa against criticising lamas.[60]

Kalu was an old man when he propositioned June and, according to her account, did so in the belief that sex with a younger woman would prolong his life. June travelled the world with him as his translator. It is my view that he respected her and, from his traditional Tibetan perspective, was honouring her with an invitation to become the consort of a high-status lama.

There are four principal sects in Tibetan Buddhism. The oldest is Sogyal's heritage, the Nyingmas. Kalu and Trungpa were from the Kagyus – the Sakyas are significant because their recently retired head, Sakya Trizin, is another lama who earned great respect in the West. The third is the Gelugs, the largest reformed and mostly monastic school, to which the Dalai Lama belongs.

There is, however, considerable overlap between the sects. There's a movement called Rime which promotes a non-sectarian agenda, and lamas are frequently affiliated with more than one sect. The Dalai Lama's background includes Nyingma lineages, and he has taught and written about the Nyingma/Dzogchen tradition.

Sogyal with the Dzogchen master, the late Chogyal Namkhai Norbu

14

CRACKS IN THE PARTY LINE

On 1 August 2017, the world's favourite holy man was the first lama to speak out publicly about Sogyal's fall from grace in an address to a Buddhist seminar in Ladakh, India.

His Holiness does not pull punches. His message nowadays appears to many of us to echo values that have been articulated for decades by modernist factions within the Buddhist community.

I feel some of these lama institutions have some sort of influence of the feudal system. That is outdated and must end – that feudal influence. Then eventually a lama institution creates lama politics. That's very bad. An individual lama's disgrace doesn't matter, but it gives a very bad impression about a monastery or a monk. Very bad. So we must pay more attention. You should not say, "This is my guru. What guru says I must follow." That's totally wrong! Buddha himself mentioned, "You must examine my teaching." Similarly if one particular lama says something, you examine whether this goes well according to Buddha's teaching or according to the circumstances in society. Then you must follow. If the lama says something; if you investigate and it's not proper, then you should not follow the lama's teaching. Even Dalai Lama's teaching; if you find some contradiction you should not follow my teaching.

As far as Gelugpa is concerned, Lama Tsonghkapa clearly mentioned: if a lama teaches something that is against the dharma it should be avoided and opposed. If the lama's teaching is in accord with the dharma it should be followed; if it is in discord with the Dharma it should not be followed. Many years ago in Dharamsala at a Western Teachers Conference, some Western Buddhist teachers mentioned some Zen masters and Tibetan Buddhist Masters had created a very bad impression among people. Then I told them; these people do not follow Buddha's advice, Buddha's teaching. We cannot do. So, the only thing is to make it public, through newspapers, through the radio. Make it public! These lamas, although they don't care about Buddha's teaching, they may care about their face. I told them at that conference, almost 15 years ago I think. Now, recently Sogyal Rinpoche; my very good friend, but he's disgraced. So some of his own students have now made public their criticism."[61]

Among Tibetans, these words must surely have caused extreme consternation, because here was their beloved leader breaking a convention that had been in place for centuries. Many Westerners saw it as too little, too late. The Dalai Lama has very little power but a huge amount of influence across a wide spectrum of the population of planet earth. So, his present stance on issues arising from the misinterpretation of guru devotion will hopefully make some blind-faith followers of manipulative spiritual teachers wake up to their error of judgement.

Many of us admire His Holiness and are convinced that his overall influence on our turbulent times has been beneficial. He's a celebrity guru who pays meticulous attention to his moral and ethical compass. But the fact remains that he knew about Sogyal's depravity for decades before he was finally forced to condemn it. We discussed it during an interview I did with him in 1997. Since his first utterance, the Dalai Lama spoke in similar terms about Sogyal at several subsequent public events. In one talk to a group of university students he warned against the perils of blind faith.[62] He also emphasised that abusive gurus should face criminal charges.[63] Sogyal fawned over the Dalai Lama, and His Holiness responded with two visits to Lerab Ling – the second of which was the temple inauguration. Sogyal was forced into a period of manic activity so he could persuade His Holiness to accept a role in Lerab Ling's inauguration. The Dalai Lama turned down the initial invitation, allegedly because of Sogyal's sleazy reputation. According to a Rigpa insider: "Sogyal was mortified when this happened and set about finding a way to make HH change his mind."

A solution to this problem emerged in the United States, where Rigpa students had raised millions of dollars to buy and develop 350 acres of land in Berne, New York, to establish an American equivalent of Lerab Ling. Initially known as the Foundation for Wisdom and Compassion, it was re-named the Rigpa Center for Wisdom and Compassion, Inc. and granted tax-exempt status as an educational organization in 1990, only to be renamed once again as the Tenzin Gyatso Institute for Wisdom and

Compassion, Inc. (TGI). This final name change had a double mission – to help the non-profit raise more money, because the Dalai Lama's name was attached to the project, and to persuade him to attend the temple inauguration at Lerab Ling. It also accorded Sogyal the recognition he craved.

The centre issued a series of elaborate newsletters, where plans for an ambitious programme of activities were described in fulsome detail. Rigpa, it seems, wanted to establish an institution equal to or even surpassing Lerab Ling in size, status and reach.

> *Intended to reach the widest possible audience, public courses, seminars and retreats will include: An introduction to the practices of meditation, loving kindness and compassion; training in methods from the Tibetan Buddhist tradition for improving health and well-being; Contemplative retreats for individuals and groups; enrichment programs for children, and teachings which are particularly geared towards family life; Inter-faith dialogues to promote deeper understanding and mutual appreciation of the world's great faith traditions; "Practical Wisdom" teachings on mindfulness, compassion and business ethics for professionals and executives; Presentations of sacred art, science and culture unique to Tibetan Buddhism. (…) a variety of seminars on spiritual care themes, such as caring for parents and being present with death; retreats for people suffering from terminal or chronic illness, etc.*[64]

From the start, things did not go according to plan. It was soon clear that, though many lamas blessed the land, nobody bothered to investigate the cost of supplying enough water on this panoramic mountaintop to support several hundred people at one time. The search for water was begun by Rigpa staff. When it ultimately appeared that professional assistance was needed, Judith Brown was persuaded to lead this project. She dedicated her energy to it as a full-time volunteer, although TGI did report that she received $15,115 in compensation in 2005. Judith is also said to be a principal donor – with a gift of $50,000. One of her first tasks was research and development for a reliable water source on the land. She also completed an environment impact statement that was presented to and passed by the local board of trustees in Berne.

There were several buildings on the land, but all of them were dilapidated and in need of extensive renovation. The road to the centre was so rough that visitors were advised to check weather conditions before setting out. "The main house was in very bad shape, it needed a lot of repairs, and there were a few pending building violations," says Linda Parker Solomon, a student of Sogyal's since 1985.

At the urging of Rigpa Europe, Judith constructed a small building on the property to house people interested in participating in the three-year retreat at Lerab Ling. It opened in 2007 at a cost of about $500,000. It turned out that Rigpa was never able to fully utilise the house as a retreat facility.

To the American sangha's surprise, when the Tenzin Gyatso Institute was dedicated to the Dalai Lama in 2007, he insisted it should sponsor several ethnic Tibetan monks to complete their education at a preeminent research institute: Emory University. This did happen, but the donors were not initially informed. The college project started gobbling up a significant amount of money from contributions that donors assumed were being used specifically to develop the centre.

When the donors eventually learned the truth, they stopped giving money; income dropped, and very few people went to the land. The last events were two picnic weekends for elderly Tibetans living in the US. Rigpa's American sangha, whose members had been so generous with their financial support, realised that their retreat centre was not going to happen.

Over the many years of its existence, the centre haemorrhaged a lot of donated money, with little to show for it. Form 990s are public documents that US non-profits are required to file with the Internal Revenue Service (IRS), and they track the large donations that were made to develop this wild, beautiful land in the Catskill Mountains. But it was never fit for purpose. Rob Hogendoorn applied his forensic skills to an examination of these 990 returns by TGI, which reveal that TGI's total net assets were reduced by 99.99 per cent between 2008 and 2018.[65]

The form 990s show that between 2003 and 2018, TGI collected almost $6.1 million in revenues and had upwards of $5 million in expenses. Its losses were catastrophic: a grand total of nearly $1.6 million between 2009 and 2018. This, bad debts, and the accelerated depreciation of the value of some assets by more than $1.8 million in 2013 and 2015 caused TGI's total net assets to plummet from more than $3 million in 2008 to $4,083 in 2018.

So where did the money go? Here are some examples: Executive director David Rand's compensation and benefits between 2009 and 2015 totalled $229,774. Between 2003 and 2015 a further $759,417 was spent on compensation, benefits and payroll taxes for unnamed employees. Other large expenses in the same period were the legal, accounting, consulting, and "other" fees ($265,557), travel ($336,071), telephone ($98,565), bad debts ($837,155), meals and entertainment ($87,661), hospitality and various events ($201,465), capped off with unspecified "other expenses" ($560,892). The total of $159,870 in "scholar program expenses" for six Tibetan students at Emory University, paid between 2011 and 2014, pales in comparison. By 2016, the Tenzin Gyatso Institute's core activity was reduced to paying president and chairman Patrick Gaffney's yearly compensation and benefits: $58,324 in 2016, $69,881 in 2017, and $61,726 in 2018.

It is not widely known that all along, Sogyal's hidden agenda for the Berne project was to create a residential facility for Tibetan refugees living in America. Two top-ranking members of the Tibetan exile administration were on the board of "special advisors" to the Tenzin Gyatso Institute. Samdhong Rinpoche was the Kalon Tripa (Prime Minister) from 2001 to 2011. Lodi Gyari (1949-2018) was the Dalai Lama's Special Envoy to the United States from 1991 to 2012. Despite their seniority, both men failed to steer the development of the Center for Wisdom and Compassion from a dream ticket idea into a concrete reality. They also appear to have ignored any semblance of due diligence in financial matters.

An overview of the TGI's form 990s tells a tale of, at best, gross financial mismanagement – and, at worst, a sustained rip-off. As a small charity, the IRS probably overlooked the anomalies in its annual reports, because it is more likely to pay attention to big ones.

In 2014 Rigpa gave up on Berne as a headquarters for TGI. European members of the Rigpa hierarchy ultimately made that decision, though many in the US sangha didn't agree. Their anger and frustration exploded when it became obvious that despite the millions of dollars donated to TGI, Rigpa chose to sell the property to a Land Trust at the price of $475,000. The trust soon re-sold this property for half that price back to the local Berne community, where it now used as a recreation area for the town. Somehow the land and its assets vanished into thin air. There is no detailed record of this final transaction in the IRS 990 reports. The donors lost all their money, and it seems likely that some people in positions of power and influence within Rigpa lined their pockets.

It is possible that the missing dollars may have been diverted into a rescue bid for Rigpa's flagship operations in France. The Rigpa Europe Association, based in France, sustained hundreds of thousands of euros in losses for years, amounting to a grand total loss of €2,104,480 between 2011 and 2017. The Lerab Ling temple sustained heavy losses, too: €333,082 in 2016, €488.421 in 2017. The Fonds Tertön Sogyal, also based in France, did no better: €158,639 (2015), €206,430 (2016), and €82,077 (2017) in losses. In effect, all through the 2010s Rigpa entities in France were bleeding money at a rate that was economically unsustainable. The proceeds from the sale of the Berne property could have helped salvage French operational liquidity, warding off the threat of bankruptcy.

Only forensic accountants could establish the facts of the matter conclusively, but the Fonds Tertön Sogyal recorded a rare "unallocated gift" of €491,800 in 2014. The Tenzin Gyatso Institute recorded a revenue of $475,001 in 'sales of assets' in 2015, while debiting $489,178 in unspecified "sales expenses" at the same time. This meant that instead of a financial gain a loss was added to its balance sheet. Fonds Tertön Sogyal subsequently paid out a similar amount in unspecified "grants": €173,440 (2015), €207,907 (2016), and €85,584 (2017).

At the time of writing, the financial reports of Rigpa Europe and Lerab Ling for 2018 and 2019 had not yet been submitted to the French authorities. This much is certain: Sogyal's downfall and death, followed by the Covid-19 pandemic, did nothing to end the financial agony in France.

Back in Europe, while the TGI saga unfolded in New York State, Sogyal was basking in the Dalai Lama's reflected glory. Following his example, many other senior lamas including my own teacher, the late Chogyal Namkhai Norbu, visited Lerab Ling, gave teachings, and enjoyed Sogyal's lavish hospitality. At the height of his renown, apart from the Dalai Lama, Sogyal was the numero uno pinup boy on the Tibetan landscape.

Despite the worldwide reverberations of the scandal, www.rigpa.org still carries a comprehensive photo gallery of Sogyal's encounters with just about every significant Tibetan lama (living and dead) who figures in the global reach of Tibetan Buddhism since the start of the diaspora.

Many rich and famous people signed up for his teachings, including show business luminaries, business moguls and politicians. He re-packaged Vajrayana/Dzogchen for popular consumption. For some time Sogyal's brand of Buddhism Lite was the flavour of the psycho-spiritual moment. It was trendy – arcane enough to make Hollywood and Manhattan feel they were members of an exclusive club – but also delivered in easy-to-digest bite-size portions. Sogyal set a bandwagon in motion, so it was probably inevitable that other lamas were eager to climb on board.

Following the eight-signatory letter, in addition to the Dalai Lama two other high-profile Tibetan Buddhists went public with their views about the revelations it contained. The first to break ranks from the red robes party line was the French monk Mathieu Ricard. He writes more in sorrow than in anger. Here's an extract from his blog post:

> *Regarding the recent letter concerning the behaviour of Sogyal Rinpoche written by some of his close disciples, I cannot judge the*

intentions of Sogyal Rinpoche or say whether he actually meant to harm his students. But I have also no reason to doubt the truth of these facts and testimonies, which describe the abuse that various people have suffered at his hands. I know two of the authors of the letter and I consider them honest and trustworthy. The behavior described in this letter and in the other past testimonies is obviously unacceptable – from the point of view of ordinary morality and especially from that of Buddhist ethics. This is all the more so, given the considerable suffering that has resulted from such actions.

I myself have visited Lerab Ling three times, not on my own behalf, but to serve as a translator either for His Holiness the Dalai Lama or for another Tibetan teacher. These short visits did not allow me to take the measure of daily life in Lerab Ling. I am not, in other words, an "insider" and, like many other people, I have been made aware of this dreadful situation only through the testimonies that have been circulated in the public domain.

Buddhist teachings describe in completely unambiguous terms the qualities of an authentic spiritual master as well as the characteristics of those that are to be considered harmful. Would-be disciples are advised not to commit themselves to any master without first examining him or her in fine detail, first from afar, then through consultation with third parties, and then by direct personal encounter – in order to make sure that the reputation enjoyed by a given master actually corresponds with reality. One is even recommended to wait for several years before entrusting oneself to the direction of a master and following his teachings. To frequent and commit oneself to a false and unqualified master is as dangerous, it is said, as drinking poison.[66]

Sogyal's popularity soared following publication of *The Tibetan Book of Living and Dying*. The spiritual seekers who turned up in their thousands at Rigpa centres around the world had almost certainly never encountered the advice Ricard mentions. Probably they adopted Sogyal as their teacher on the spot and without investigation.

Mingyur Rinpoche has an awesome reputation as a Vajrayana adept, meditation master and scholar. He's the VIP lama who walked out of his monastery in India without warning to spend three years as a penniless wandering yogi. His response to the letter is written in general terms, but his message is clear both in context and content.

Here's an extract:

It should go without saying that when schools, businesses, and other public institutions are expected to adhere to a code of conduct and the laws of the land, then spiritual organizations should be role models of ethical behaviour. And teachers even more so.

Throughout history, one of the most important roles of Buddhist teachers and the Buddhist sangha was exactly this. They modeled ethical behavior to the communities that they served.

Vajrayana Buddhism is thought of as a precious treasure by Tibetans. It is our spiritual heritage and our gift to the world. Now that the teachings and practices of this tradition are spreading across the globe, it is important that we understand the tradition and how to work with its powerful teachings.

…The core of the Vajrayana tradition is that we strive to embody pure perception. We view our thoughts and emotions – even the difficult ones – as manifestations of timeless awareness. We see every person as a Buddha, and we treat them as such. We view the world that we live in as a pure realm, enlightened just as it is.

This tradition of treating everything and everyone as though we are meeting the Buddha face-to-face is our main practice in the Vajrayana. It is the life blood of our tradition and the very highest ethical standard we could aspire to. In this day and age, with confusion and conflict all around us, the world needs this more than ever.[67]

The letter to Sogyal exposed a fault line within Tibetan Buddhism. On one hand we have the Dalai Lama, Mingyur Rinpoche and Mathieu Ricard making statements from a modern ethical perspective – and on the other, died-in-the wool Nyingma traditionalists speaking from convictions rooted in what can only be described as medieval superstition. Khenchen Namdrol pointed the finger directly at two of the eight signatories:

Matthew was my friend and student. Actually, I really thought of him as having a very good and kind heart. I thought of him as a good person and I have known him for many years. I have given him many profound Dharma teachings and of course he has probably been Sogyal Rinpoche's student even many more years than that and received many teachings. So, just because he may have thought he was physically harmed on one occasion and was offended by it. Is it really worth it? To do what he has done as a retribution? Is it really worth it? I think it is more like... it is so kind of unusually surprising. It's more like the rising up of the Maras, the demonic forces. And this is well known in Dharma that these obstacles come when something is going really well. And so I think that it is somehow the magical play of non-human entities more than the humans that we are pinning it on. There is more to this.

And also Damcho, in terms of her, she was also close with me. I thought she had an excellent character. She seemed to have tremendous faith in the teacher and when I hear that her name is on this list... It is impossible to even imagine. How could it be the same person? It is hard to even believe. Unbelievable! So that's why I think that this is maybe the magical manifestation of Mimayan, non-human entities. Trying to destroy the doctrine in general Buddhism, in particular Nyingmapa and especially the Rigpa Sangha. And so what we need to do now is: neutralize this. Just neutralize. Go into evenness and with faith towards the master and Dharma, lift ourselves up and be even stronger than ever before with faith in this doctrine of the Dzogpa Chenpo. More than ever before and to inspire others with our examples in this way.[68]

The irony of these apparently opposing views is that both Mingyur Rinpoche and Khenchen Namdrol offer the same solution to the dilemma, causing so much painful heart-searching: faith in the dharma and the effectiveness of Vajrayana/Dzogchen.

Another elderly senior Nyingma lama, Shenpen Dawa Norbu Rinpoche, also advised along similar lines. One of his comments appears to challenge Western analytical thinking – and suggests a low opinion of the dharma students he is addressing:

It is best not to criticize other teachers because you do not have the insight or the wisdom to do so. Your judgement is based on intellectual understanding and you do not have the depth of awareness or clairvoyance to see the many different lifetimes that a teacher has accumulated and practiced.

Apparently in support of Sogyal's modus operandi, Shenpen adds:

There are many stories of bodhisattvas behaving erratically in order to purify our perceptions – shouting, beating and even killing others – these are examples of countless ways to show how perceptions unfold.[69]

Unfortunately, we could not ask Shenpen to justify these remarks because he died shortly after he made them.

Observers like the co-authors of this book, Tahlia Newland, the shadowy Sogyal Truth, plus several who operate under the radar, realised as the months following publication of the letter passed that the Rigpa hierarchy was reacting to the backlash in exactly the same way as when confronted with a crisis in the past. Retreat to the bunker, ride out the storm and maintain business as usual. It became clear that radical reform was not on the agenda.

Marianne Jurgaitis, the mother of Sogyal's son Yeshe, with her lover Pedro Beroy, a Rigpa loyalist and senior advisor, in 2011.

Inauguration of the ill-fated Tenzin Gyatso Institute in New York state 2010. Rigpa luminaries include Sogyal, Tsoknyi Rinpoche, the Dalai Lama's representative in America Lodi Gyari, Patrick Gaffney, Pedro Beroy, David Rand, and Kimberley Poppe.

15

Another Letter

Frustrated at Rigpa's intransigence, seven of the original eight signatories sent a second letter in January 2018.

To get a clear picture of the dynamics involved in the wake of the original letter, it makes sense to read the complete text of the second one.

> "…*True teachers are kind, compassionate, and tireless in their desire to share whatever wisdom they have acquired from their masters, never abuse or manipulate their students under any circumstances, never under any circumstances abandon them, serve not their own ends but the greatness of the teachings, and always remain humble. Real trust can and should only grow toward someone who you come to know, over time, embodies all these qualities."*

The Tibetan Book of Living and Dying, *page 134*

January 11, 2018

Dear Sogyal Lakar,

We join with many members of the Rigpa sangha, and the greater Buddhist world, who wish that you would explain your actions that we attested to in our July 14, 2017 letter, so that reconciliation and healing can begin.

Our original letter six months ago was to you, our Buddhist teacher, asking for clarification on a number of matters. First, are your sexual relations with many of your female students in accordance with the Dharma? Second, are your physical beatings and emotional abuse of us and other students in accordance with the Dharma? And third, is financing your sybaritic lifestyle by using donations from students in accordance with the Dharma? If those actions are not in accordance with the Dharma, we asked you to refrain from them now and in the future. We expected answers to our questions.

The teachings you have shared in the past thirty years, including writing *The Tibetan Book of Living and Dying*, have benefitted us and so many people around the world. We do not believe that this benefit is an excuse for you to abuse students sexually, emotionally, physically, and financially. Should you choose to explain your actions to us, we will listen to you intently – not through your proxies or other Buddhist teachers. If you concur that your actions have harmed students, we believe the first step towards healing is for you to publicly admit, and apologize, to the many who you have harmed. We are waiting.

Instead of responding to our original questions, it seems that you and Rigpa are engaging in a massive public relations effort to deflect attention from your actions. First you replied to our letter by saying that you were very sorry for our having misunderstood your intentions. You did not deny your actions but deflected blame by implying it was due to our own ignorance. Rigpa has continued in this vein by promoting Orgyen Topgyal's comments made in Lerab Ling, Rigpa Paris, and online that our attestations of your behavior guaranteed that we were samaya breakers and bound for the hell realms. Rigpa also released on September 23, 2017 the video of Khenpo Namdrol telling the gathering at Lerab Ling that the eight of us are agents of demonic forces, accused us of the heinous crime of causing schism in the sangha, which is morally equivalent to killing one's parents, killing an arhat, or drawing the blood of a Buddha.

Then, on December 19, 2017 we received a packet of communication from Rigpa US, Rigpa UK, Rigpa's law firm Lewis Silkin, and An Olive Branch, requesting our participation in an investigation into the veracity of our attestations, and to respond within 10 days (over the Christmas holiday). In our original letter to you, which is a matter between a teacher and students, we did not include our views on Rigpa, nor on the enablers who supported your abusive behavior. In fact, we took responsibility and apologized in our letter for our own support of you and how it may have harmed others. Our intention with the letter was solely focused on the issue of your behavior that harmed others.

We did not expect, nor need any communication from Rigpa or their lawyers because you can speak for yourself.

Three days after we received the packet of communication, Rigpa announced publicly to the greater Rigpa Sangha that we would participate in the so-called investigation and speak to Rigpa's lawyers. We were neither consulted as to whether we wished to participate with Rigpa's law firm, nor did we give our consent to said participation. This suggested to us that Rigpa was not intent on truly listening, but instead, managing their public image and in fact saving themselves from scrutiny by legal authorities. Despite all of that, some of us still considered speaking to Rigpa's lawyers with a hope that it might bring about some kind of healing for Sangha members.

Then, on January 2, 2018 you and Rigpa announced the establishment of a Vision Board to guide Rigpa's future activity. You said that Orgyen Topgyal guided the decision-making, and that Khenpo Namdrol was named as a principal advisor. Relying upon Orgyen Topgyal and Khenpo Namdrol, following their defamatory remarks about the eight of us, indicates what you and Rigpa think about our motivation and character and the content of the July 14 letter.

Our July 14, 2017 letter stands as an attestation to your sexual, mental, and physical abuse of students and misuse of donations for the Dharma.

We regret that neither you, nor Rigpa's leaders, have acknowledged the abuse and trauma that you have caused, so that deep healing can begin. We hope that you and Rigpa will reconsider your approach and be truthful and act in accordance with the Buddha's teachings.

In the spirit of transparency and to avoid confusion and misinformation, we will share this letter with various people who have expressed an interest regarding these matters. Regarding our communication with Rigpa, Lewis Silkin, and An Olive Branch, they will be receiving a letter shortly.

We deeply regret the necessity of our letters. We, like so many others, have seen greatness in you. We pray that you can live up to the level of integrity of which we know you are capable. Please take responsibility for your actions and begin the path to healing. Please seek the counsel of His Holiness the Dalai Lama and mend this stain on your reputation that is causing so many to lose faith in you, the lineage, and the noble Dharma.

We were sad to hear of your ill health and hope you recover completely so that you can fully enter your retreat.

Signed,

Michael Condon

Gary Goldman

Matteo Pistono

Graham Price

Sangye

Joanne Standlee

Mark Standlee

Damcho, the Australian former nun, was the missing signatory. She was deeply affected by the aftermath of the original letter and is understood to have made a statement about the abuse she suffered to the police in London. Damcho returned to her home country.

As far as I know, the second letter was ignored.

Several developments are mentioned in the second letter – notably the commissioning by Rigpa of an independent inquiry conducted by the UK law firm Lewis Silkin, chosen for their experience in investigating the film star Kevin Spacey's sexual activities while he was Director of the Old Vic theatre in London. Rigpa could not avoid this expensive exercise, nor could they duck the barrage of scepticism it generated.

Very few people in the worldwide "get-real-about-Sogyal" community had faith in the genuine independence of the inquiry, despite Rigpa stipulating this. The lead investigator, Karen Baxter, also endorsed this in her letter of agreement. This document was supposed to be confidential but was in fact distributed among interested parties.

You have made it clear that the investigation should be objective and impartial. You have asked that we ensure that due respect and sensitivity is to be shown to those who feel they have been harmed. You have made it clear that the fact that Rigpa engages us as a client should not be allowed to influence or bias us in any way. We are happy to proceed on this basis.

Co-author Mary Finnigan was one of several people who assisted Karen Baxter with her investigation. Asked in July 2018 when her report would be concluded, she could not give a definite date but hoped it would be published "within the next few weeks."

Inevitably there was unease among the eight signatories, living as they did in fear of legal reprisals. Karen acknowledged that she had encountered "suspicion" during the course of her work. Rigpa went through another of their duck-and-weave exercises, trying initially to restrict publication to "recommendations." Under pressure from significant witnesses, they eventually agreed to make the entire report public.

The establishment of a "Vision Board" to guide the future development of Rigpa was another development mentioned in the second letter that was greeted with scepticism bordering on derision by Sogyal's critics. Its members were chosen by divination, supervised by the ultra-traditional Nyingma lama, Orgyen Topgyal. Significantly, Dominique Side was not among them.

Rigpa announced its remit in their customary damage-limitation style, carefully avoiding any mention of concern for Sogyal's victims:

The Vision Board is made up of seven of Sogyal Rinpoche's longstanding students who share a deep understanding of the vision of Rigpa. Their task will be to oversee the culture of study and practice, care for the Rigpa community, nurture teachers, and strengthen links with other Buddhist teachers and organizations – all in the open and inclusive spirit that Rigpa has sought to cultivate over the last forty years.[70]

Every public communication following Sogyal's "retirement" has been focussed solely on introverted priorities. But astute observers were not fooled by the unctuous language – it was obvious to us that Rigpa only cares about its own survival.

Tahlia Newland hit the nail on the head on What Now?

Rigpa has announced its Vision Board: Valerie Baker, Mauro de March, Seth Dye, Patrick Gaffney, Verena Pfeiffer, Philip Philippou and Vinciane Rycroft. These are all long-term students, many of whom likely experienced and/or observed the kind of behaviour the 8 attested to in their letter, and some who have actively helped to cover up this kind of behaviour for decades. Instead of their resignation in acceptance of their role in facilitating a culture of abuse, they have been enshrined as leaders of the community.[71]

The bare-faced cheek of this exercise in deception, self-interest and denial is almost beyond belief – despite the fact that (alongside other activists like Marion Dapsance, Tahlia, the German monk Tenzin Peljor and Tenzing, the aristocrat from Sikkim) the authors have witnessed similar manoeuvres by Rigpa bigwigs for many years.

In France, a long-standing criminal investigation by the senior gendarme Laurant Carbonneaux was resurrected following the release of the first letter. His evidence was passed on to the prosecutor's office in Montpellier, which is also assisted by the lawyer Jean Baptiste Cesbron. Carbonneaux's original investigation was launched following rape allegations against Sogyal by a former member of Rigpa – but it did not result in charges due to an absence of corroborative statements. Reluctance to give evidence on the part of abuse victims from Buddhist organisations has been a long-standing source of frustration to the police and investigative journalists.

In the UK, faced with complaints about Rigpa over many years, the Charity Commissioners finally initiated enquiries aimed at setting up a Statutory Investigation. I was interviewed by the senior investigator, David Hughes-Jones, along with several other observers, former Rigpa insiders, and victims. Boxed in by bureaucracy and the complexity of Rigpa's multinational activities, the process was still grinding on when this book first came out in 2019. One update request yielded the following response:

The difficulty here is that the Charity Commission is not a prosecuting authority. That means that any decision we make to open a statutory inquiry can be legally challenged.

We are currently considering the extent to which we can exercise our statutory powers to address the concerns put to the Charity Commission.

A critical factor in determining whether it is appropriate in this case to exercise our statutory powers will be our ability to rely on evidence provided by witnesses. The law requires us to set out our reasons when deciding to exercise certain powers. It is difficult to see how any concerns might be progressed without relying on some of the information and testimonies provided by witnesses.

We are now actively seeking the consent of individuals to the use, and potential disclosure, of evidence provided to the Commission.

At the same time, we are also examining what powers are available to us outside a statutory inquiry.

The implications of this were worrying, because at least two of the people who gave credible evidence to the Commissioners would probably not allow their names to be disclosed. On the upside, David Hughes-Jones expressed his determination to hold Rigpa to account.

Sogyal made public statements justifying the fact that he has never taken legal action against the authors or anyone else who has published material about his misconduct. He cites the Tibetan practice of lojong as his motivation. It involves breathing out blessings and breathing in negativity. The real reason Sogyal has never sued is much more likely to be the fact that revelations about his behaviour are true. However, in December 2017 Lerab Ling announced that it was suing the lawyer Jean Baptiste Cesbron for defamation, following comments by him published in the newspaper *Midi Libre*, alleging that Rigpa is a cult.[72]

"In the Buddhist tradition, we do not respond when we are attacked," explained Rigpa spokesman Dominique Hilly. But Lerab Ling Director Sam Truscott let the cat out of the bag when he confessed that as a result of the *Midi Libre* article, "It has become difficult to work with our usual partners, the Montpellier tourist office and local communities." Truscott acknowledged that the sustainability of Lerab Ling was under threat. Another spokesperson admitted that attendance at events at Lerab Ling had decreased. So, Buddhist tradition goes out the window when cash flow is affected, but in this instance at least Rigpa told the truth rather than hiding behind their usual smokescreen.

Meanwhile, other victims of abuse by Tibetan lamas appear to have become emboldened by the courage of the eight signatories.

Witness statements were published on social media pointing the finger at a Belgian self-styled lama called Robert Spatz, who is currently appealing a five-year suspended prison sentence relating to years of power and sexual abuse, child abduction and money laundering.

In Switzerland, a former student of the ethnic Tibetan lama Namkha Rinpoche blew the whistle on him on Facebook and then told her story of emotional, physical and sexual abuse to the Swiss prosecuting authorities. Her experiences were corroborated by a Dutch woman, who spoke about her abuse by Namkha on Dutch national radio and television.

In the United States, the community around the lama Norlha Rinpoche called time on his sexual activities and forced him into retirement.

The loudest noises, however, came from the headquarters in Canada of the worldwide Shambhala organisation, set up by the pioneer lama, Chogyam Trungpa Rinpoche, and inherited by his son Mipham, also known as The Sakyong. Mipham, enjoyed status equivalent to royalty for many years and, it transpires, took advantage of his position to obtain sexual favours from women students, allegedly at times when drunk and allegedly at times forcing them to submit.

The Sakyong followed Sogyal's example and "retired" from his role, in order to "enter a period of reflection and self-examination." But in contrast to the Rigpa elite, the Shambhala governing body, the Kalapa Council, resigned *en masse* after it became obvious that they were in charge for decades of an organisation that apparently turned a blind eye to multiple exploitations, including child abuse.

The fault lines at Shambhala are long-standing, broadly distributed across senior membership and in essence a continuation of the hedonistic, freewheeling style of its founder, Chogyam Trungpa. His descent into depravity has been chronicled by many people, including his wife, Diana Mukpo, whose memoir revealed some, but not all, of the horrors that occurred in the mid-80s, towards the end of Trungpa's life. Shambhala was supposed to be a fresh start, with high ideals around "enlightened society" – but it went badly wrong.

The whistle was eventually blown by Andrea Winn, a second-generation Shambhalian who says she was sexually assaulted as a child by several men within the organisation, including one senior figure. Andrea launched an inquiry, which became known as Buddhist Project Sunshine, aiming to shed light into the murky corners of Shambhala and, as a result, obtain justice and healing for the victims involved. She says she was resisted by the upper echelons of the organisation at every step along the way. The full truth did not emerge until she published Phase Two of her investigation. In July 2018 new levels of misconduct became known, which were expected to lead to criminal charges. The mess at Shambhala was internationally reported – in the *New York Times* and the UK's *Guardian*.[73]

A year after publication of the eight-signatory letter it was not quite business as usual at Rigpa – more like business aimed at a fresh demographic. People who had perhaps heard about the latest trend in self-improvement known as Mindfulness training – or maybe even taken part in a course offered by an employer worried about the fall-out from work-related stress.

Mindfulness training certainly owes a lot to Buddhism, but it is one segment of a practice palette – basic calm-abiding meditation minus the more comprehensive levels of emptiness, visionary experience, and insight, which unfold into deep realisation. It also ignores study.

The Rigpa websites were recalibrated to appeal to a constituency that might like a holiday in the south of France or southwest Ireland, with some meditation as value-added. Headline references to Sogyal have been removed. Prior to the letter, Rigpa was already peddling dumbed-down dharma; nowadays occasional visits by Tibetan lamas figure in the programmes, but most activity is directed by senior students under rubrics like Finding Peace, What Meditation Really Is and Discovering the True Nature of Love.

One factor that brings up the red mist for campaigners like my co-author and me is that VIP lamas, including Dzogchen Ponlop Rinpoche, Ringu Tulku and Tsoknyi Rinpoche are still accepting invitations to teach at Rigpa. The red-robed mafia shows no sign of abandoning one of its primary power bases, regardless of intense moral and ethical pressure.

The main Rigpa portal, www.rigpa.org, now states that The Rigpa Code of Conduct and the Shared Values and Guidelines of the Rigpa Community were adopted by all the boards of the Rigpa entities in June 2018. What it does not make clear is the fact that these institutional caveats were introduced in an attempt to sanitise their public image, following the July 14, 2017 letter. Even more significantly, Tantric gurus are excluded from the clauses relating to sexual activity.

Dzongsar Jamyang Khyentse added 16 new photos.
20 hrs

I thought this might come in handy for Rinpoches like myself who are not omniscient, not omnipotent, and not well trained; who don't give enough preparatory training on the prerequisites to their students; and who get carried away by their own self-agendas and, from time to time, by their hormones.

MAKE LOVE NOT HEADLINES! SCREW WITHOUT GETTING SCREWED!

Bender and Boner Law has over 70 combined years' experience in the Tibetan Buddhist tradition. We are sensitive to the special needs of Gurus and Rinpoches who desire to save all sentient beings yet also wish to have fulfilling sex lives.

Let one of our ironclad consent forms protect you from fears of future litigation. Our in-house psychologists are on call 24/7 to assess your potential partners for any unsuitable moral quirks and/or tendencies to play victim.

If you've already made a few mistakes, (and who hasn't?), don't worry! We can still save your reputation, your assets, and your ass. Free initial consultation. Call us before it's too late! See our website at

http://www.theyconsented.com

Dzongsar's Facebook post before it was deleted

16

Damage Limitation

Dzongsar Khyentse Rinpoche is another younger-generation lama who has mastered the dark art of popular appeal. He had a long-standing friendship with Sogyal and his claim to fame is that he made a successful movie called *The Cup*. It says something about 21st century culture that, apart from the Dalai Lama, the two Tibetans who have attracted the largest worldwide followings have movies in their CVs – in Sogyal's case, Bertolucci's *Little Buddha*.

Dzongsar's pitch appears to be ultra-hip and modern. He's fond of self-deprecating jokes. Soon after the publication of the first letter to Sogyal he posted a 16-page spoof contract on his Facebook page. It was greeted on social media by howls of derision and horror at the insensitivity of it and the bad taste. It was swiftly taken down.

Dzongsar also published a 10,000-word essay aimed at his followers – and members of the Rigpa community suffering the anguish of betrayal. If you can grit your teeth to read, it contains some useful advice about how to approach Vajrayana theory and practice. It also includes content that reveals his underlying conservatism and scornful dismissal of contemporary liberal values.

> *If you are uncomfortable with the non-dual groundlessness of Buddhism – you might just as well follow one of the Abrahamic religions. These are the religions that follow a clearly grounded dualistic path and say things like "don't eat pork, do eat fish, and women must wear burqas." If the label 'religion' is altogether too embarrassing for your elitist so-called progressive minds, you might try some kind of quasi-atheistic secularism, coated with moralistic ethics and bloated with dogmatic liberal self-righteousness. Or you could blindly allow*

yourself to be swallowed up by existentialist angst, then get annoyed with those who get blissed out on hope.

Dzongsar agreed to be co-opted into the Rigpa damage-limitation exercise. His contribution was probably the most gruelling – he embarked on an international charm offensive with a series of personal appearances organised by Rigpa in Berlin, Lerab Ling, Paris and London. These took the form of long, rambling monologues punctuated by questions and answers, aimed at neutralising the bad odour that hangs over Tibetan Buddhism after the Sogyal revelations. In common with his fellow members of Rigpa's red-robed fraternity, his principal objective was to try to repair the reputation of Vajrayana Buddhism, which had taken its most severe nosedive since the start of the Tibetan diaspora in the 1950s. In London, the Dzongsar talks were spread over two days and tickets were snapped up within hours of going on sale.

Informed opinion on the message they conveyed is sharply divided.

Some observers, including co-author Rob Hogendoorn, saw the series as a propaganda exercise exhibiting a total lack of empathy with Sogyal's victims. Writing at the time, he noted: "For practising Buddhists much of Dzongsar's discourse can be highly embarrassing: his performances do not exactly amount to solid advertising for Rigpa and its Vision Board – or for Tibetan Buddhism as a whole. Members of the Roman Catholic clergy may well act similarly when confronted with sexual abuse, but not so ostentatiously. They know better than that. Indeed, Dzongsar Khyentse's habitual self-centeredness and tendency to keep his audiences amused may well be regarded as tasteless."

A long-time Buddhist practitioner and former member of Rigpa was inclined to give Dzongsar the benefit of the doubt. She asked to remain anonymous:

Basically his main agenda was to explain the Madhyamika Teachings and an authentic Vajrayana. At the same time he was clearly trying to support the Rigpa Sangha, not necessarily the people in management at the top.

I guess people will hear it all in different ways. Because I know what his private opinion of Sogyal is, I could appreciate his comments about Vajrayana based upon a clear understanding of Madhyamika. He doesn't spell things out but relies on the students using their intelligence. No doubt there will be several people who will find that confusing and accuse him of dodging the questions.

> *I thought his talks were successful in turning things around from the original flat denials to acceptance that wrongdoing had taken place.*

Tenzing Abrahams is a grandson of the late king of Sikkim. He has known Sogyal and Dzongsar personally for many years. He regards both as traitors to the true values of Vajrayana Buddhism. So much so that when Dzongsar was speaking at Conway Hall in London, Tenzing decided to challenge the lama to debate issues that he believes have brought Tibetan Buddhism into disrepute.

Tenzing says he was promised a ticket to the event by his friend, the former top model Penelope Tree – a long time Dzongzar devotee. He crept into the hall while Dzongzar's talk was underway. Before he could sit down, he was approached by a couple of bouncers. At that moment he stood up and moved towards Dzongsar on the platform, shouting in strong language.

Accounts of what happened next vary according to which eyewitness is telling the story. Tenzing insists he was pushed by Rigpa bouncers – and that he did not intend to create a disturbance. But there's no doubt that his intervention caused considerable consternation in the audience, with some people screaming. The incident was recorded in the official video but was later deleted. The Rigpa bouncers surrounded Tenzing, dragged him to the ground outside the building and immobilised him while they called the police.

The cops who turned up were bemused to find a young oriental aristocrat apologising for wasting their time, while pinned down by several Western men. They gave Tenzing a lift home. Dzongsar sat silent throughout the incident. Tenzing recorded the rough treatment he received from allegedly nonviolent Buddhists on his mobile but has declined to make it public.

So, what conclusions do we draw from this brave but ill-conceived protest? The authors feel that Tenzing could have planned his attempt to debate with Dzongzar much better but that overall it probably succeeded in making some hitherto brainwashed Rigpa people wake up to the fact that a groundswell of extreme distaste for the behaviour of Sogyal and other lamas will not subside any time soon. Tenzing believes someone tipped off the event organisers about his intention to challenge Dzongzar. He insists that he should have been given the chance to discuss issues which need to be taken seriously.

Sogyal in full Nyingma ceremonial attire

Mary Finnigan and Rob Hogendoorn

17

The Report

As the months since the commissioning of the Independent Investigation passed with no news about when it would be concluded, stress levels within the Rigpa elite must have reached fever pitch. So much so that in July 2018 they decided to stage another video presentation from Lerab Ling. Once again Dominique Side was corralled into action, together with Sam Trusscott and Claudia Thurn, the Director of Practice.

Almost certainly aware that Karen Baxter's report would be critical (to put it mildly) of the Rigpa leadership, they decided to come clean about the impact on the organisation of the eight-signatory letter.

The underlying theme was business as usual, but they admitted there had been a 50% drop in attendances, resulting in a severe financial crisis. They glossed over the way they dealt with restructuring their activities as a collaborative process, involving consultation with all concerned and advice from senior members like the banker, Pedro Beroy. But the unvarnished truth is that 67 people lost their jobs, and the programme of events was drastically cut back. Dominique reiterated that Lerab Ling was going ahead with the defamation lawsuit. Sogyal was referred to as Rinpoche several times, and considerable emphasis was placed on the fact that 400 people turned up for the Lerab Ling open day.

They did their best to stick to the spin, but all three looked worried and uncomfortable. The mood music was identical to the pious claptrap they have been spouting for years, which goes something like: "We are the good guys bringing the precious dharma to people in need of spiritual sustenance... All this bothersome stuff is a distraction to be overcome, so we can carry on with our good work."

It is safe to assume that other Rigpa centres worldwide were going through similar upheavals.

However, one astute observer pointed out that the Terton Sogyal Trust in the UK declares assets of circa £1,200,000. Also, Rigpa entities in the UK, Holland and Germany have substantial cash reserves. Lewis Silkin is one of the most highly regarded legal firms in Europe, so the bill for Karen Baxter's services probably ran to six figures. I doubt if Sogyal contributed to the cost from his personal fortune.

At this point it seems appropriate to spare a thought for the people who have devoted their mental, spiritual, and physical wellbeing, their energy, their time and their money to Sogyal and Rigpa. A sizeable constituency is heartbroken and experiencing an acutely challenging journey into recovery. Some may never recover.

The Buddhist jungle drums thrummed with a persistent rhythm as the projected date for the publication of Karen Baxter's report came and went. Speculation on social media revolved around reasons for the delay – with emphasis on the probability that Rigpa's "Investigation Committee" had seen it and was so shocked by its content, they were trying to find excuses to avoid making it public.

But there was no escape route, and their reaction was justified, because when the report finally reached the public domain on 5 September 2018 it was clear that Rigpa had taken another colossal hit.

Karen Baxter promised to be impartial and she stuck to her remit with forensic precision. Before launching into the details of her research, she established the basis for it according to UK civil law. It differs from criminal law, which has "beyond all reasonable doubt" set in concrete. Civil law, however, works on a basis of "the balance of probabilities."

Karen is scrupulously fair in her assessment of the evidence and points out from the start that "not all the allegations against Sogyal Lakar are upheld." But also, on page four of her 50-page report, she presents her two most damning conclusions, prior to unpacking how she reached them:

> *Some students of Sogyal Lakar (who were part of the 'inner circle' as explained in the body of the report) have been subjected to serious physical, sexual and emotional abuse by him.*

> *There were senior individuals within Rigpa who were aware of at least some of these issues and failed to address them, leaving others at risk.*[74]

These two statements must have induced sighs of relief from the eight signatories to the July 14 letter – and groans of despair from the Rigpa elite. The signatories were vindicated, and the threat of legal reprisals was lifted.

For the latter there was the realisation that their cover was blown and all the years of denial, ducking and weaving, spin-doctoring and obfuscation were a waste of time, money, energy and misdirected loyalty.

Shortly after the Janice Doe lawsuit in 1994, a Rigpa insider who managed to hang on to her/his common sense, decided to confront the dominant troika (Gaffney, Side, Philippou) with misgivings which s/he had been composting for some time. This person remains friends with people loyal to Sogyal – and has requested anonymity. S/he presented a case in the form of a document outlining a litany of concerns. These included:

- Sogyal would destroy his reputation if he continued his debauched behaviour.
- Sogyal's behaviour would cause dissent and fracture the Rigpa sangha.
- Sogyal's behaviour would damage Rigpa and its satellite entities.
- Sogyal's behaviour would seriously harm Tibetan Buddhism in the developed world.

This person requested that the document should be included in records of the meeting. S/he was told that this would not be allowed and that all mention of her/his concerns would be deleted from the minutes and supressed. This person continued to raise issues with the troika and other senior figures and was consistently ignored. Eventually s/he gave evidence to the Lewis Silkin investigation and was accepted by Karen Baxter as a credible witness. The July 14 letter confirmed everything that s/he had flagged up over many years.

Karen Baxter conducted her analysis of the situation within Rigpa with meticulous attention to detail and legal objectivity. She concealed the identities of her witnesses and rigorously applied the yardstick of "balance of probability." However, Rigpa insiders instantly recognised evidence given by Gaffney, Side and Philippou. Karen Baxter points up anomalies and obfuscations from all three, together with a reluctance to engage in direct language. She singles out Dominique Side as an intractable loyalist who, despite the overwhelming evidence, still gives Sogyal the benefit of the doubt. Dominique insisted that the accusations against Sogyal were exaggerated – accusations that include graphic descriptions of extreme violence inflicted on members of his inner circle.

For example, on page 18 of the report:

Mid-way through the retreat there was a major event – Buddha's birthday. We had to practise all day and had been preparing for several days. We took everything to the house and practised together – it started around 4 pm and went on until around 2 am. During this, Sogyal was the most wrathful I have ever seen. Everything and everyone was annoying him. He was hitting everyone, pulling hair. Witness E and I were his main targets, and he hit us repeatedly with the backscratcher and with leather-bound parchments. My scalp was bleeding and my ear ringing from having been hit on the side of the head. He hit me 10 or 15 times and there was nothing soft or painless about it. It stings, it hurts, it knocks you over. If you try to move away he will call you out and make you come closer. I was in complete shock and petrified. I was in a state of anxiety – my instinct was to run but those around me were convincing me to stay. I felt I had no choice. My brain stopped working – it was damage control to try to stay alive. We were on call, day and night. We would try to pre-empt any scenario that would anger him and do anything to try to avoid irritation. I saw Witness F being beaten a lot ... Witness F was regularly hit – he would use his backscratcher to hit her... It was unnerving to watch [another student being beaten]. You would have a sense of relief that it's not you and you would be terrified. Stepping in would make it worse for both of you."

Witness F: "On one occasion he was hitting me, [and three other students] with a broken wooden hanger. He hit each person repeatedly and was so tense that he bit through his own lip while doing it and drew blood. My initial assumption was that the blood on his face had come from one of the people he was hitting. [One student] was knocked unconscious. If one of his girlfriends was at their limit, he would hit me instead. Between 2006 and 2010 I was beaten over two hundred times; if he was in a bad mood he would beat me every day, or more than once a day. At one stage he had fallen out with [his girlfriend] – he would meet her daily at her chalet, come back to his chalet, slam the door and punch me in the guts. He was just taking out his frustrations; it was nothing to do with me. He did the same thing every day for ten days. On one occasion I asked him if he had remembered to take a calendar that he wanted to give as a gift. He responded by grabbing me by my ear – it ripped all down the back and was bleeding."[75]

In conclusion Karen Baxter made 12 recommendations:

Assuming that the Rigpa leadership concludes that the appropriate overall course is to put in place structures and procedures to ensure that its work as an organisation can continue in the future without the risk of harm, I recommend the following:

1. Sogyal Lakar should not take part in any future event organised by Rigpa or otherwise have contact with its students;

2. Rigpa should take steps to disassociate itself from Sogyal Lakar as fully as is possible (having regard to any legal arrangements which may for the time being connect the organisation with him);

3. Rigpa leadership in each country (being the trustees or equivalent) and the Vision Board should, as necessary, be refreshed in order to ensure that:

a. its members are unconnected with the harmful events referred to in this report and so can credibly lead the programme of changes required;

b. its members are all publically committed to the concept that abuse will not be tolerated by anyone, or against anyone, within Rigpa (including teachers); and

c. wherever possible, the leadership should include some members who are unconnected with the student body, for example lay trustees as such would be recognised in the United Kingdom.

4. Professional management should be appointed at each major Rigpa centre. Wherever possible, the management team should include some members who are not part of the student body. Care should be taken to ensure that all members of management are able to perform their responsibilities and are not inhibited in doing so, for example, as a consequence of considering themselves bound to demonstrate 'unwavering respect' towards the guru.

5. An appropriate risk assessment addressing the whole range of the organisation's activities should be conducted and regularly refreshed. The risk assessment should specifically address teaching practices which are, or have been, associated with the Dzogchen Mandala – careful, well-guided judgments will need to be made on the future use of such practices in the organisation's work. For the avoidance of doubt any practice amounting to abuse of a student should never be tolerated.

6. A comprehensive and written safeguarding policy should be put in place to ensure that:

a. Sexual relationships between teachers and students are either prohibited entirely, or subject to specific safeguarding measures to ensure there can be no abuse of power;

b. Any 'lama care' that is deemed to be necessary is carried out in a way which ensures the health and safety of those providing these services is adequately protected;

c. Mechanisms for the confidential reporting of concerns are clear and can be easily found by those with concerns;

d. Reports of any incidents and allegations are recorded and stored in a secure and proper way;

e. Incidents and allegations are promptly investigated in accordance with the policy with appropriate follow-up action taken;

f. Consideration is given to reporting serious incidents to relevant law enforcement authorities and/or regulators; and

g. The management and leadership of each Rigpa entity is aware of and properly trained in its responsibilities.

7. An abuse helpline outside of Rigpa should be set up, in addition to the internal reporting mechanisms made available.

8. To the extent that it has not done so already, Rigpa should review its fundraising activities to ensure that these are compliant with local laws and regulations. This review should specifically include contexts in which Rigpa events such as retreats may be used as an opportunity for third parties such as external speakers to raise funds for other causes and/or invite gratuity payments on their own behalf. There should be absolute clarity on the proper uses of all such funds.

9. A clear approach to the engagement of speakers and teachers should be established which ensures that they are aware of relevant policies, including the safeguarding and fundraising policies, before having contact with students.

10. So far as is consistent with the wider financial responsibilities of Rigpa, a fund should be created to provide professional counselling to those affected by abuse.

11. An appropriate programme of communications related to the above steps should be undertaken with the letter writers, students and the wider Rigpa community. In addition to a first communication setting out Rigpa's commitment to a safe and secure environment for all students and the steps to be taken in achieving that, regular updates should be given until the programme of changes has been completed.

12. Rigpa's leadership should consider (taking further advice as necessary) the extent to which it is obliged to report any of the matters set out in this report to law enforcement authorities or relevant regulators in each applicable jurisdiction.[76]

Newsletters distributed to the Rigpa membership and www.rigpa.org have been examined in detail by both authors of this book. In December 2018, it was clear from the contents of the newsletters and public statements on the website that Rigpa has failed to implement all Karen Baxter's recommendations – except for an ambiguously worded Code of Conduct and a Grievance Procedure.

For example, there are no external appointees in the Rigpa leadership. Although the troika are said to have relinquished their "governance" roles, there are no unequivocal references to their present status within the organisation. Patrick Gaffney was said to be receiving treatment for prostate cancer. Dominique Side appears to have been discreetly airbrushed out of the limelight, but she is still listed on internal Rigpa communications as a leader of practice retreats. They are both still teaching. There's no mention of professional management. There is no mention of a fund being set up to provide counselling for Rigpa people traumatised by Sogyal or the revelations in the July 14 letter.

References to Sogyal's status within Rigpa are significantly avoided, apart from the original "retirement as Spiritual Director." In contradiction to Karen Baxter's recommendations 1 and 2, updates from Sogyal about his health figure in membership communications. And far from disassociating itself from Sogyal, the main Rigpa website still features him. The suggestion that the present administration might like to consider reporting Sogyal to law enforcement authorities must have been received like a cup of cold vomit. No mention is made of fund-raising reform or an external help line. All the measures extant in December 2018 were "in house" within Rigpa.

In December 2018, the Buddhist commentator Matthew Remski published a blog post, quoting "reliable sources," revealing that a group of senior students had written a letter to Rigpa's Vision Board requesting that Sogyal be reinstated as Spiritual Director. According to Remski, the letter "is gathering signatures." He said 17 people had signed it and alleged that he had redacted their names. As of mid-December 2018, there was no independent confirmation of Remski's story – nor had it been denied by Rigpa.[77] Comments on social media were scathing, revolving around themes like, "What in the name of all the Buddhas is the matter with these people?"

Perhaps the most distasteful aspect of the (allegedly) post-Sogyal Rigpa is the fact that the Vision Board and other levels of management in Rigpa entities around the world are still controlled by members of the "Inner Circle." These are the people who enabled, concealed and participated in Sogyal's corruption for decades. There has been speculation that they (probably including the troika) deliberately threw Sogyal under the bus in order to save the business – and their own livelihoods. I favour the view articulated by Tahlia Newland that Sogyal remained as puppet master and that his core group of loyalists obeyed his diktats until he died.

In September 2018, Sogyal's latest health bulletin revealed that his cancer has spread to "two early-stage tumours" on his liver. I have encountered several people who regretted their decision to refuse chemotherapy advised by oncologists treating primary cancer. Sufferers have been known to survive secondaries, but this is rare. Sogyal turned down chemo first time around in favour of traditional remedies, but to stand a chance of staying alive he admitted he had to undergo it following the discovery of new tumours. His initial refusal significantly reduced the chances of success. He tells his adoring fans not to be alarmed, but it is a hollow reassurance because most people must know the prognosis is not good.

On May 16, 2019, health bulletin number three was posted on Sogyal's Facebook page. Cocooned in the same old gush about prayers and devotion, he admitted that chemotherapy was an uncomfortable experience and that he would soon be undergoing another series of tests. It generated predictable responses from the party faithful, but this time the comment tally was well down – in the 400s rather than the previous 1,000s.

All communications that emerge from Rigpa are carefully crafted to avoid the A word. Abuse is not in the vocabulary. The V word is also avoided. There are no victims. Only "people who may have experienced harm." The programmes of events at the various entities are angled towards attracting tourists – time out in idyllic surroundings with value-added meditation. Fine at Lerab Ling or Dzogchen Beara – but not so wonderful in a claustrophobic basement in central London. Rigpa's Autumn/Winter 2018 London programme featured short courses, drop-in meditation and only one ethnic Tibetan lama – the young, inexperienced Gelug reincarnation, Ling Rinpoche.

But alongside Rigpa's global damage-limitation exercise there was a vigorous debunking campaign conducted by Tahlia Newland and contributors to the What Now? blog – and by Sogyal Truth on Twitter. All of this is available for reference via online searches. The guest writer Jo Green on What Now? is a maestro analyst and a talented writer who shines a merciless light on Rigpa's manipulative communications. For example, a satirical treatment of a French police raid on Lerab Ling starts with a quote from a newsletter, written by Rigpa's mistress of spin, Catherine Paul:

Lerab Ling is undergoing a preliminary investigation conducted by the French authorities into its activities. As part of this process, on September 19th, the lead investigator accompanied by a group of gendarmes visited Lerab Ling. Although it was an unsettling surprise for the community, they were met with kindness and openness.

Jo Green continues:

Yes, while some in Rigpa were busy weaving a giant rug to sweep everything under, the French authorities were taking all these matters very seriously indeed. For a group of armed police officers to be authorised to do a raid on Lerab Ling, investigations must have progressed quite a long way. How nice that "they were met with kindness and openness." I can almost picture the scene now…

'Yes Inspector, if you just sit yourself down there, we can bring out the wads of cash and count it for you, whilst your officers have a coffee. Someone from admin will be along in a minute with that file of reports of abuse that we compiled over the years, and I'll jot down Sogyal's address in case you want to pop over and have a chat with him. Are you all right there or would you like a cushion?'

Jo Green entertains, but critical appraisal is as sharp as broken glass:

Over the last year the leadership of Rigpa has been engaged in a huge survival project: making the changes that must be made so as not to lose their charitable status in different countries and thus their right to exist. That is the "outer" appearance. Meanwhile, at the "secret" level they are engaged in a project to not give a millimetre, not accept any criticism, or any demotion of "Rinpoche" and reassure the faithful that this is the case.[78]

They are playing a risky game. The French state bestowed Lerab Ling's crucial status as a "religious community" and it can take it away. France is also unique in having the "About Picard" law, designed to protect vulnerable people from exploitation by religious groups who behave like cults. Everything Rigpa says that is evasive and manipulative goes towards building a case against them under that law. They would be wise to get real and get real fast.

By autumn 2017 the trickle of complaints about sexual, financial, emotional and psychological abuse involving both Western and ethnic Tibetan Buddhist teachers had escalated into a phenomenon that could no longer be ignored by mainstream news media. It gained momentum in parallel with the #MeToo movement, revelations about Hollywood mogul Harvey Weinstein's obsessive sex life – and exposés involving members of the British parliament. As a result of this latest phase in feminist confidence, two UK cabinet ministers resigned.

I had been determined for years to extend awareness of Sogyal's misbehaviour into a more comprehensive demographic. My journalism in the *Guardian* and Mick Brown's features in the *Telegraph* Magazine certainly had impact within the Buddhist community but did not threaten the status quo at Rigpa. After publication of the July 14 letter, I was approached by Oliver Harvey, Chief Feature Writer at the UK's biggest selling tabloid newspaper, the *Sun*. I thought I had achieved my goal. But although Oliver wrote the story and pestered his editors to run it, it was eclipsed by Hollywood and Westminster.

This turned out to be a temporary setback. On September 22, 2018, The *Sun* ran the story as a double page spread in the print edition and as an extended item online, which included video material from the Canadian documentary, *In the Name of Enlightenment*.[79] Oliver Harvey produced a bravura piece of tabloid journalism, topically pegged to the UK Charity Commission investigation, loaded with quotes, sprinkled with shock horror, and thoroughly researched. Such is the power of the *Sun* that the online version went viral in English-language publications across the world, including the *New York Post* and other American media. This was a breakthrough, because until this happened the Sogyal saga had been ignored in the US.

C'est pourtant pas compliqué

BOUDDHISME ET TRADITIONS
Le nirvana bien terrestre du lama violeur

CLAUDE ARDID

« Oui, ma fille a été violée à plusieurs reprises par Sogyal Lakar. » Guy termine son témoignage. La présidente du tribunal correctionnel de Montpellier lui demande de compléter son récit. Il raconte alors son périple au cœur du Rigpa Lerab Ling, « sanctuaire de l'activité éveillée », une congrégation bouddhiste implantée au nord de Lodève, dans l'Hérault. Il détaille ses retraites spirituelles, sa proximité avec Sogyal Lakar, dit « le Précieux », le lama fondateur du site. Il dit tout jusqu'au drame : « C'est par une lettre que ma fille m'a appris qu'elle était sous son emprise mentale. Il en avait fait son pantin. Je lui ai proposé de déposer plainte. Mais une adepte du bouddhisme, même violentée, ne se révolte pas contre son maître. »

Assis derrière Guy, Jean-Baptiste Cesbron – avocat de l'Union nationale des associations de défense des familles et de l'individu victimes de sectes (UNADFI) – acquiesce. C'est lui qui a **Une authentique** révélé le scandale en accordant une **machine à fric** interview au *Midi libre*. Il évoque des témoignages d'« étudiants », tous victimes de Sogyal Lakar, « *des abus physiques, sexuels, émotionnels et psychologiques* » de celui qu'ils vénéraient. Cesbron n'a fait que son métier. Mais il est sur le banc des prévenus avec *Midi libre*. Jugés ce jour-là pour diffamation. L'avocat aurait laissé supposer que la congrégation était une « *secte* ». « *Faux*, rétorque-t-il, *mon seul but était de dévoiler les pratiques pénalement répréhensibles d'un lama qui a agi en toute impunité pendant des années.* »

Cesbron présente encore une lettre de l'ancien assistant de Sogyal Lakar. Il y écrit notamment : « *En 2014, lors de la retraite des anciens à Lerab Ling, il nous a demandé d'être généreux en offrandes : pas de chèques, pas de cartes de crédit, que du cash! Qu'est devenu cet argent? Personne ne le sait...* »

L'affaire est tellement grave que l'assistant finit par déposer plainte auprès de la gendarmerie. Panique chez les bouddhistes. Mais rien ne bouge. Le dalaï-lama, qui a inauguré le centre quelques années plus tôt, se contente d'une déclaration lapidaire : « *Sogyal était mon ami, désormais il ne l'est plus...* » Quant à Matthieu Ricard, proche du dalaï-lama, il botte en touche : « *C'est aux disciples de démasquer l'imposture. Ce n'est pas notre rôle d'œuvrer en justiciers. Le bouddhisme n'est pas organisé de façon hiérarchique, comme c'est le cas, par exemple, de l'Église catholique.* » Mais il finit quand même par qualifier d'« *inadmissibles* » les agissements de Sogyal Lakar.

LES SECRETS DE LA LÉVITATION

Inadmissibles, mais le « maître » continue de dispenser son savoir à Lerab Ling. Une sorte de Disneyland du bouddhisme, lové dans la causse du Larzac. Vingt-cinq mille visiteurs et 4 millions d'euros de chiffre d'affaires annuel, une authentique machine à fric. Ce n'est qu'en 2016, craignant les foudres de la justice, que « le Précieux » finit par dételer au bout du monde.

« *N'attendez rien du bouddhisme*, conclut Jean-Pierre Jougla, ancien avocat, éternel pourfendeur des sectes cité par la défense. *Le bouddhisme, c'est une religion comme les autres, mais c'est aussi une société féodale où personne ne remet en cause les agissements du chef. Une société où la levée de l'impôt et le droit de cuissage sont encore de mise. Mais l'avouer, ce serait jeter le trouble dans la tête des 600 000 bouddhistes français. C'est une honte que cet avocat soit aujourd'hui sur le banc des accusés !* » Délibéré le 17 juillet. ●

French satirical weekly Charlie Hebdo's coverage of the June 2019 court case in Montpellier, headlined: "The rather earthly nirvana of the rapist lama." Claude Ardid's story begins with a witness's testimony: "Yes, my daughter has been raped several times by Sogyal Lakar."

Sogyal in Bad Saarow, Germany, 2016

18

Breakthrough

To his everlasting credit, in November 2018 David Hughes-Jones emailed everyone who had helped with his research, to let us know he had been successful in raising the Rigpa inquiry to statutory level. Shortly afterwards, the UK Charity Commission issued a press release giving details of the statutory process.

> *The Charity Commission, the independent regulator of charities in England and Wales, is today announcing that it has opened a statutory inquiry into Rigpa Fellowship (279315). The inquiry was opened on 8 November 2018.*
>
> *The charity, which is based in London, has objects to advance the Buddhist religion, and provides religious education, training and activities.*
>
> *The Commission has been engaging with the charity since August 2017 over serious concerns about adult safeguarding. The regulator's concerns have escalated in the course of this engagement, prompting the opening of a statutory inquiry.*
>
> *The inquiry will examine the charity's governance, policies and practices with regard to adult safeguarding, particularly in relation to:*
>
> - *its response, general handling and disclosure to the Commission and other agencies in relation to serious adult safeguarding incidents*
> - *its responsibility to provide a safe environment for its beneficiaries, staff and other charity workers in the delivery of its programmes*

More generally the inquiry will examine the charity's:

- *recruitment and supervision of its employees, volunteers and other charity workers*
- *financial controls and their application*
- *responsibility to maintain its reputation as a charity which can be entrusted with public support and the confidence of its beneficiaries, staff and volunteers.*[80]

It is the Commission's policy, after an inquiry has concluded, to publish a report detailing what issues the inquiry looked at, what actions were undertaken as part of the inquiry and what the outcomes were.

David Hughes-Jones must have made a Herculean effort to persuade key witnesses to accept the possibility of their names being made public. He is a modest individual – an archetypal discreet public servant – but to people striving to protect the integrity of Tibetan Buddhist teachings he is a hero.

If Rigpa's track record since the July 14 letter is an accurate yardstick, the present administration will apply maximum smoke and mirrors, obfuscation, ducking and weaving, lies and distortions in their efforts to retain their charitable status and avoid the potential for the entire house of cards to come tumbling down.

In April 2019, the Charity Commission for England and Wales confirmed that Patrick Gaffney has been disqualified as a trustee of all charities for a period of eight years, because he was responsible for misconduct and/or mismanagement in the administration of the Rigpa Fellowship. This announcement appeared on the Charity Commission web site in advance of the publication of their report on their Statutory Inquiry into Rigpa UK. They declined to give further details but said that Patrick's disqualification is connected to the Inquiry.

Disqualification by the Charity Commission of one trustee prior to the publication of a report on their Statutory inquiry is highly unusual – but in Rigpa UK's case one was followed by another.

On September 20, 2019, the Commission announced that Susan "Bunny" Burrows had been disqualified as a trustee for life.

The Commission found that Bunny had known about instances and allegations of "improper acts and sexual and physical abuse" against students. It was found she had either "failed to recognise" or "sought to downplay" the seriousness of allegations and was responsible for misconduct and/or mismanagement at Rigpa.

Amy Spiller, the watchdog's head of investigations, said: "Serious failings in the leadership of this charity led to people it was supposed to help being harmed and let down.

"Trustees hold important positions of trust and are rightly expected to take all appropriate steps to keep people safe. The appalling abuses and failings that occurred here run counter to everything people associate with charity.

"I hope this will bring some comfort to those so badly affected by what went on at Rigpa Fellowship," she added.

Bunny was one of Sogyal's original followers in 1973. In the squatting days she was Patrick Gaffney's girlfriend. But as Sogyal's profile escalated and Patrick moved with him into a multinational arena, Bunny was left behind in London. Her loyalty to Sogyal was unwavering, but like so many Rigpa students afflicted with blind faith, she paid a high price for her misguided devotion.

Rigpa was subjected to howls of derision on social media when it announced that Bunny had resigned as a trustee a few days before she was disqualified. It is beyond doubt that she knew what was coming.

As the backwash from the July 14, 2017 letter gathered momentum, it became increasingly obvious that Rigpa outfits around the world were struggling to survive. The most lucrative feature of any guru-centric organisation is the availability of the charismatic leader to strut his stuff. With Sogyal a cancer-stricken fugitive and members cancelling their subscriptions in droves, financial meltdown became a real threat. Lerab Ling in France and Dzogchen Beara in Ireland turned themselves into holiday destinations with value-added meditation, but Rigpa Australia was forced to put its most valuable real estate on the market, a huge modern house at Bluey's Beach, New South Wales, built at vast expense as a bolthole for Sogyal and his harem during the northern hemisphere winter months.

The agony piling onto Rigpa did not stop with the French police and UK Charity Commission investigations. Both cases, either separately or combined, represent a potential to scupper the organisation. But another damaging development took place in the Netherlands, under the guidance of my indefatigable co-author, Rob Hogendoorn. Spotting an opportunity to influence key figures in the ethnic Tibetan Buddhist hierarchy, 12 survivors of sexual abuse by Tibetan lamas launched an online petition, requesting that the Dalai Lama accept a collection of victim statements in person.

By the time His Holiness arrived in Rotterdam on September 14, 2018, more than 1,000 people worldwide had signed the petition – and he agreed to a personal encounter with four of the survivors. With sexual misbehaviour trending on the news agenda, the Associated Press news agency carried the story.[81] It appeared in numerous publications around the world, including the two usually reticent Buddhist journals, *Tricycle* and *Lion's Roar*. By the end of November 2018, the petition had been signed by 2,500 people.[82]

Reports from the survivors' delegation following the meeting, suggested that at first the Dalai Lama was underwhelmed by their testimonies, but as the exchanges between them unfolded his attitude became more receptive. At a press conference the following day His Holiness made what can only be seen as a PR blunder. Asked what he had learned from the meeting, he replied that he already knew about the sex abuse allegations, so it was "nothing new."[83] That admission triggered another wave of headlines. The Dalai Lama's truthful response is typical of his character – it almost certainly earned approval within the Buddhist community but did not play well to an uninformed public.

However, news reports did not highlight the fact that HHDL condemned sexual exploitation and abuse unequivocally. He repeated advice given during the 1990s that if offenders refuse the mend their ways, victims should go public with their complaints. His final remark to the delegation made it clear that he intended to deal with the problem. "You have given me ammunition," he said, before posing for photographs with the four with his usual bonhomie.

Mary Finnigan and Rob Hogendoorn

19

THE END OF AN ERA?

When Sogyal Lakar turned up in London during the latter days of the sex 'n' drugs 'n' rock 'n' roll revolution, most people who were drawn into his orbit did not investigate how Tibetan society functioned prior to the Chinese takeover in 1950. We were not interested in social history – we were dazzled by the mysterious, exotic, and alien phenomenon of Tibetan Buddhism. Some of us were also refugees from the formulaic, claustrophobic and – let's face it – boring Christian churches that sought to impose a strict moral code on their congregations.

Some but not all of us were fugitives from the drug culture. We had blown our minds on psychedelics, exploring altered states of consciousness previously accessible to only a small, priestly/monastic/privileged elite. Going to church on Sunday did not involve visionary experience. Going to a Tibetan temple in India or Nepal – or even a sitting room in north London – to participate in, rather than merely witness, a long ritual certainly did, so it was easy for us to fall in love with Vajrayana Buddhism. We parked our critical faculties at the temple door along with our shoes and nosedived into a complex and extremely potent yogic tradition – a synthesis of indigenous shamanism, Indian tantra, mainstream Buddhism and rigorous scholarship.

Many of us encountered skilful teachers who handled our naïve enthusiasm with care, kindness and caution. Teachers who offered a balanced diet of study and meditation, who insisted on strong foundation practices before suggesting we might like to visualise ferocious deities brandishing weapons while dancing on corpses in a halo of flames. We needed to understand the symbolism and the energy involved in deity practice – and that experiences along the path were another layer of illusion, more subtle, more vivid and very effective, but not an end in themselves. We were taught to view these signs of practice as indicators of contemplative progress, but that the real purpose is to go much deeper – beyond concepts and into a state of profound insight. We were dilettante Buddhists when we embarked on our Tibetan journey. Some of us stayed that way. Others accepted the challenge presented by serious commitment to a system that effectively re-calibrates mind, body and spirit.

Inevitably the halcyon days did not last forever. I have difficulty remembering the exact point when I woke up from the beautiful dream and a reality check kicked in. I think it happened when Felix, the young man who helped to squat Sogyal's first London base, phoned me one day during the late 1980s with concerns about several lamas who were having casual sex with their students. His hope was that I would take a journalistic interest in this situation because some of the women were distressed and confused. Quite the opposite, he said, to what is supposed to be happening with Buddhism.

At first, I was appalled at the idea of exposing our beloved lamas as sex offenders. I knew about Sogyal and had heard lurid rumours about the exploits of his role model, Trungpa Rinpoche in America, but I found it impossible to accept that sexual exploitation was happening across the lama landscape – with a few exceptions, mostly found within the reformed monastic Gelugpas. But I couldn't ignore the nagging awareness that Felix was probably right, so eventually I started to ask awkward questions, and people who knew what was going on started to answer them.

Foremost among my early whistle blowers was the former Gelugpa monk, Stephen Batchelor. Gifted with a formidable intellect, exceptional common sense and an endearing personality, Stephen had renounced Vajrayana in favour of Zen Buddhism, eventually formulating his own (extremely controversial) secular Buddhism best known via his book *Buddhism Without Beliefs*. Stephen wised me up to the misogyny that was hard-wired into Tibetan culture. The fact that pre-Chinese Tibet was a feudal medieval society, where women were regarded as inferior beings, came as a surprise to me.

"Senior lamas could choose any woman they fancied," said Stephen.

"*Droit de seigneur?*" I queried

"More like *droit de cuissage*," he replied with a fiendish grin.

The most awful aspect was that Tibetan women considered it an honour to be chosen for sex by a high lama and had no idea they were being exploited. Often, they were passed around like commodities and discarded when no longer desirable. Thankfully, one positive change occurred – especially among the young – with the post-1959 diaspora, when exiled Tibetan women encountered the politics of liberation.

As the process of discovery unfolded, it became obvious that lamas who did not sleep with their students were a minority. Shocked and disillusioned, I wrote the first of several letters to His Holiness the Dalai Lama, naming names and pleading for an explanation. I doubt that this letter got past his secretariat because I did not receive an answer.

The fantasies I had woven around all things Tibetan unravelled via information from level-headed friends like Stephen and from my own research. And while this was happening, I experienced a slow awakening. I was no longer in love with the magic and mystery of Tibet, the external paraphernalia of ritual practice was no longer a playground – it acquired meaning. This was a breakthrough in my understanding of the positive effects on daily life that result from consistent time on the cushion. I knew that I would be forever grateful for my encounter with the dharma – but simultaneously I was also happy to locate my confidence as a Western woman with the capacity to recognise the smell of corruption.

Then I did what journalists do. I talked about the fact that I no longer regarded the lamas as infallible. I criticised them as human beings, with human strengths and human weaknesses. As men who could not resist the temptations of the flesh – and as a boys' club keenly aware of the need to protect their own interests. I wrote and broadcast about Tibetan politics and religion in newspapers, on radio and on the internet. My fresh perspective coincided with the explosion of interest in Tibetan Buddhism that occurred during the late 1980s. It became multinational big business, and there was no doubt in my mind that many lamas were being spoiled rotten by the adulation accorded them by Western devotees.

I decided to focus my attention on Sogyal Lakar. Partly to atone for the fact that I failed miserably at the level of discriminating wisdom when I helped him at the start of his career. But mostly because by the late 80s I knew beyond a scintilla of doubt that he was a charlatan.

Two people whose judgement is based in meticulous scholarship and contemplative insight alerted me to his lack of qualifications and experience. The late John Driver and Ngakpa Chogyam (Ngakchang Rinpoche) sounded the alarm during the 1970s. My colleague Rob Hogendoorn, while researching for this book, confirmed that Sogyal had never been effectively trained as a lama.

In addition, as a frequent attendee at his teachings, I became aware that I had my own doubts about Sogyal. But like so many of us caught in the web of magic and Shangri La mystery, I did not give them adequate attention.

As always in samsara, there was a downside to my newly established clarity. I thought it would be welcomed by the fellow dharmites – but to say that I misjudged their likely reactions is a massive understatement.

Almost without exception, people I had known for years within the Tibetan Buddhist community were horrified by my campaign to shine light into the murky corners of the lama landscape. They retreated into denial. They excoriated me on the internet. They accused me of breaking samaya and, worst of all, ignoring the taboo against criticising lamas. One of Sogyal's henchmen tried to bully me. I lost friends and made enemies.

This went on for years, while I stuck stubbornly to my right to be right and, despite the opprobrium, I carried on going to teachings. My daily maintenance practice was trimmed to basics, and I branched out into Five Rhythms Dance and Hatha Yoga. A few members of the Buddhist cognoscenti were supportive, including lamas Tsultrim Allione and Jampa Thaye, Ngakchang Rinpoche and Stephen Batchelor. I collaborated for a while with another whistle-blower, the French author/academic Marion Dapsance.

Then Rob Hogendoorn came into my life and I found an ally I could trust and respect who had been following a parallel path for almost as long. We pooled our resources and expertise. Rob is a fiercely determined researcher – he enjoys teasing out corroborative evidence from arcane sources – while my passion resides in weaving disparate threads into coherent, credible stories. Rob's digital skills outstrip mine by the distance between Rotterdam and Devon. He has a steady, very Dutch temperament – in contrast with my volatile Anglo-French DNA. We are good friends and excellent teammates.

Rob got to the eight-signatory letter a few minutes before I did. He was on the phone to me as I opened the first of several files emailed by mutual friends, who knew that it represented a hugely significant moment for both of us. We had hung onto our positions on the moral high ground despite vitriolic criticism, threats, ridicule and vilification. We were vindicated. It was exhilarating, but also very sad because we now knew a lot more about the level of suffering that Sogyal inflicted on his brainwashed acolytes.

The release of the letter coincided with a step change in women's rights. A new constituency of courageous feminists from all walks of life blew their whistles loudly and defiantly about sexual exploitation and abuse that had been swept under the rug for generations. Surfing this wave of enlightened self-interest, during the initial backwash from the letter, Rob and I felt that at long last the Tibetan Buddhist establishment would be forced to accept that they have something to learn from us Westerners in the realm of moral and ethical values.

Along these lines, Tahlia Newland took a lead role in an initiative aimed at reaching out to ethnic Tibetan lamas who teach around the world. A list of 40 with published contact details was compiled and the eight-signatory letter was translated into Tibetan. Each lama received a copy of the letter plus a polite request for feedback. Four months after these were despatched only two lamas, Dagpo and Ato Rinpoches, had responded.[84]

So here we are, in the third decade of the 21st century and – with a few exceptions – Tibetan lamas are still aloof, unyielding, and rigidly adherent to the Red Robes code of silence. Sogyal still has a devoted worldwide following, illustrated by the fact that his Facebook post announcing that his cancer had spread attracted 1,200 responses, 130 shares and 346 comments along lines of:

In these incredibly difficult times you remain steadfast and continue to hold all of us in your heart. Thank you for being the perfect example to us Rinpoche, for helping me to find meaning even in the midst of my own difficulties. All my love and prayers, C…..

I suppose there is no need to hurry. Buddhism has thrived for 2,600 years through many tumultuous upheavals. It has adapted to many different cultures, shape-shifting but never deviating from its core message. All these changes happened on slow timelines. And they happened exclusively in Asia until the first decade of the 20th century. Integration into contemporary culture in the developed world is of a far greater order of magnitude. It would reek of hubris on our part to suggest that we made anything other than a small contribution.

A 2018 photo of Sogyal following his cancer diagnosis and surgery

20

DEATH OF A SALESMAN
(Apologies to Arthur Miller)

Sogyal Lakar died on August 28, 2019. The announcement was made on his Facebook page by his devoted dakini, Jackie Lee.

> *I have some very, very sad news to give you. Sogyal Rinpoche's health deteriorated today after he suffered a pulmonary embolism and he left this world around 1 pm here in Thailand. The doctors did everything they could but could not restore the function of his heart. Although his passing was sudden, in a way, all the same it was very peaceful and serene, and he was surrounded by close and loving students.*
>
> *Rinpoche is now resting in meditation. Several Lamas are supporting us with precise guidance at every step, and especially Sakya Gongma Trichen Rinpoche. Please during this time focus on Narak Kong Shak and the Heart of Vajrasattva, along with the Hundred Syllable Mantra, and especially this will be an important moment to focus on Guru Yoga practice and on uniting our mind with our beloved master's wisdom mind.*

This was the first public reference to the fact that Sogyal had been hiding in Thailand since the publication of the July 2017 letter. When the announcement was published on Sogyal's Facebook page, it attracted 2,000 comments – most of them expressing profound sorrow in highly charged language. It followed an increasingly dire series of bulletins which chronicled his rapidly declining health.

Sogyal on July 25 2019. (Still trying to sound optimistic):

> *Since the time of my first diagnosis, I have been following closely the advice of my doctors and recently undertook a procedure which successfully removed two small cancerous spots on my liver. At the same*

time, tests and scans were done to determine whether the rest of my body was free from cancer. It has emerged, however, that cancerous cells have been detected in some of the fluid inside my body.

Since receiving this news, I have consulted several oncologists to determine best treatment options, and received advice from my masters. It seems the best option is to follow a new course of intravenous chemotherapy. I am also considering adding complementary support with Tibetan medicine. The chemotherapy will start in the coming days, and will be repeated every two weeks.

I am very tired and need a lot of rest. The fluid impacts my breathing and so from time to time I am assisted with extra oxygen, which helps. The pain and discomfort are not too bad. I am in good spirits and remain confident that the power of the practices being done, in conjunction with the excellent medical treatment I'm receiving, will lead to complete healing.

Jackie on August 27:

I'm writing to you today as one of Sogyal Rinpoche's care team, to share some news about the current status of Rinpoche's health.

Rinpoche is presently in hospital, being closely monitored on account of complications arising from his condition, particularly in relation to his breathing. At times, he has been admitted to the Intensive Care Unit for closer supervision and support. The doctors and medical team, who are all experts in their field and show exceptional kindness and respect, are doing everything they can and remain confident that he will recover sufficiently to be able to return home soon. At the same time, it is important to know that Rinpoche's condition is fragile and serious, and therefore your prayers, love, practice, and support are needed now more than ever. As someone who has been close to Rinpoche, supporting him through his illness, I can tell you this really does make a difference.

Since Rinpoche is in a fragile condition now, susceptible to infection, and in need of quiet and rest, it is probably wisest that few people visit him now, until he regains strength. On behalf of the care team, I will endeavour to keep you all informed, until Rinpoche is well enough to resume communication himself.

The next day it was all over for Sogyal in living, breathing, physical form. His life may have ended, but Rigpa did not give up on him. Quite the contrary, in fact. Almost before the corpse was cold, planning was underway for funeral rites that are probably unique in the 2,500 year history of Buddhism. More than one observer speculated that Sogyal himself may have ordered the transcontinental extravaganza that Rigpa organised at, what seems with hindsight, barely credible short notice.

"He was terrified of dying," said one of my anonymous Rigpa sources, "so he may have given instructions for the maximum amount of ritual practice possible." Here was a man who claimed a level of insight and clarity that enabled him to teach others how to die well. But when it came to his own encounter with the Grim Reaper, he was probably incapable of applying that knowledge for his own benefit.

In view of the suffering he caused when alive, his fear makes sense from an ultra-traditional Tibetan Buddhist perspective. Heading off into the after-death bardos with a guilty conscience would be a scary prospect for a man burdened with a superstitious dread of the wrathful deities and the horrors of the Vajra Hell.

Maybe Jackie Lee, or others close to Sogyal as his health deteriorated, knew he was aware that he had racked up a rock pile of karmic debt during his dissolute lifetime. Or perhaps he clung to the belief that he had done nothing but his best for his students, that he had no need to feel regret and/or remorse. Those of us outside the innermost circle will never know for sure.

What we do know is that from the moment Sogyal drew his last breath the Rigpa elite embarked on the most ambitious public relations campaign in the entire history of an organsation that specialised in persuasive spin doctoring. To sceptical observers, the aim appears to have pivoted on sanitising Sogyal's reputation as fast and as ostentatiously as possible. They may not have a living guru any longer, but what they did have for a limited period was a corpse.

In the Tibetan Buddhist tradition, great masters who leave their physical bodies are said to manifest signs of their profound realisation during the immediate after-death state. It is said that the area around the heart remains warm, or that rainbows appear in the sky or that they sit for some time in the meditation posture.

In Sogyal's case, on August 31, 2019 his private office team issued a statement, giving more detail about the status of his mortal remains.

From the time when he passed away on August 28th, Sogyal Rinpoche has remained in a state of meditation (thugdam) at his residence in Thailand. Yesterday, Tulku Rigdzin Pema, a close disciple of Dilgo

Khyentse Rinpoche and a highly accomplished and knowledgeable master, arrived and confirmed Rinpoche's profound meditation. Today, three days after his passing away, Rinpoche left his meditative state, and Tulku Rigdzin Pema performed all the necessary rituals and prayers. He also noticed a gentle fall of rain at that time, which he considered a very auspicious sign.

We checked out Tulku Rigdzin Pema. There's no record of him available via internet search, but we did manage to establish that he is a member of the Sechen community near Kathmandu and is said to specialise in authenticating statues and making stupas. This hardly fits the Rigpa description – but that of course is not intended to be accurate. Its more like fairy dust sprinkled on the remaining devotees in order to maintain enchantment and cash flow.

Sogyal's Flying Circus was officially unveiled on Sepember 20,2019 in a brief announcement from the private office:

Following advice from a number of highly respected lamas, and taking into consideration the wishes of Sogyal Rinpoche, his family and close students, several private ceremonies will take place in remembrance of Sogyal Rinpoche in the coming months. The ceremonies will take place in Bangkok, France, Bodhgaya and Sikkim. Most events will be private and will only be open to family and close students.

The Rigpa interpretation of "private" turned out to be somewhat wide of the mark, because at every venue retinues of monks were commissioned and paid to perform elaborate rituals – and the events were live-streamed to Rigpa students all over the world. Once again it was obvious that despite all the online information, all the media coverage and public disapproval from the Dalai Lama, there were still thousands of people locked into deep devotion. There's no doubt that the late Sogyal Lakar was a successful cult leader.

They transported the pickled corpse (referred to in Tibetan as kudung) of Sogyal the violent rapist in a leak-proof coffin from the Wat Thong Nopakhun temple in Bangkok to Lerab Ling in France, Sechen Gompa in Bodhgaya, India, Chorten Gompa in Gangtok, Sikkim and finally to his cremation at Tashi Ding in west Sikkim. The proceedings started on September 17, 2019 and ended on December 2.

The live stream of the cremation showed a densely packed crowd of devotees from many countries, a long procession of monks chanting, ringing bells, blowing horns and banging drums in full regalia, together with several members of the Rigpa elite who probably escorted the coffin on its transcontinental journey.

Notable absentees included the majority of senior lamas, apart from the elderly Dodropchen Rinpoche who, we are told, has agreed to lead the search for Sogyal's reincarnation. The cost of the funeral must have run into mind-boggling figures. Who paid? Was it Rigpa, by this time in serious financial difficulties? Or did Sogyal bequeath a hefty sum in order to guarantee a lavish send-off?

Unless another well-informed whistle blower emerges from Rigpa, we will probably never know.

The high-profile lamas who boycotted the cremation did, however, stand by their man with more than 20 effusive eulogies published on sogyalrinpoche.org. This and other Rigpa websites refer to his death as "entering Parinirvana." This is hyperbole in very bad taste, because the word Parinirvana is associated with the passing of an enlightened Buddha. By no stretch of the imagination could anyone familiar with Sogyal's track record apply it to him.

The use of this term appears to be another aspect of the carefully choreographed campaign to sanitise Sogyal's reputation via adulatory language and exaggeration – probably aimed at preparing the Rigpa faithful for his reincarnation. When, rather than if, this happens, the unfortunate child deserves sympathy for the time when s/he inevitably finds out about her/his predecessor's disrepute.

The eulogies were another example of this – which also highlight the ongoing refusal by the Tibetan Buddhist establishment to own up to his grotesque behavior. The Dalai Lama was forced to distance himself from Sogyal by the eight-signatory letter, but the Central Tibetan Administration did not follow his example:

The eulogies unleashed a tornado of sound and fury on social media, which in turn generated two online petitions demanding recognition of Sogyal's abusive behaviour. The American lawyer Charles Carreon set one up on Change.org under the headline: "Dharma teachers: Please retreact you homages to Sogyal." It was addressed to the lamas who posted eulogies, who were named individually. It attracted 747 signatures.

Together with several other outraged people, Rob Hogendoorn wrote to the Central Tibetan Administration, demanding a retraction and an apology to Sogyal's victims. Somewhat to their surprise, it worked. The CTA removed their homage and issued an apology.[85]

The International Dzogchen Community, one of the largest Tibetan Buddhist organisations, was also confronted with objections from its membership after adding an appreciation of Sogyal to the eulogy collection. It was switfly withdrawn.

In the months following Sogyal's death, the organisation he left behind went through paroxisms of reappraisal and doubt. Most of the high-profile senior students disappeared into the woodwork. Dominique Side relinquished her role as Mother Superior of the Lerab Ling congregation but rematerialised discreetly as leader of a Dzogchen retreat. Phillip Phillipou melted away – leaving Patrick Gaffney as the sole survivor of the original leadership troika. Sam Truscott resigned as Director of Lerab Ling – hardly surprising given the centre's dire organisational and financial straits. Rigpa's mistress of spin, Catherine Paul, also abandoned ship. So now the organisation no longer benefits from her capacity to apply smoke-and-mirror techniques to soften the impact of factual information. "People who feel they may have been harmed," for example, rather than "people who were abused."

When the charismatic founder of a personality cult is no longer around to attract big audiences, their organisations invariably suffer financial decline. This is true of Bhagwan Shri Rajneesh organisation (later rebranded as Osho), for example, and for the Dzogchen Community founded by the late Chogyal Namkhai Norbu. This was also the case for Rigpa – no Sogyal equals substantially reduced cash flow.

Rigpa's two residential centres Lerab Ling and Dzogchen Beara were already in serious trouble when along came the coronavirus to make matters a lot worse. Public gatherings of all descriptions were banned as most countries around the world went into lockdown. Religious institutions were closed, along with entertainment venues and holiday locations. The travel industry collapsed. Online teachings by famous lamas, including the Dalai Lama, came nowhere near replacing the revenue generated by personal appearances.

Along with most other Buddhist organsations, Rigpa offered online teachings and practice sessions. It also embarked on restructuring its gobal entities into a federation, with the aim of spreading the cost of keeping Lerab Ling and Dzogchen Beara up and running. Many years earlier, a similar approach was adopted by Chogyal Namkhai Norbu's Dzogchen Community, with major centres financially supported by smaller groups around the world. Interestingly, Rigpa UK was not represented in the federated model. At the time of writing, one can only speculate why this happened, but it may have had something to do with the fact that Patrick Gaffney was being lined up to teach again – after keeping his head well below the parapet for more than a year after Sogyal died.

Sure enough, in June 2020 online teachings by Patrick Gaffney were flagged up on social media – followed shortly aftewards by an indignant item in the UK's *The Times* newspaper[86] and a howl of derision in a tweet by Sogyal Truth. Rigpa UK was quick off the mark with a press release.

Rigpa UK Statement, 4 June 2020

The Trustees of Rigpa Fellowship (also known as Rigpa UK to members) have been informed that Patrick Gaffney has been invited to teach online by some international Rigpa centres. Rigpa UK has not been and will not be involved with this teaching. Mr Gaffney resigned from Rigpa UK in 2018 and is no longer associated with Rigpa UK. In 2019, the Charity Commission disqualified him from being a charity trustee for eight years. Rigpa UK is an independent charity registered in England and Wales with the Charity Commission and not legally part of Rigpa International. The Trustees continue to co-operate with the Charity Commission in respect of its statutory inquiry into the charity.

Sogyal Truth hit the nail on the head, describing Rigpa UK's statement as "Orwellian double speak." It's a safe bet that lots of Rigpa UK members tuned into teachings by the man Sogyal designated as his "spiritual heir."

An attempt at reinvention of the Rigpa formula for success was launched in June 2020 with an announcement to members of forthcoming events.

The old guard was back in business – with Professor Philippe Cornu in pole position. The lineup included two Tibetan stalwarts – Ringu Tulku and Jetsun Khandro – together with Patrick Gaffney and Dominique Side, the two lynchpins who more than anyone else supported and concealed Sogyal's long track record as a violent sexual abuser. The two who knew beyond doubt that Sogyal had no personal insight into the profound experience generated by sustained Vajrayana/Dzogchen study and practice.

This online series, running from July to October 2020, was promoted as "financial support for Lerab Ling and Dzogchen Beara, in extreme financial difficulty because of the coronavirus pandemic." Lerab Ling and Dzogchen Bera were financially unsustainable for some time prior to the pandemic. They had already curtailed their programmes and shed staff following the mass exodus of members in the wake of the eight-signatory letter. By June 2020 Rigpa was reeling under the impact of a triple whammy – the letter, Sogyal's death, and the virus.

The Sakyadhita conference of Buddhist women held in Australia in June 2019 was another painful episode in the post-Sogyal period of decline. His former personal attendant Damcho Dyson (aka Michelle Tonkin) spoke in detail about her experiences. Here's a transcript:

Like many others, I met him at a time when I was yearning for a way to make sense of suffering after my life was derailed by a series of traumas. When I felt like I had nothing left to lose, Sogyal's bestselling book, The Tibetan Book of Living and Dying, *provided me with great support and tools.*

I didn't want to fall back into the confusion and suffering of my life and so reasoned that I should surrender my ego to the teacher and follow him and the lineage of the Buddha's teachings that he was transmitting. I'd already noticed the benefits of meditation and contemplation, so dismissed a number of the concerns that arose in those early days.

As a community, Rigpa had a culture in which faith and devotion – rather than rigorous study – were emphasized. The few who openly questioned Sogyal's manner of teaching were made an example of through a publicly humiliating dialogue that could completely hijack a teaching session. We were told by Sogyal and his senior students that these so-called training sessions were "activity teachings" and Sogyal's erratic and tantrum-like behavior was "crazy wisdom," and the way to view it correctly was to cultivate "pure perception."

I blindly trusted in the authenticity of Sogyal and his methods. By the time I moved to Lerab Ling, Rigpa's main center in France, I was inspired to take monastic ordination and aspired to surrender myself to the teacher and be trained in the manner of the great saints of the past. Therefore, when Sogyal first "corrected" me by striking me across the top of my head with a wooden back scratcher, I took this as a blessing.

Over the years, I became closer to Sogyal, and he gave me greater and greater responsibilities for his household and personal affairs. Now as his personal attendant, the frequency and severity of private beatings and public humiliations increased. For many of us in the "inner circle" it was not uncommon to have multiple lumps on our skulls or split scalps from beating. He once ripped my ear.

We all saw that his worst moods were caused by problems with the young attractive females – students he'd groomed for sexual relationships – that were on call to him 24/7. Only later was I to hear from some of them personally that they had been raped. They had been coerced into the relationship by being told they were engaging in consort practice, karmamudra.

Yet somehow, we kept each other afloat by reflecting on the karma we might be purifying, and the ego-clinging that we were loosening.

In 2008, six years after taking ordination, I started having waking and sleeping flashbacks of his beatings and verbal abuse, and began to feel physically ill at the sound of his voice. Sogyal sent me to Rigpa Therapy which was supposedly a fusion of Western psychology and the buddhadharma. I was grateful to have someone I could talk through my challenges with, but the therapist manipulated me too, telling me that the beatings and trials were nothing to do with Sogyal but rather with some past issues with a family member that needed to be purified.

Two years later, two visiting teachers could see that something was not right for me. They encouraged me to speak to them – something that we were always warned against as "no one will understand." The first told me that I was too close to the fire and so was being burned. He encouraged me to slowly and skillfully take a step back. A few weeks later, the second told me, "This is abuse."

Upon hearing those three words, I finally saw the entire history of my "training" for what it truly was. Over the coming months, I secretly planned how I could run away from Lerab Ling. When I finally did – at the end of 2010 – and went into hiding in India, I was publicly discredited and shamed by Sogyal. It was at least three years before the traumatic flashbacks and nightmares eased, and more years before I could turn to a professional therapist for help.

In 2017, I joined seven other current and former Rigpa students who wanted to hold Sogyal to account for his behavior. Each of us had different stories and when we spoke together, we realized that the damage went far beyond our individual experiences. Our open letter outlined the main concerns regarding Sogyal's misconduct in relation to sexual, physical, emotional, financial and psychological abuse of students; and the ways in which his actions had tainted people's appreciation for the practice of the dharma.

Since co-authoring this letter, I have heard many more extreme and profoundly disturbing accounts of Sogyal's abusive behavior and can state that what has been published in the press and the official investigation merely scratches the surface.[87]

The Director of Rigpa Australia, Dr Kathryn James, was in the audience when Damcho spoke. It was a wake-up call, which led her to admit that she had been hit by Sogyal. Her confession was the basis for a two-part report and an editorial in the Australian newspaper the *Newcastle Herald*.[88] Dr James was the first and, so far in 2021, the only senior Rigpa official to own up to experiencing his violent behaviour.

Damcho, aka Michelle, spoke again during an online seminar on sexual abuse framed by religion, organised by the London-based organisation Inform in July 2020. Her powerful speech, delivered by pre-recorded video from her home in Australia, revealed two hitherto unpublished incidents involving members of Sogyal's harem.[89]

In one case the woman involved stoically endured beatings and humiliation until she cracked. We heard that this happened regularly. She would run away, then be enticed back with promises of love and support. The other was even more distressing – the woman was constantly beaten or dragged around by her hair. Michelle described how this woman's vitality ebbed away until eventually she was taken into residential psychiatric care. Michelle's speech can be accessed on YouTube.

Rob Hogendoorn and I participated in the seminar – Rob from the registered attendees and me as a guest speaker. Here's a transcript of my talk, one of several five-minute slots covering Christianity, Islam, Yoga, Buddhism and witchcraft.

> *I'd like to thank Michelle for speaking direct, stark-reality truth and for being one of the eight people whose open letter in July 2017 brought about Sogyal's fall from grace.*

> *I first met Sogyal in the spring of 1973. Along with other people who shared my interest in meditation, I found him a place to teach – a house in Kilburn, London which we squatted in the name of the Nyingma tradition of Tibetan Buddhism.*

> *I do not refer to Sogyal as Rinpoche. It is a title accorded to lamas in recognition of their contemplative realisation and scholarship. Sogyal was a charlatan who was never trained as a lama. But we did not know this in the 1970s. We were naïve, ill-informed and enthusiastic. We felt lucky to be involved with a charismatic Tibetan guru.*

> *It soon became obvious that our new found teacher had an insatiable sexual appetite. He hit on virtually every pretty woman he*

encountered. It did not occur to us then that this behaviour was not compatible with the power imbalance inherent in his role as a lama.

The late John Driver first sounded an alarm about Sogyal. John was a respected Tibetan Buddhist scholar-practitioner. I am a journalist, so after John's alert, I applied my professional skills to finding out more about Sogyal's background.

His ascent into guru superstardom occurred after the publication of The Tibetan Book of Living and Dying, *and his role in the movie* Little Buddha. *His organisation Rigpa went global.*

In 1994 a woman known as Janice Doe sued Sogyal for sexual abuse and battery. This was the first time we heard about the beatings he inflicted on members of his inner circle. By the early noughties I had built up a dossier on Sogyal, But it lacked corroborative evidence – until Mimi Durand told me about her experience of rape and violence as a member of Sogyal's harem.

My essay Behind the Thangkas went live on the internet in 2011. Thangkas are sacred paintings. They hung in Sogyal's chalet at Lerab Ling. When an orgy happened they were taken down to reveal pornographic images.

Soon afterwards Sogyal's depravity was exposed in the Canadian documentary In the Name of Enlightenment. *And soon after that I met Rob Hogendoorn. We discovered that we worked well as a team – so we wrote* Sex and Violence in Tibetan Buddhism.

Sogyal fled to Thailand after the publication of the eight-signatory letter. He died of cancer there on the 28th of August last year, steeped in scandal and publicly disgraced by His Holiness The Dalai Lama. Thousands of students abandoned Rigpa between 2017 and 2020. But thousands stayed loyal to Sogyal, the cult leader who had brainwashed them into blind faith adoration.

So what of his legacy? Rigpa's public presentation emphasises business as usual. Their schedules include teachings by ethnic Tibetan lamas and also with eye-watering chutzpah – by Patrick Gaffney and Dominique Side. The two innermost disciples who knew beyond doubt about Sogyal's behaviour –who enabled it, condoned it and concealed it. Who lied about it in public and in private, for more than 40 years.

But behind the scenes Rigpa is in big trouble. Most of its national groups are close to insolvency – and the Charity Commission for England and Wales is due to publish a report on a statutory inquiry into Rigpa UK. Two senior Rigpa insiders – Patrick Gaffney and Susan Burrows -- have been disqualified as Charity Trustees, in advance of the report.

It is my view that Rigpa will not recover from the corruption it refused to acknowledge – and should be disbanded. To its everlasting shame Rigpa has never apologised to Sogyal's victims.

Rob Hogendoorn has applied his research skills to an in-depth survey of Rigpa's finances. Senior figures within the organization have admitted that Lerab Ling and Dzogchen Beara are in deep financial trouble, so Rob's analysis will not come as a big surprise. It will also be difficult for them to challenge his findings.[90]

Many organisations established by Sogyal and his coterie have tax-exempt status. This enabled us to examine the financial statements of 14 organisations, which fall into three broad categories: membership, service providers and investment funds.

To frame our discussion of Rigpa's finances, we share some aggregate numbers that give an idea of the overall scale of its international operations: according to their own profit-and-loss accounts, these 14 organisations collected more than €54.2 million in revenue between 2012 and 2017. Because the same organisations spent almost €55.6 million in expenses, the aggregate result in these six years was a deficit of almost €1.4 million.

For more than five years to September 2020, a steady decline of interest in Rigpa has translated into decreasing proceeds from donations and fees. Between 2012 and 2017, income dropped faster than Rigpa's expenses – in particular labour costs – so that deficits mounted. Between 2012 and 2017 the organisations that operate the retreat centres Lerab Ling in France and Dzogchen Beara in Ireland ran into a total deficit of 1,807,619 euro. The year 2015 was a low point, Rigpa's financial *annus horribilis*: the aggregate result of the organisations we looked into was a deficit of €1,360,937. Over time, attempts to compensate for the accumulating deficits through appeals to the generosity of members and supporters became futile: the losses mounted up, while the donations lagged behind.

The faltering results pointed to significant flaws in Rigpa's earning capacity and cost containment – long before Sogyal went into hiding and died in Thailand, and long before the Covid-19 lockdowns in the Spring of 2020. Indeed, its annual report for 2017 already noted that Lerab Ling's somewhat contradictory economic model – based on three pillars: frugality, generosity, and prudent management of resources – was seriously undermined by two consecutive years (2016 and 2017) recording significant deficits of €333,082 and €488,421. The Rigpa Europe Association in France, which provides Lerab Ling with the "free use of the temple, the accommodation building for the nuns and monks, as well as the neighbouring land," also lost a further €545,135 in 2017.

The results of the two organisations that operate Dzogchen Beara were worrying too – they lost €606,404 in 2018. On March 19, 2019, the Irish newspaper *The Southern Star* published an interview with Malcolm MacClancy, the director of Dzogchen Beara in Ireland. At that time the concrete frame of their Tibetan temple had just been weather-sealed. MacClancy announced that the temple would be inaugurated in the summer of 2019. The cost of this grandiose vanity project was estimated at €3.6 million, only €1.9 million of which had been raised by Rigpa members and supporters.

MacClancy enthused that "the temple – with its magnificent copper roof, is going to be a jewel for Ireland, but also for the Beara Peninsula. It will attract many visitors." When asked how many members Rigpa as a whole has – and how many would be visiting the temple, MacClancy could not answer. Since then, the building work has ground to a halt, while the temple is being decorated with faux Tibetan ornaments made of packing material. It seems highly unlikely that it will be completed. And even more unlikely that Buddhist practitioners and tourists will travel to a remote corner of south west Ireland to marvel at an empty concrete shell. One must wonder if Peter Cornish, the original owner, now regrets handing the Beara retreat centre over to Rigpa.[91]

The most recent financial statements of the organisations that operate the French and Irish retreat centres had not been released by March 2021. But it seems likely that the significant statistics will reveal a dramatic decline. When the European lockdown began, Lerab Ling's revenue deficit for 2020 was estimated at more than €1.3 million. Dzogchen Beara faced an income reduction of more than €1 million. Rigpa's current leadership intervened by pausing other fundraising initiatives in favour of an urgent request for help to secure the survival of the retreat centres. This was in fact their umpteenth bailout appeal. Also, it was decided that all income from impromptu online streaming events would go towards support for the two residential centres.

By August 2020, MacClancy made public that Dzogchen Beara had laid off 70 percent of its staff – which cost around €500,000 in 2018. Lerab Ling announced that 40 out of a total of 58 paid staff would be dismissed by the end of September. During the previous three years, the French retreat centre spent nearly €1.3 million on wages and social security.

Massive redundancies and financial pledges notwithstanding, Lerab Ling still faced a €520,000-plus deficit by the end of 2020. It expects to have around one million euros in the bank at the close of the year. But Lerab Ling has also incurred a debt of more than one million euros. Dzogchen Beara, in turn, stands to lose €140,000 in 2020. As MacClancy said: "This is a deficit that remains for this year and we don't have any way to get these funds apart from the generosity of the sangha."

During a streamed event in August 2020, Rigpa officials acknowledged that attendance has dropped "year after year," while the community ages.

They underlined that Lerab Ling's support base needs to become more local and regional, while "online connections" gain importance, albeit yielding less profit. Participants in the online meeting were told that Lerab Ling used to rely on big events for the sangha in order to generate income but these required a lot of resources: But they were told "we are not flexible, which means that if we don't have an event we still have to keep the people and the resources in place."

The challenge, as Lerab Ling's current leadership sees it, is to provide for its upkeep with much lower costs and a much smaller staff, while retaining the resources and flexibility to host big international events.

A newly formed Steering Group proposed recently that Rigpa should function as a federation:

> *Led by Rigpa's Vision, all decisions will be taken for the benefit of Rigpa as a whole, and decisions will be made by consensus. The federation will be implicit, respecting different cultures, age groups, et cetera, and will have representation from all of the different bodies in Rigpa. So, everybody is included, and nobody is left out. And responsibility will be shared for services between the different Rigpa bodies, and these services include curriculum, programme, finances, et cetera. And very importantly, its operations, decision-making processes, everything else will be completely transparent.*

This seems to be a tall order – and it is also doubtful that a federation can be *implicit*. Either it is a federation or it isn't. In legal terms and in charitable status there's no grey area. Only about 1,500 members and supporters worldwide tuned into the Sangha Connection streaming event in May 2020 – and only 350 people responded to the urgent appeal for financial support. The Rigpa sangha's average age is 58. Even if "donations have never been lacking at crucial moments in our history," the capacity of Lerab Ling's remaining well-wishers to absorb deficits of hundreds of thousands of euros every year must be finite.

Also, it is doubtful whether Rigpa members and supporters are willing to risk the survival of their national organisations in order to save Lerab Ling and Dzogchen Beara – especially when their own revenues are faltering.

Between 2013 and 2019, income from retreat and practice fees at the Rigpa Fellowship in the United Kingdom, fell 90 percent. After Sogyal's demise, income from membership fees dropped by 25 percent. In 2019, it was reported that the Fellowship borrowed money from the bank "to aid cash flow." Also, the trustees began "de-restricting funds" in a deposit account, to help "the charity navigate the uncertain climate and help update the building." It was hoped that generating income from "residential and commercial rent and venue hire" might provide further relief. But turning its main objective "to advance the Buddhist religion" into a sideshow might threaten its tax-exempt status.

National tax authorities would probably also question the legal implications of funds being transferred from one tax-exempt entity to another to cover foreign organisations' structural deficits. The tax-exempt Rigpa Foundation in the Netherlands, for instance, has acquired about one million euros in donations for a new centre. Beyond the legal issue of a possible misappropriation of funds, it remains to be seen whether the Dutch tax authorities allow the Dutch Rigpa branch to make its liquid assets available to secure the survival of Lerab Ling and Dzogchen Beara.

References by the current leadership to Rigpa Germany, the German Tertön Sogyal Stiftung, and its spiritual care centre, Sukhavati, are conspicuous by their absence. The Tertön Sogyal Stiftung owns Sukhavati's enormous new building in Bad Saarow, built at a cost of around nine million euros. It opened its doors in 2016. Between 2015 and 2017, Rigpa Germany itself lost €404,522, part of which was spent on Sukhavati.

We have not examined the financial statements of the Tertön Sogyal Stiftung – which is the German branch of a total of four trusts worldwide – and Sukhavati, but it's hard to see how they would have escaped unscathed from the cumulative effect of pre-existing malaise, the disgrace and death of Sogyal, and the Covid-19 crisis. The willingness of German members and supporters to bail out French and Irish retreat centres may have reached its limit some time ago. Indeed, Rigpa's current leadership seems to anticipate precisely such concerns by insisting that Rigpa as a whole is merely an implicit federation: the decision to call it that may be no more than a sales pitch, couched in pseudo-organisational jargon, to urge foreign donors to donate generously to the two retreat centres in dire financial straits. Any such ploy does have a precedent: internal references and payments to the Rigpa International Association in France continued long after the organisation was dissolved on February 4, 2006.

When supply fails to create demand and loss of revenue, overspending, deficits, and problems of liquidity continue to impact the two retreat centres, a sale of assets may become inevitable. According to their 2017 balance sheets, five of the 14 organisations held some €24 million in real estate. Its real worth is what remains after the borrowed capital used to buy and develop the properties has been paid back. Then again, some of Sogyal's vanity projects may not be easily marketable. A Tibetan temple's value may be incalculable to some, but little more than the cost of demolition to others.

We asked investment analyst Chris Gilchrist (my husband) to assess Rigpa's financial status. He was not fooled by the complexities of the organisations's multi national business model:

It looks like Rigpa did what any smart corporate empire builder would do: hold the land and assets in one entity in a jurisdiction and conduct the trading activities through other entities. The assets can be pledged for loans without donors in the trading entities knowing about it, charges can be levied to the trading entities for their use of the assets (land and buildings), assets can be shuffled, so can investments, and when stuff hits the fan, trading entities can be shut down and any losses need not be made up from the entities holding the assets. I would also guess that the entities holding the assets pay members of the inner circle in ways the faithful donors do not entirely understand.

In America, the Tenzin Gyatso Institute's balance sheet for 2010 inflated the value of its land and buildings, along with the (supposed) development thereof, against the purchase value ($405,000) to almost $1.9 million. A few years later, these assets were devalued by $1.4 million and sold for $475,000 – even though in the interim the institute spent more than $5 million.[92] Likewise, the securities listed on the balance sheets of the three investment funds we checked – nearly €1.3 million in 2017 – may be worth significantly less than their book value, especially when sold in haste.

The temples at Lerab Ling and Dzogchen Beara may suffer a similar fate. The various membership organisations, service providers, and investment funds that constitute Rigpa as a whole are highly interdependent. So, the most pressing concern might be which one will be the first domino to fall? But with Chris Gilchrist's analysis in mind, it may end up that the tangible assets (land and buildings) are safely ring-fenced. Which in turn might mean that none of the loans keeping the show on the road will be repaid.

The fact that financial mismanagement on the scale revealed by this research went unchecked for so long pivots on one dominant factor. Until his death in 2019, Sogyal was an autocrat whose diktats were set in concrete. Nobody dared to challenge him until the gang of eight dropped their bombshell in 2017. The extreme extravagance of his lifestyle, his vanity projects and his harem were not negotiable. Even his funeral rites had to be the most flamboyant and the most extravagant in living memory.

There's a lot we don't know about Rigpa's *modus operandi*. We don't know, for instance, if Sogyal ever paid taxes, anywhere. Although he is said to have been a French national, it's possible that Rigpa organisations around the world covered all Sogyal's living expenses. Indeed, as a traveling salesman he may have avoided income and wealth taxes the whole of his life. We also don't know anything about his personal fortune.

It remains unclear if Sogyal acknowledged Yeshe, the son he fathered with Marianne Jurgaitis, as his heir. Sogyal's alimony arrangements are unknown too. Jurgaitis lives in New York City with Pedro Beroy, a current member of the Rigpa Vision Board. We haven't been able to determine who – or what – are Sogyal's beneficiaries. No executor was announced publicly. Only Sogyal's tax returns or his Will would provide answers to these questions. We have no access to either.

But we do know quite a lot about Pedro Beroy. His online CV, for example: "Pedro is a partner of AP Structured Finance with more than 25 years of experience in financial markets. Between 1995 and 2011, he worked for Credit Suisse in New York as Managing Director, he was a member of the Global Fixed Income Operations Committee, Chief of Longevity Markets, Latin America Structuring and Coverage Manager."

And from the Rigpa's Terton Sogyal Foundation web site: "Pedro Beroy has been a Rigpa student for the last seventeen years. He is currently a partner of AP Structured Finance. Prior to his current role, Pedro spent sixteen years at Credit Suisse in the Investment Banking Division with diverse responsibilities in trading, structuring and sales. He was a Managing Director based in New York and a member of the Fixed Income Operating Committee. Pedro headed Credit Suisse's global fixed income activities in the Longevity Markets Group. Prior to that role, Pedro was responsible for the Latin America Structuring and Coverage Group. Pedro holds a Master in Business Administration from the Amos Tuck School at Dartmouth College and a degree in Civil Engineering from the Universidad Politecnica de Catalunya in Barcelona. He is the president of the Tertön Sogyal Foundation, a member of the Rigpa International Investment Board and a member of the Rigpa Endowment Investment Committee."

Pedro appears to be a heavyweight money man with an impressive track record. He is currently employed by an organisation that specialises in "credit solutions to our clients requiring financing alternatives outside of those offered by traditional commercial banks." This is financial code for obtaining loans for companies that cannot get money from banks, often because of the questionable nature of their business or the people running them. The questions we ask are: "What in the name of all the Buddhas has he been doing for the last 17 years at Rigpa?" How come he was blind to the implications of Rigpa's gross financial mismanagement? And if he did know about them, why did he fail to sort out the problems?

Although we have no proof to support our hunch, there's a murky aura around Pedro's position as a money expert Rigpa management figure, who is also in a relationship with Marianne Jurgaitis and *de facto* stepfather to Yeshe. What appears in Rigpa bookkeeping may not correspond with the actual value of its worldwide holdings.

It has been established beyond doubt that Rigpa was a corrupt organisation while Sogyal was alive. Their massive PR campaign since July 2017 claims root-and-branch reform, obeying all the rules of ethical conduct. But anyone with a background in persuasive copywriting can see through the spin. To long-time observers it is obvious that behind the public façade very little has changed.

Sogyal's reputation is being sanitised, in preparation for the appearance of an infant suitable for recognition as his reincarnation.

The Sogyal mega-loyalists Patrick Gaffney and Dominque Side are enthroned as dharma teachers – and the red robes mafia is still supplying lamas to maintain Rigpa's credibility as a Tibetan Buddhist resource.

In December 2020 Rigpa embarked on another in a series of attempts to sanitise their reputation and curry favour with their remaining membership. Their Sangha Survey is an initiative that would never have been allowed by the late dictator, Sogyal Lakar – so in that sense it represents a significant break with the past. It was not a resounding success. Although the reaction to it from the present elite is presented with the usual soft-focus gloss on Rigpa websites, the fact remains that only a small portion of the membership who received the survey bothered to respond.[93] Rob Hogendoorn analysed the results.

In 2021, Rigpa claims 117 centres in 24 countries. The survey was sent to the 3,900 "sangha members" everywhere who "currently accept to receive emails from Rigpa." Of those, 444 members responded within 24 hours, 756 more members responded within 19 days – which amounts to a total of 31%. It's reasonable to assume that these 1,200 members are the remaining true believers. That's an average of 50 committed respondents per country, 10 per Rigpa centre.

However, the survey results indicate that the place of residence of the respondents is heavily skewed towards France (22 % = 264) and Germany (17% = 204). This is hardly surprising: these are the two countries where Rigpa's largest operational facilities – the French retreat centre Lerab Ling and the German spiritual care centre Sukhavati – are found. These centres stand apart, because they accommodate resident students and the largest remaining staff of semi-professionals and volunteers, who are economically dependent on their centres' survival.

Also, the survey indicates that 74% of the respondents strongly agree that having a physical, local centre is important to them, while 86% of them are likely to attend a physical, local centre sometimes (24%) or regularly (62%). These findings indicate, for all intents and purposes, that French and German students' will tend to focus on the economic survival and upkeep of their own physical, local centres rather than Rigpa centres elsewhere in the world.

The survey does not bode well for Rigpa's other retreat centre, Dzogchen Beara. Only 48 of the survey's respondents (4%) reside in Ireland. The new temple there is under construction, with secure funding for roughly half the estimated building costs. Dzogchen Beara accommodates resident students and spiritual care too, but on a smaller scale. And it is less accessible than the French and German centres.

Between 2011 and 2021, the French, German, and Irish branches of Rigpa sustained heavy financial losses. The recent updates by Rigpa's financial management team underline that the Covid-19 pandemic made a bad situation much worse. Their economic sustainability is at stake, and it seems unlikely that the remaining members will continue to foot the bill of loss-making ventures in far-off places. Or that struggling centres will place their institutional interests second to those of struggling centres elsewhere.

The demographic of the respondents to the survey also serves to illustrate Rigpa's predicament: 16% of the respondents are aged 40-49, 28% 50-59, 36% 60-69, 13% 70-79, and 2% over 80. Of the members in this ageing group, 35% have been involved for 20 to 29 years, while 10% have been involved for more than 30 years. Only 1% of the respondents are aged between 20 and 29.

Rigpa's remaining committed members are in an older age group, whose enthusiasm for the cause is not being replaced. This demographic affects not only Rigpa's sources of income, but also the presence of readily available volunteers. A faltering organisation with an ageing membership is hardly a major attraction for young recruits.

The survey shows that the remaining members lean heavily on teachings on video (83%), and audio (54%) and online programmes. In fact, the respondents profess the greatest preference for online video teachings. This is remarkable, since Sogyal's most trusted advisor Orgyen Topgyal took the Dalai Lama to task for giving teachings and empowerments via the internet during the pandemic, saying that such a practice degenerates and destroys the dharma. According to Topgyal, the teacher and student should be physically together.[94] For all of the respondents' insistence on the importance of "authentic lineage and teachings," (4.66 on a scale of 1 to 5), their preference for online learning (4.32 on a scale of 1 to 5) clashes with the orthodox Tibetan perspective.

Since the pandemic forced many Buddhist teachers and organisations to look for new sources of revenue, the market for online Buddhist teachings is highly competitive. Now that interested parties experience relatively cheap and easily accessible online teachings, it may be hard to rekindle their interest in more expensive, less accessible on-site, in-person teachings in foreign countries. It's hard to see how expansion of the online programme could become enduring and profitable and enough to provide for the repayment of the mortgages and upkeep of the expensive centres in France, Germany, and Ireland.

Sogyal's capricious and often brutal antics entertained and bonded the remaining, ageing true believers – who evidently had no trouble ignoring his sexual and other abuses. Online teachings by teachers other than Sogyal will be less "entertaining," and certainly less bonding. This seems especially important, because 88% of the respondents to the survey strongly agree that "a sense of community and friendship" is important for their involvement with Rigpa.

Around two thirds of the respondents to the survey feel "clear and resolved with respect to the allegations and investigation findings against Sogyal" (66%), and "feel safe to bring up a disagreement, complaint, or ethical issue in my sangha" (63%). It's obvious that the one thing most respondents have in common is that they were long-term apologists for Sogyal's abusive behaviour. The "feelings" of this group are in stark contrast to the sense of outrage and betrayal felt by Sogyal's victims, disillusioned Rigpa members who left the organisation, and critical observers.

21

Post Mortem

Rigpa has managed to survive a series of disasters, including the Janice Doe lawsuit, the findings of the Lewis Silkin investigation and the Charity Commission for England and Wales, a French police investigation, damning testimony from whistle-blowers like Mimi Durand, Damcho Dyson aka Michelle Tonkin, Sogyal Truth, Dominique Cowell, Sangye Ngawang and Joanne Standlee, my online blog Behind the Thangkas (2011 to 2018), the documentary movie *In The Name of Enlightenment*, worldwide broadcast and print media exposes, the eight-signatory letter, public disapproval from the Dalai Lama, Sogyal's illness and death, and the coronavirus pandemic. But with financial collapse on the horizon how much longer can they sustain the myth?

Regardless of evidence of huge debts and very little income, in December 2020 the Rigpa elite launched a morale-boosting initiative aimed at their remaining membership. They were told that the "sacred" house at Bluey's Beach in Australia no longer needed to be sold, that work on the Dzogchen Beara temple in Ireland was going ahead and that the Paris centre would be refurbished. These are expensive ventures – so who is footing the bill? Hardly surprising that details of the necessary resources were not included in the pitch.

As the Charity Commmission for England and Wales's statutory enquiry progressed, there was considerable interaction between the Commisssion and Rigpa UK's trustees. Fully aware that it could lose its charitable status, Rigpa UK did everything it could to distance itself from Rigpa worldwide and to clean up its act. Comprehensive safeguarding proceedures were published on its web site and it rebranded itself as a separate, self-governing entity. It sacked its salaried staff, including former head honcho Paul Brusa, and replaced two of its four trustees. It issued what the sharp and well informed commentator Jo Greene described as a "laughable" disclaimer of any involvement in Patrick Gaffney's online teachings from Lerab Ling in France. Former trustees Gaffney and Burrows were disqualified prior to the release of the Commission's report on its inquiries, so the rump of Rigpa's administration knew that their survival was on a knife edge. This bout of frenzied activity paid off.

In November 2020 the Charity Commission published its report.[95] It is hypercritical but, no doubt to the great relief of Rigpa, stops short of removing the cherished charitable status. The Charity Commission's Chief Executive Helen Stephenson went straight for the jugular:

> Today's findings make for very difficult reading. The fact that students were subjected to abuse by somebody in a position of power is shameful, and I am appalled that this was able to happen in a charity where people should have felt safe.
>
> People were let down because senior figures not only failed to listen and act on concerns, but also failed to properly address the problems with the charity's safeguarding culture once these came to light.
>
> I hope that our findings bring some comfort to those so badly affected by what went wrong at Rigpa Fellowship.

The report by lead investigator David Hughes-Jones and his team highlighted a catalogue of safeguarding and managements failures, together with criticism of the attitudes displayed by the two primary Sogyal enablers – Patrick Gaffney and Susan "Bunny" Burrows.

> The inquiry found that some students had been subjected to mental, physical and sexual abuse by Sogyal Lakar. The inquiry also found that there were senior individuals within the charity who were aware of at least some of these issues and failed to address them, which exposed the charity's beneficiaries to the risk of harm.
>
> Mr Gaffney discussed physical acts by Sogyal Lakar towards others, saying he wouldn't characterise these as violent. He said these were only occasional. Mr Gaffney stated that he had never received any complaints from those who had been on the receiving end of such acts. In the meeting, Mr Gaffney appeared unable or unwilliung to recognise the serious nature of the allegations that had been made and the lack of appropriate action taken.
>
> At a meeting with the inquiry on 23 January 2019 Ms Burrows was specifically asked whether anyone at all had previousky told her of instances of abuse concerning Sogyal Lakar and she stated "absolutely

not" and indicated that she had no knowledge of the allegations against Sogyal Lakar until the letter dated 14 July 2017 was published.

On 18 November 1994, the charity published a document which commented on the Janice Doe case. This charity circular was signed by several key Rigpa figues including Ms Burrows. It is therefore apparent that Ms Burrows must have been aware of the Janice Doe allegations.

Ms Burrows appeared unable or unwilling to recognise the serious nature of the allegations that had been made and the lack of appropriate action taken.

Patrick and Bunny strung together a collection of barefaced lies when giving evidence to the Lewis Silkin investigation and to the Charity Commission. People who know her would agree that Bunny is not a nasty person, just profoundly misguided. Blindsided by guru devotion, she allowed herself to be embroiled for more than 40 years in a conspiracy of silence around Sogyal's increasingly deranged behaviour.

During the last years of his life Sogyal was almost certainly certifiably insane. Rigpa's former IT supremo Sangye Ngawang mentions in the Dutch film *Guru in Disgrace* that Sogyal "saw himself as a king" – a delusion of grandeur confirmed in the same movie by Joanne Standlee. Joanne also says that Sogyal reckoned he was a "mahasiddha." This refers to someone who is a fully realised yogi – the ultimate accolade in Tibetan Buddhism. As his mental health deteriorated, his personal appearances became increasingly theatrical, featuring grand entrances in elaborate robes and fancy hats, with musical accompaniment.

By this time there was nobody within Rigpa who dared to challenge Sogyal's behaviour. To do this would risk physical attack with any hard object within reach. Backscratchers were his favourite weapon or a woodbound Tibetan book or perhaps a coffee mug. Joanne Standlee is on record describing how Sogyal knocked a "thin young girl" unconscious – and refused to allow an ambulance to be called. Although the eight-signatory conspiracy eventually stripped the emperor naked, he managed to escape criminal prosecution for serious crimes – rape and battery for example – by bolting to Thailand and then dying.

So how does this dismal saga play out on the wider landscape of diaspora Tibetan Buddhism? It is clear that its overall reputation is severely tarnished and that even the saintly aura around His Holiness the Dalai Lama does not hold up to detailed scrutiny. There are many disillusioned admirers who disapprove of his failure to condemn Sogyal's behaviour until forced to do so in 2017.

More damaging revelations emerged in late 2020. The hitherto squeaky clean Foundation for the Preservation of the Mahyana Tradition (FPMT) was knocked off its perch by a sex scandal. The FPMT is a monastically inclined, globally successful Tibetan Buddhist organisation affiliated to the Dalai Lama's Gelugpa sect. It was founded by my first teacher, Lama Thubten Yeshe, and managed to avoid public controversy until one of its senior teachers, the monk Dagri Rinpoche, was outed as a serial sex pest. There have also been reports of sexual exploitation by high-ranking lamas from the Kagyu sect, along with allegations of bullying and intimidation by their followers.

Last-minute insights manifested just before this edition went to press.

Back in the day when Rigpa was in a state of peak hubris, the hapless former director of Lerab Ling, Sam Truscott, and his cronies launched a libel suit against the lawyer Jean-Baptiste Cesbron and the local newspaper, *Midi Libre*. They did this because Cesbron gave an interview to the paper in which he referred to Rigpa as a cult.

Cultish behaviour is taken very seriously in France, so Lerab Ling was worried that the local Tourist Office might stop recommending visits to the centre. When the case came to court, it was dismissed. Apparently determined to carry on banging their heads against a brick wall, Lerab Ling appealed. In May 2021 it was declared inadmissible by the Montpellier Appeal Court. Jean-Baptiste Cesbron has mixed feelings about the outcome:

"Although this is a huge satisfaction for me, I remain very bitter about the pain of the many victims, who, in fact, were denied a lawsuit against Sogyal Lakar, and/or against the Lerab Ling congregation," he wrote in an email to his supporters.

Also just before our publication deadline, Ngak'chang Rinpoche, the British lama formerly known as Ngakpa Chogyam, gave us permission to quote from the fourth unfinished volume of his memoir, *Goodbye Forever*.[96] This is significant because the quotes were transcribed from recordings of conversations between Chogyam and the highly respected Nyingma lama, the late Chimed Rigdzin Rinpoche, during the mid-1980s. By Tibetan standards, his comments are uniquely outspoken. They corroborate Rob Hogendoorn's analysis of Sogyal's early life in Tibet and India, and CR Rinpoche pulls no punches in his criticism of Sogyal. For example (in his idiosyncratic English):

> *This Lakar Sogyal only 'Sogyal name' having. Sogyal only 'Sônam Gyaltsen'. Many Tibetan 'Sônam Gyaltsen' name having. Sogyal from 'so' and 'gyal' coming – first syllable each name, then Sogyal making. Nothing else coming! This Lakar one big fraud! Much arrogance.*

> *Much greed. Much stupid. Much bad mind. Nothing knowing. No study. No retreat.*

And dismissing Sogyal's alleged credentials as a *terton* (hidden teachings finder):

> *And this 'Lakar Sogyal' – only son from rich trader family coming! Lakar family rich from tobacco, buying and selling! In Tibet people saying 'Lakar-gold and Lakar-gold are sex together having. This way Lakar-gold children making – and more gold coming. This all from evil tobacco business coming. This business too bad! Very bad! Very great evil. Lakar Sogyal pocket searching and cigarette case finding. This hidden treasure revealing. What else this Sogyal Lakar discovering? Nothing! Maybe penis in trouser discovering – then many young girl vagina discovering. If Törtön, then must be Térma finding. No Térma finding – what purpose coming? Only bla-bla nonsense saying.*

Chimed Rigdzin Rinpoche was a revered scholar, yogi and teacher. And – it seems – a prophet.

> *When no Térma activities beginning – no Térma activities concluding. Only great shame beginning – then money-making concluding and sex concluding. Future time – after Chhi'mèd Rig'dzin died maybe – great shame for this Lakar Sogyal coming. Many peoples shame saying. Maybe newspaper shame saying. Maybe even Dalai Lama shame saying – maybe… maybe possible. Then dead.*

These words were uttered in the mid-1980s.

It is true that the mystique around the sexual yoga component of Tibetan tantric Buddhism triggered a range of naïve expectations during its transition into the developed world. It is also true that, according to tradition, the physical union of male and female energy was a peak experience, with details of the practice reserved for adepts who had reached high levels of equipoise and non-attachment. The Dalai Lama said (probably with tongue in cheek) that you are ready for sexual yoga when you can drink urine or fine wine with the same level of indifference.

The days are long gone when Tibetan Buddhism was flavour of the month with celebrities, socialites and politicians. The challenging contemplative disciplines developed by hermit yogis in pre Chinese Tibet are now often replaced by New Age-style programmes, like Finding Inner Peace in a Turbulent World. Or the Secular Mindfulness movement, which cherry-picks a psycho-emotional fix from Buddhist meditation techniques. Sogyal spearheaded the trend with his brand of Buddhism Lite.

Amost all the lamas who maintained the integrity of the tradition are dead, which is bad financial news for the insititutions they established around the world. Western disciples do not attract thousands of paying customers to their teachings, and online versions forced upon us by Covid 19 are even less lucrative. Rigpa is not the only Tibetan Buddhist organisation facing cash flow problems.

But all is by no means lost. Across planet earth today there are individuals and organisations dedicated to the appreciation of authentic Tibetan tantric Buddhism. Individuals and organisations that devote their existence to maintaining the very best, the most useful and the most profound teachings that have been passed down through centuries from generations of realised masters to students who in turn transmit them onwards.

The translator of Tibetan texts Sarah Harding describes esoteric Buddhism as "the precious crown jewel of spiritual practice in Tibet." She writes on the Tsadra Foundation web site:

The esoteric or secret quality of the tantras, however, is only revealed by direct contact with masters who embody an awakened state of mind. Then the practitioner sees directly the living teaching, and is in turn seen by the guru in his or her unique capacities and needs. It is this relationship that powers the development of spiritual growth. For that reason the direct instructions transmitted within such relationships are the most prized of all the Buddha's doctrines.

Which of course means that people who "embody an awakened state of mind" need to be alive and active in order to sustain the transmission. In 2021 they are thin on the ground. Where are the masters who measure up to the standards set by the late Dudjom Rinpoche for example? Or the late Lama Thubten Yeshe? There are plenty of young "reincarnations" but so far none of them appear to personify the qualities displayed by their predecessors.

But those of us who care about the survival of one of one of human kind's great spiritual heritages live in hope – and maybe a small portion of expectation. The historical Buddha Sakyamuni attained enlightenment sitting under a tree 2,500 years ago. His legacy has withstood innumerable permutations, interpretations and violent assaults ever since. Our wish for the future is that it will continue to do so. And that we will not witness the rise to prominence of a Sogyal Lakar ever again.

REFERENCES

1. International Commission of Jurists. (1997). *Tibet: Human Rights and the Rule of Law*. Geneva: International Commission of Jurists, p. 30.

2. Buswell, Robert & Donald Lopez Jr. (2014). *The Princeton Dictionary of Buddhism*. Princeton: Princeton University Press, p. 847.

3. Chapter 2 and 3 are based on Rob Hogendoorn's "The Making of a Lama: Interrogating Sogyal Rinpoché's Pose as a (Re)incarnate Master," a paper presented to the panel, From Rape Texts to Bro Buddhism: Critical Canonical and Contemporary Perspectives on the Sexual Abuse Scandals in Western Buddhism, during the annual meeting of the American Academy of Religion in Denver, 17-20 November 2018.

4. Sogyal Rinpoche. (2008). *The Tibetan Book of Living and Dying* (Revised and updated edition). London: Rider, p. xvi.

5. Dilgo Khyentse Rinpoche & Orgyen Tobgyal Rinpoche. (2017). *The Life and Times of Jamyang Khyentse Chökyi Lodrö: The Great Biography by Dilgo Khyentse Rinpoche and other stories*. Boulder: Shambhala, p. 181.

6. Jackson, David (2003). *A Saint in Seattle: The Life of the Tibetan Mystic Dezhung Rinpoche*. Boston: Wisdom Publications, p. 197.

7. See note 4, p. 4.

8. See note 5, pp. 199-200.

9. Gyatso, Tenzin, the fourteenth Dalai Lama. (2000). *Dzogchen: The Heart Essence of the Great Perfection*. Ithaca: Snow Lion, p. 9.

10. See note 4, pp. 4-5.

11. See note 5, p. 228.

12. Author unknown, (Fall 1989). "Sogyal Rinpoche." *Snow Lion Newsletter*, 4 (2), p. 2.

13. See note 5, p. 26.

14. See note 5, p. 235.

15. See note 5, p. 238.

16. See note 5, pp. 27, 372.

17. Penth, Boris & Harald Golbach (2008). *Sogyal Rinpoche: Ancient Wisdom for a Modern World*. Hilversum: Boeddhistische Omroep Stichting. This documentary can be watched on YouTube: https://www.youtube.com/watch?v=sHCQoxfx4nI (retrieved 12 April 2019).

18. See note 16.

19. See note 16.

20. See note 4, p. 45.

21 Finlay, Victoria. (1997, May 16). Joyful Road to Death. *South China Morning Post*, p. 25.

22 Avedon, John (1998). *In Exile from the Land of Snows: The Definitive Account of the Dalai Lama and Tibet Since the Chinese Conquest*. New York: Harper Perennial, p. 74.

23 Gyatso, Tenzin, the Fourteenth Dalai Lama. (2004). *Freedom in Exile*. London: Abacus, p. 152.

24 For the full story of David Bowie's pivotal year in Beckenham, see: Finnigan, Mary. (2016). *Psychedelic Suburbia: David Bowie and the Beckenham Arts Lab*. Portland, Ore., Jorvik Press.

25 For an extensive discussion of life at Kopan Monastery in those years, see: Hulse, Adele. (2020). *Big Love: The Life and Teachings of Lama Yeshe: Volume 1: 1935-78*. Boston: Lama Yeshe Wisdom Archive.

26 Mackenzie, Vicki. (1998). *Cave in the Snow: Tenzin Palmo's Quest for Enlightenment*. New York: Bloomsbury.

27 Dapsance, Marion. (2021). *Alexandra David-Néel: Spiritual Icon, Feminist, Anarchist*. Portland: Jorvik Press.

28 Bärlocher, Daniel. (1982). *Testimonies of Tibetan Tulkus: A Research among Reincarnate Buddhist Masters in Exile: Volume I: Materials*. Freiburg: Universität Freiburg, pp. 682-684.

29 Marol, Jean-Claude. (January-February 1978). "Le Seau d'Eau." *l'Originel*, 3 (9), pp. 16-20.

30 See note 21, p. 25.

31 Author unknown. (18 January 1986). "Healing, Death & Dying." *The Age*, p. 120.

32 Sogyal Rinpoche. (1977). *View, Meditation & Action*. London: Orgyen Cho Ling, p. 3.

33 Author unknown. (23 November 1982). "Compassion Lecture." *Santa Cruz Sentinel*, p. 3.

34 Author unknown. (3 November 1983). "Tibetan Lama to Talk About Death and Dying." *The Press Democrat*, p. 21.

35 Schwartz, Larry. (10 February 1986). "Tragedy in Life of the Laughing Lama." *The Sydney Morning Herald*, p. 6.

36 Brinkley-Rogers, Paul. (26 May 1983). "Lama on dais at dedication in Bisbee." *Arizona Daily Star*, p. H-2.

37 Sogyal Rinpoche. (1990). *Dzogchen And Padmasambhava*. London: Rigpa Fellowship, p. 97.

38 Best, Bruce. (21 January 1986). "Death is as Natural as Laughing, says the Buddhist Cleese fan." *The Age*, p. 1.

39 Morphew, Clark. (25 September 1993). "Tapping into Tibetan understanding." *News Journal*, pp. 13-14.

40 See note 16.

41 See note 4.

42 Verhoeven, Jaap. (2021). *Guru in Disgrace*. Akaash Films. The documentary can be watched here: https://vimeo.com/ondemand/guruindisgrace (Retrieved April 10, 2021).

43 Lattin, Don. (10 November 1994). "Best-selling Buddhist author accused of sexual abuse." *Free Press*.

44 Finnigan, Mary. (10 January 1995). "Sexual Healing." *The Guardian*, p. 19.

45 Finnigan, Mary. (19 February 1995). BBC Radio Four: "The Sunday Programme."

46 Brown, Mick. (2 February 1995). "The Precious One." *The Daily Telegraph*, pp. 20-28.

47 Kjolhede, Bodhin. (1993). "The Dharamsala Conference." *Zen Bow: Special Supplement*.

48 Lachs, Stuart & Rob Hogendoorn. (2021). "Not The Tibetan Way: The Dalai Lama's Realpolitik Concerning Abusive Teachers." Open Buddhism. See: https://openbuddhism.org/not-the-tibetan-way-the-dalai-lamas-realpolitik-concerning-abusive-teachers/ (Retrieved April 19, 2021).

49 For the archived version of Tibetanlama.com, see: https://web.archive.org/web/*/Tibetanlama (retrieved 12 April 2019).

50 Goodwin, Debi. (2011). *In the Name of Enlightenment: Sex Scandals in Religion*. Toronto: Cogent/Benger Productions. The documentary can be watched on YouTube: https://www.youtube.com/watch?v=yWhIivvmMnk (retrieved 12 April 2019).

51 Emery, Elodie. (2011). Pas si zen, ces bouddhistes. *Marianne, 756*, pp. 72-77.

52 In 2020, Oane Bijlsma published her story on Rob Hogendoorn's website Openbuddhism.org: Bijlsma, Oane. (2020). My Time in Rigpa. Retrieved July 28, 2020 from https://openbuddhism.org/my-time-in-rigpa/

53 See note 48.

54 Dapsance, Marion. (2016). *Les dévots du bouddhisme*. Paris: Max Milo Editions.

55 Mostert, Dirk. (14 June 2017). *Brandpunt: Misbruik in de boeddhistische gemeenschap*. Hilversum: KRO-NCRV. The documentary can be watched (with subtitles) on YouTube: https://www.youtube.com/watch?v=-Rxljr7KGIE (retrieved 12 April 2019).

56 Brown, Mick. (23 September 2017). "Bad Karma." *The Daily Telegraph* (Magazine), pp. 22-27.

57 Downing, Keith. (2014). *The Divine Madman: The Sublime Life and Songs of Drukpa Kunley*. CreateSpace Independent Publishing Platform.

58 Bijleveld, Menno. (3 July 2018). "Sogyal Rinpoche in disgrace: Part 4: Sangye Nawang." The interview can be watched on YouTube: https://www.youtube.com/watch?v=hW8VqIGQk9s (retrieved 12 April 2019).

59 Author unknown. (30 July 2004). "Sogyal Rinpoche justifies hitting student." The audio can be heard on YouTube: https://www.youtube.com/watch?v=_LcMeNBWj6Q (retrieved 12 April 2019).

60 Campbell, June. (2002). *Traveller in Space: Gender, Identity, and Tibetan Buddhism*. London: Continuum.

61 Author unknown. (2017). "Dalai Lama speaks out about Sogyal Rinpoche." The video can be watched on YouTube: https://www.youtube.com/watch?v=0wP4rsM7AZQ (retrieved 12 April 2019).

62 Gyatso, Tenzin, the Fourteenth Dalai Lama). (2019). Interaction with College Students. Retrieved 18 November, 2019 from https://www.youtube.com/watch?v=ghhFkuzLojw

63 Peljor, Tenzin. (2017). The Dalai Lama on Abuse by Buddhist Teachers or Gurus. Retrieved October 11, 2019 from https://buddhism-controversy-blog.com/2017/10/10/the-dalai-lama-on-abuse-by-buddhist-teachers-or-gurus/

64 Author unknown. (2004). "Rigpa: The Center for Wisdom & Compassion" (Case Statement). Berne: Rigpa Center for Wisdom & Compassion.

65 The form 990's of the Tenzin Gyatso Institute filed with the Internal Revenue Service can be retrieved through the Nonprofit Explorer of ProPublica: https://projects.propublica.org/nonprofits/organizations/133576181 (retrieved 12 April 2019).

66 Ricard, Matthieu. (29 July 2017). "A point of view." Retrieved 12 April 2019 from https://www.matthieuricard.org/en/blog/posts/a-point-of-view--2.

67 Yongey Mingyur Rinpoche. (26 October 2017). "When a Buddhist Teacher Crosses the Line." *Lion's Roar*. Retrieved 12 April 2019 from https://www.lionsroar.com/treat-everyone-as-the-buddha/

68 Lewis, Craig. (2017). "Khenchen Namdrol Rinpoche Speaks Out Over Public Criticism of Sogyal Rinpoche." Retrieved from https://www.buddhistdoor.net/news/khenchen-namdrol-rinpoche-speaks-out-over-public-criticism-of-sogyal-ripoche. The quotes were taken from a video that since has been removed.

69 Shenpen Dawa Norbu Rinpoche made these remarks in a letter addressed to "Dear Dharma Friends" distributed through Facebook on 18 January 2018 (retrieved on 12 April 2019).

70 Author unknown. (2018). Rigpa Press Releases. Retrieved 12 April 2019 from https://www.lerabling.org/lang-en/rigpa-press-releases-3-jan-2018.

71 Newland, Tahlia. (2018). "Latest News from Rigpa: How the future looks." WhatNow? Retrieved 12 April 2019 from https://whatnow727.wordpress.com/2018/01/04/latest-news-from-rigpa-how-the-future-looks/.

72 Guiraud, Sophie. (2017, December 12). Centre bouddhiste Lerab Ling de Lodève: "La parole se libère". *Midi Libre*. Retrieved from https://www.midilibre.fr/2017/12/09/centre-bouddhiste-lerab-ling-de-lodeve-la-parole-se-libere,1600455.php

73 Newman, Andy. (2018). "The 'King' of Shambhala Buddhism Is Undone by Abuse Report." *The New York Times*. Retrieved 12 April 2018 from https://www.nytimes.com/2018/07/11/nyregion/shambhala-sexual-misconduct.html. Marsh, Sarah. (5 March 2018). "Buddhist group admits sexual abuse by teachers." *The Guardian*. Retrieved 12 April, 2019 from https://www.theguardian.com/world/2018/mar/05/buddhist-group-admits-sexual-abuse-by-teachers.

74 Baxter, Karen. (22 August 2018). "Report to the Boards of Trustees of: Rigpa Fellowship UK, and Rigpa Fellowship US." London: Lewis Silkin LLP, p. 4.

75 See note 62, p. 18.

76 See note 62, pp. 49-50.

77 Remski, Matthew. (2018). "Senior Rigpa Students Ask for Sogyal Rinpoche to Be Reinstalled: Sources." Remski's post can be read here: http://matthewremski.com/wordpress/senior-rigpa-students-ask-for-sogyal-rinpoche-to-be-reinstalled-sources/ (Retrieved April 10, 2021).

78 Green, Jo. (17 October 2018). "Missing the Connection." WhatNow? Retrieved 12 April 2019 from https://whatnow727.wordpress.com/2018/10/17/missing-the-connection/.

79 Harvey, Oliver. (22 September 2018). "The Bad Buddha." *The Sun*. Retrieved 12 April 2019 from https://www.thesun.co.uk/news/7319165/celeb-guru-sogyal-rinpoche-sexually-abused-women-dubbed-dakinis/.

80 Author unknown. (29 November 2018). Press release: "New Charity Inquiry: Rigpa Fellowship." Retrieved 12 April 2019 from https://www.gov.uk/government/news/new-charity-inquiry-rigpa-fellowship.

81 Corder, Mike. (2018). "Dalai Lama meets alleged victims of abuse by Buddhist gurus." Associated Press News. Retrieved 12 April 2018 from https://www.apnews.com/b6c4535313234fa4b5cc41a97c41da98.

82 Abrahams, Matthew. (15 September 2018). "Buddha Buzz Weekly: Sept. 15, 2018." Tricyle: The Buddhist Review. Retrieved 12 April 2019 from https://tricycle.org/trikedaily/buddha-buzz-weekly-sept-15-2018/.

   Littlefair, S. (17 September 2018). "Dalai Lama meets with survivors of abuse by Buddhist teachers." Lion's Roar. Retrieved 12 April 2019 from https://www.lionsroar.com/dalai-lama-meets-with-survivors-of-abuse-by-buddhist-teachers/.

83 Mees, Anna & Bas de Vries. (2018). "Dalai lama over misbruik: ik weet het al sinds de jaren 90." NOS. Retrieved 12 April 2019 from https://nos.nl/artikel/2250536-dalai-lama-over-misbruik-ik-weet-het-al-sinds-de-jaren-90.html. The Dalai Lama's remarks can be watched through this link.

84 Newland, Tahlia. (21 October 2018). "An Email to Lamas." WhatNow? Retrieved 12 April 2019 from https://whatnow727.wordpress.com/2018/10/21/an-email-to-lamas/.

85 Jensen, Karen. (2019). Sogyal Rinpoche Eulogies Make Victims Disappear, Critics Charge. *Tricycle: The Buddhist Review*. The article and letter of the Central Tibetan Administration can be read here: https://tricycle.org/trikedaily/sogyal-rinpoche-eulogies/ (Retrieved April 10, 2021).

86 Author unknown (2020, June 15). "Abuse guru's aide to give online talks." *The Times* (iPad edition).

87 Wicks, Jack. (2020). Michelle Tonkin speaks at inform seminar 22 July 2020 [trigger warning]. YouTube. The video can be watched here: https://youtu.be/uX8BCHhJxiY (Retrieved April 10, 2021).

88 Author unknown. (2019, December 12). Editorial: Reality behind 'mindfulness'. *Newcastle Herald*; McCarthy, Joanne. (2019, December 13). Buddhist leader says fallen guru hit her. *Newcastle Herald*, p. 2.; McCarthy, Joanne. (2019, December 14). Disgraced guru left dark trail. *Newcastle Herald*, p. 14.

89 Wicks, Jack. (2020). Michelle Tonkin speaks at inform seminar 22 July 2020 [trigger warning]. Retrieved July 23, 2020 from https://www.youtube.com/watch?v=uX8BCHhJxiY&feature=emb_logo

90 This analysis is based on the financial statements submitted to national tax offices by fourteen tax-exempt organizations affiliated with Rigpa International (in Australia, Canada, France, Germany, Ireland, Netherlands, United Kingdom, and the United States of America). The listed amounts have not been consolidated and audited by forensic accountants, so they ought to be seen as approximations to the best of our knowledge.

91 Its founder Peter Cornish documented Dzogchen Beara's history in: Cornish, Peter. (2014). *Dazzled by Daylight*. Garranes: Garranes Publications.

92 Rulison, Larry. (2015, February 7). Land Deal Has High Point. *The Times-Union*, p. C6.

93 Author unknown. (2020). Rigpa Sangha Survey. Rigpa.org. The survey can be read here: https://www.rigpa.org/rigpa-sangha-survey (Retrieved April 10, 2021).

94 Wangyal, Lobsang. (2020). Tulku Orgyen Tobgyal criticises Dalai Lama for online teachings. *Tibet Sun*. See: https://www.tibetsun.com/news/2020/05/28/tulku-orgyen-topgyal-criticises-dalai-lama-for-online-teachings (Retrieved April 10, 2021); Wangyal, Lobsang. (2020). Tulku Orgyen Tobgyal apologises to Dalai Lama for criticising online teachings. *Tibet Sun*. See: https://www.tibetsun.com/news/2020/05/31/tulku-orgyen-tobgyal-apologises-to-dalai-lama-for-criticising-online-teachings (Retrieved April 10, 2021).

95 Author unknown. (2020). Decision: Charity Inquiry: Rigpa Fellowship. Charity Commission. The entire report can be read here: https://www.gov.uk/government/publications/charity-inquiry-rigpa-fellowship/charity-inquiry-rigpa-fellowship (Retrieved April 10, 2021).

96 Ngak'chang Rinpoche *Goodbye Forever Volume IV*. The text here is an abbreviation of a complex conversation, including Tibetan technical terms. It will appear in full when published by Aro Books.

www.ingramcontent.com/pod-product-compliance
Lightning Source LLC
Chambersburg PA
CBHW052020290426
44112CB00014B/2315